The
LAST
WORD

An imprint of HarperCollins*Publishers* Ltd
1 London Bridge Street
London SE1 9GF

www.harpercollins.co.uk

HarperCollins *Publishers*
Macken House, 39/40 Mayor Street Upper,
Dublin 1, Ireland, D01 C9W8

This edition 2023

1

First published in Great Britain by
HQ, an imprint of HarperCollins*Publishers* Ltd 2023

Copyright © Amy Price with Sharon Hendry 2023

Amy Price and Sharon Hendry assert the moral right to be
identified as the author of this work.

A catalogue record for this book is available from the British Library.

HB ISBN: 978-0-00-858792-5
TPB ISBN: 978-0-00-858793-2

MIX
Paper | Supporting
responsible forestry
FSC™ C007454

This book is produced from independently certified FSC™ paper
to ensure responsible forest management.
For more information visit: www.harpercollins.co.uk/green

Printed and bound in the UK using 100% renewable electricity
by CPI Group (UK) Ltd

The LAST WORD

Setting the Record Straight About My Daughter, Katie Price

AMY PRICE
WITH SHARON HENDRY

ONE PLACE. MANY STORIES

CONTENTS

DEDICATION

This book is for my family. Without them, I would never have been a complete me.

To my funny, hardworking, supportive husband Paul: You are always in a muddle and rush, but you have looked after me as best you could. I know my illness has been a hard road and we have had to accept it together. You have been there with me, *for* me, in every meeting without fail – I, the logical one, accepting the inevitable outcome and you, the positive one, having hope even when the news is bleak. I adore you – who knew we would put up with each other for over 38 years? No one thought it would last. It did, and I'm so grateful for every single second of it.

To my son Daniel – 'Dan the Man': I couldn't have wished for a more wonderful, strong-minded, thoughtful and clever son. You've been supportive of us as a family, always there for us but especially me – we have a special bond. You are a wonderful father to your children and I love you with all my heart. I am so very, very proud of you and what you have achieved. I know you will continue to look after our family forever. You are the building block and the wisdom. In the months I have been ill, you have shined through, helping me like no other person. We have had many a deep conversation about how you could support me – and Paul, your dad, when I am gone. I am grateful and so lucky to have such a wonderful son.

To my daughter Kate – 'Katrina', 'Doll Doll': You are a kind, generous, caring daughter to me; so vulnerable and fragile and yet when I look into your eyes, I can see you understand and love me wholeheartedly. Hard work, yes you are, but iridescent with a personality that shines through. You are always late, but you arrive with a smile on your face so magical that I forget I was supposed to tell you off. Kate, you have given me so many ups and downs in life and experiences I would never have had without you – both good and bad. Being your mum has been a total learning curve but I have loved every moment – and I am very proud of you, especially watching you become a wonderful mother yourself. I love you dearly. You are so misunderstood but I understand you well. You are like a perfect peach – now, at last, ready to ripen with age, beauty and wisdom – and you will.

To my baby daughter Sophie – 'Sophie Wophie', 'Doll Doll', my double: Like me, you love the simple things in life – nature, music, the sea and driving around the countryside together with a coffee, marvelling at nature and playing music at the same time. We cry too, emotional but happy tears. How wonderful that we can cry and laugh at the same time. Sophie, you have always been a breath of fresh air. You have spoiled me and encouraged me to enjoy and embrace the simple things in life, especially when I have felt ill and we have gone out on trips (even in dad's 'In the land of the Toyota car'). And we have enjoyed life. You are not materialistic but instead you are a Mother Earth person like me. And you won't admit it yet, but I know you will become spiritual and embrace my love of yoga. You too are a wonderful mum and you have blossomed with motherhood. I am so very proud of what you have achieved, too, going from a hairdresser to gaining a master's degree in history. How proud I am of this. You will have your own Amy's Cottage one day – I promise.

To my grandchildren: Junior, you are caring and I know you love me wholeheartedly. I love your texts of encouragement and love. When I'm feeling low, they cheer me up. You will always be successful and so talented. Make your own way in life and ensure that the decisions you make are your own and not influenced by other people. Stay true to yourself. Then there is Princess, my double, Kate's double. I love the fact you have my curly hair. You text me all the time asking me how I am and what I am doing – I am so lucky you care like you do. Princess, you will be a shining star too. You shine now, and I know you will continue to do so. You know your own mind, and you need to trust your own decisions.

My little Jett, you are a little farmer and my gardener with an angelic face and a heart full of love, you are so caring. Bunny, the mischievous one, who helps me in the garden too and loves my vegetable patch: always in trouble and headstrong, you are sharp as a razor and a mini-Kate. Amalie, the amazing footballer with your large sparkling eyes, and Betsy with your wonderful smile that illuminates your face, your wonderful singing and piano playing – you all have my curly hair and call me Nanny Big Hair. I love that!

Albert, my 'Tom Thumb', you are my youngest little grandson with strawberry-coloured hair that's going curly to my delight and big saucer eyes. When your mum stays with us, we all snuggle up in bed with you while drinking coffee and chomping digestive biscuits. You have a gentle personality and I'm sure you will have a kind heart. Will you be a footballer, Grandad asks. 'No,' your mum says, 'A *polo* player'.

I wonder what life will offer you all? I wish I could be there to find out but it's enough now for me to imagine.

Then there is Harvey. For the first 13 years of your life, I was with you and your mum constantly as we tried to understand you while juggling your hospital appointments with the school runs. We encouraged you to learn and adapt to your medication even though we were sometimes anxious. Would you talk, walk, interact, have facial expressions; would you be able to love and feel emotion? Would you be able to feel and say, 'I love you, Mum.' Well, as I write this you are 20 years old and that is an achievement in itself. I cannot tell you how much I have learned from you, Harvey, and how your bravery has made me brave. You have held my hand and helped me walk. You have touched the oxygen tube under my nose and told me, 'Get well Nanny'. I am so proud of you, the man you have become. You will have a great future because you are so talented with your art and your music. And one thing is for sure – you love your family and absolutely adore and cherish your mum. Your love for her is unconditional – no barriers, just love. We all love you dearly, Harvey, and are so proud of you – me especially. I love you so much.

To the Royal Brompton & Harefield Hospital whose

research department and transplant team have looked after me during this awful illness: Professor Phil Molyneaux, Toby Maher, his wife Maggie, and the research team – you really are exceptional people who have encouraged me to take chances, and have kept me alive as long as possible, allowing me the opportunity to try research drugs. The transplant team has also been fantastic, especially the transplant co-ordinator Debbie Burns, who encouraged me to get on the transplant list against all odds because of my age. My thanks to the consultants, Professor John Dunning and Dr Martin Carby, Dr Anna Reed, Dr Vicky Gerovasili, Dr Kavita Dave, and all the wonderful nurses. And to the wonderful people who've become part of my transplant family by walking this road with me – namely to Jackie and Anita who are still waiting for transplants – we've kept each other's spirits up and I couldn't have done it without you. Thank you. Thank you.

To St Barnabas Hospice: Thank you to all the amazing staff who have supported me with my end of life care.

To my friends: You have all been there for me through thick and thin. These moments, along with those shared with my family, have made my life complete.

With love,
Amy x

FOREWORD
by Kate Price

Whenever I think of my mum, my mind fills with music, laughter and the image of her big green eyes. For as long as I can remember, we've been joined at the hip and as a young girl I recall her being so full of life. I watched her singing and dancing around to songs by Madonna, Luther Vandross, Alexander O'Neal and George Benson. She played them on this little ghetto blaster which was her pride and joy. For the rest of my life, I know a smile will spread across my face when I hear those tunes and picture her beautiful, happy face.

When I sing and dance around with my own kids, I think about all that my mum has passed on to me and all that was passed on to her from my nan. In that sense, I think life is an incredible, complex, magical merry-go-round.

Mum has always been the spirit and soul of everything and I definitely get a lot of my personality from her. She is fiercely protective of her family and closest friends and I used to cringe (and still do) at some of her opinions because she tells the honest truth and doesn't care what people think. Unfortunately, she is always right.

What you see is what you get with my mum and if she doesn't like you she won't give you the time of day – just ask some of my exes. She's definitely a force of nature and I know I get that from her. She's still the one person I look up to because I know I've learned from the best: Mother Price. We're very, very close and she still tells me off to this day. When I'm around her, I revert to being a teenager. It's like *Kevin & Perry Go Large* – 'That is so unfair,' is often all I can say when she's having a go at me, which is quite often. The truth is, I don't feel she has ever treated any of her children differently even though I'm the one who gives her more trouble because of the problem I have with choosing the right men – it's always men!

I am touched that she has put her heart and soul into this book, a legacy for me and our whole family. From the moment I stepped into the public arena, the media constructed an image of me which is not the whole truth. My mum is setting the record straight because she knows me better than any other person on this planet. In fact, she knows me better than I know myself. I can only thank her for all the love she has invested in this book and hope that her perspective on our family gives people a chance to form a more accurate picture and understand how certain patterns have formed – it's certainly been interesting and sometimes tough for me to contemplate.

My mum has been alongside me at every single stage of my life, including the darkest moments imaginable. She certainly has evidence to back up what she says because she has seen my life unfold first hand. She isn't a vindictive person and always wants the best for everyone. But if she has to stand up for the people she loves in order to protect them, she will.

My career has been unusual and at times it has exposed my family to upset, for which I am sorry. But I have never felt judged by my mum and she has always been there for me – especially when Harvey was born. We found out a few years ago that her illness was terminal and I have tried to get my head around it, but when the time comes to say goodbye it won't be easy. It's been very, very hard seeing her struggling to breathe and trying to talk, because she has always been and still is a warrior. She is starting to get very weak now and I know that unless she gets a lung transplant, her death is just around the corner. I can't put into words how much I am going to miss her. My life will never be the same again when she's gone, so I'd like to tell her something now that I hope she has known all along: I love you so, so much.

Kate xxx

PROLOGUE

My name is Amy Price. In many ways, I'm just an ordinary mum, wife and granny. I adore dogs, horses and yoga – and I love to stroll by the sea close to my cosy little South Coast bungalow. But in all honesty, there's never been much of a chance to enjoy a completely normal life because I also happen to be Katie Price's mum – a role that came with a lot more than I bargained for when her decision to become a topless model attracted the full attention of Britain's 'celebrity machine' almost overnight.

And now there is the terrible inconvenience of my mortality. It's a really hard thing to say out loud, but I'm dying you see. Out of the blue, I was diagnosed with the incurable illness idiopathic pulmonary fibrosis (IPF) in 2017 and given five years to live. It causes scarring to the lungs and makes it difficult to breathe so in many ways it limits my everyday life, restricting my ability to do all the ordinary things I have always taken for granted – like cooking a meal, having a bath and playing with my grandchildren. Nowadays, every day is like running a marathon and my heart beats fast with exertion just walking back and forth to the bathroom. My lungs constantly require the portable oxygen tank that has of late become my trusted companion, trailing along behind me wherever I go.

Socializing, travelling and even talking for long periods feel like mammoth tasks and more recently, I have succumbed to using a wheelchair outside my home. I suppose it won't be long before I finally take up Kate's offer (she has always been known as 'Kate' in our family) of a pink mobility scooter. But I haven't given up on walking just yet – or life for that matter. In many ways, edging closer to death has sharpened my mind, forcing me to look back over my life in an attempt to try to make sense of the forces that have shaped my family.

Early on, I asked the incredible team taking care of me at Harefield Hospital to put my name on the lung transplant list and it is in my nature to remain hopeful. But by the time you read this, there is a strong chance I won't be here and that's why this book had to happen, why I had to set the record straight once and for all. The world of fame needs heroes and villains to keep its audience entertained and I am weary of seeing my daughter cast as the bad guy. For years, I've looked on from the side lines but now it's time to reveal the REAL Kate – along with the impact her life in the limelight has had on our entire family. My greatest wish is that my daughter will one day find the peace she deserves but I can't pretend I'm not scared of leaving her behind – *terrified* even. I've always been her rock you see, the person who really knows what makes her tick. I'm the first person she calls when she's in trouble, which means my phone has been quite active over the past few decades.

To the outside world, Kate is her own worst enemy, a grown woman who should know better than to set the scene

again and again for her own demise through failed relationships with inappropriate men, a self-absorbed surgical quest
for the perfect body, wild spending and even wilder partying. My daughter is seen by a large percentage of the British
public as a free-falling fame junkie who gets the publicity she
deserves, a reality TV caricature who has veered between the
highs of national treasure and the lows of being compared to
the serial killer Myra Hindley.

Somewhere in this narrative, the essence of Kate has been
lost (even to herself) but as her mum, *I* have never lost sight
of my daughter's inner world. This book – which will serve as
my last testament to her and her siblings, and to my grandchildren when they're old enough to read it – is of course
written with love and conveys the strong bond between us, but
it is not a simplistic defence of her behaviour because, frankly,
her critics sometimes have a point. But what they don't know,
what they've *never* known, is the truth. Through the column
inches of the tabloid press and reality TV cameras, they have
constructed an idea of my daughter based on *what* they have
seen, but only me and her closest family understand *why* they
have seen it.

For years, we have looked on – often powerlessly – as Kate's
relationships have repeated toxic patterns of coercive control
and domestic abuse. We have watched her turn to drugs and
ever more drastic measures to protect herself against the pain
of childhood traumas and a longing to reconjure the lost
relationship with her dad. She has defended her vulnerability with alter egos like Jordan, but it can still be seen in her
needy men, treacherous friendships and even an obsession

with caring for animals. At times, Kate's tough armour has served her well, turning her into a formidable campaigner for her disabled son Harvey and countless other people like him. She has also survived bankruptcy, multiple divorces, a close shave with prison and attempted suicide on more than one occasion. Kate has shrugged off these traumas as if they were inconvenient headaches, but as she approaches middle age, I see the mask slipping and wonder how she will weather the storms without me and her regular visits to my appropriately named 'Pop In House'.

This book is also an intergenerational tale about families and especially mothers – the legacy we leave our children. Advances in psychology now tell us that nature and nurture sit side by side, making us all a combination of our genes and the environment the dice rolls us. Writing this book has highlighted some interesting – and occasionally disturbing – patterns in our family, like control and abuse, which have sadly been repeated through the generations. It has also revealed new patterns, formed through the distorting glare of the media and celebrity culture. What began as a chance for me to set the record straight will, I hope, also serve as a deeper historical record for my family, and a salutary tale for others. Countless fans and foes have no doubt lived out their own hopes and fears through my daughter's soap opera-style antics over the years, but few could ever imagine the real price of fame and its impact on an ordinary family. It's either a sunny day or an extremely grey one.

Since time immemorial, human beings have wanted to leave their mark on society and counteract the unthinkable reality of mortality with something everlasting. Early civilizations left etchings on cave walls but by the nineties and noughties, in the age of 'mega celebrity', reality TV was where it was at. Sadly, my daughter unwittingly became the poster girl of that millennial culture at a time when it knew no boundaries. Lad mag culture was at its peak and journalists acted with impunity amid the ferocious circulation wars between the tabloids. All that would be unthinkable now, and is thankfully being questioned in the aftermath of events like #MeToo and phone hacking. But Kate was caught up in it; she became a creation of many industries – even publishing – where she spawned the idea of the celebrity novelist. Her material success was extraordinary, but the personal cost was perhaps greater still. I had never felt it more keenly than when I walked into the Portland Hospital on 13 June 2005 as she was about to give birth for the second time.

I was there to offer love and support to my daughter, who was understandably frightened after the traumatic birth of her first child Harvey. At Harvey's birth, I was by her side, able to stroke her hair and tell her, 'You can do this' as the labour pains came thick and fast. This time I was being pushed aside by a stooge from a management company carrying a camera, who explained that she would be the one accompanying my tearful daughter to the operating theatre. Kate, her husband and the camerawoman were all gowned up as I followed them to the lift but I wasn't allowed to step inside. I'll never forget watching the tears slide down my daughter's cheeks as the steel doors slowly shut tight and the lift descended. As I turned to seek my own emotional support from my husband

Paul, another camera was thrust in my face and someone began asking me inane questions like, 'How do you feel about all this?' The truth was, I felt it was wrong and could see that my daughter just wanted to be with her husband. But I didn't say how I really felt because I was on camera.

Reality TV isn't real at all – it masks the truth. A baby boy called Junior was entering the world for the first time that day, but it felt like the focus was on creating some drama and the production team began to make a big deal out of the fact that Kate had been in surgery more than 40 minutes, which wasn't a drama at all. In the end, my daughter could have been giving birth to a doll for all the natural bonding that was allowed to happen in the glare of the cameras during those first precious moments of Junior's life. It's hardly surprising she went on to develop crippling post-natal depression. But this was her life now and it had been heading that way ever since we made a fateful trip to Australia in 2004 and met a man called Peter Andre. Somehow, the boundaries between public and personal had become vastly compromised. Yet – on reflection – there was already a strong precedent for this in our family, as the pages of this book explain.

Chapter 1

MY MERMAID MUM

The story of why my family is unique begins with my mum, Esther Cohen. Esther was a rebel of sorts. While some women were conforming to the cold reality of WW2 by taking up roles as munitions workers and air raid wardens, she was contributing to the war effort in a rather different way. Each morning Esther would leave her family home in East London and head for the financial district where she climbed onto a bench placed behind a human-sized goldfish bowl so that she looked as though she was inside it, dressed as a topless exotic sea creature – a mermaid. Interested onlookers could slot coins into a pair of binoculars fixed on a wall opposite the tank and plunge themselves into a deep-sea fantasy, complete with fish and seaweed props.

Esther's long, red, curly hair was part of the attraction, and she would allow it to tumble down across her chest, combing it seductively while flicking her mermaid's tail across the make-shift seabed. I remain puzzled by some of the finer details of this attraction, but presumably it was the brainchild of some canny entrepreneur who recognized that men traumatized by war needed a little soft porn escapism.

My dad, Harvey Junior Charlier, was one such soldier who was tempted to take a peek at this beautiful, glass-encased creature and remove himself momentarily from the horrors of war. Harvey had come to Britain with the American army. Like many men subjected to too much trauma, he would never talk to me about his experiences of war, but I managed to deduce that he used to go on piggyback missions in planes, clear paths for incoming troops and take part in operations that involved blowing up bridges. He was a handsome guy and people said he looked just like Bing Crosby – so his nickname was Bing.

Harvey was later walking and bumped into Esther on the pavement outside the conference centre where she performed. He instantly recognized her walking along the street (no doubt it was her red tresses that gave her away) and he approached her and said he'd seen her through the binoculars in the tank. They soon started going out together as often as possible, having a wonderful time in London at tea parties and nightclubs. Her lit cigarette obviously destroyed the illusion of being under water so, not surprisingly, Esther was sacked from her mermaid gig for smoking behind the fishbowl, leaving her all the time in the world to dive headfirst into a love affair with Harvey. I suspect she was more than a little miffed about losing the job, though, because she had become bored with her previous work as a waitress and had found the work as a mermaid unusual and interesting.

In those early days, Esther was under the watchful eyes of her older brothers Leslie, Henry, Alec and Billy, who were all very protective of her. If she hadn't found work, she would have been stuck in the house helping with domestic chores as at this time there was a large family living at home – knowing mum, this would have been stifling. She clearly wanted the freedom to provide for herself and taste some independence in what was very much a man's world. Jobs for women were limited, and while the waitressing role would have been accepted by the family, I doubt the topless mermaid shifts would have been. My grandparents would have gone berserk if they had known what their daughter was up to, and I suspect this made it all the more enticing for my mum who liked to challenge the norms. As a child of a Jewish family, Esther had learned to stick up for herself at school; she found an ally in another Jewish girl called Valerie. Together they stood up to the bullying by fellow pupils and were not afraid to question the authority of teachers. Esther and Valerie tended to do what they wanted rather than what they were told to do, but I don't know how Esther would have explained away meeting Harvey when she introduced him to the family. I do remember her telling me that he was readily accepted because of his kindness and generosity. Apparently, he would provide rationed food and silk stockings for my mum and nan. Mum once confided in me that he had even gifted her silk underwear monogrammed with her initials, which I thought sounded very extravagant indeed.

Harvey was striking – well dressed and well groomed – but he wasn't Esther's first love. She had already married a man called Charlie Carter when she was 17. But Charlie had been deployed to Australia in the army and Esther needed to make ends meet so she took a job as a waitress in Brighton where she served food and refreshments to exhausted pilots and other soldiers stationed in Brighton or on leave from active duty. Brighton was bombed heavily during the war, and there was a general atmosphere of having to take each day as it came, never knowing what it might bring. During the evenings, Esther would frequent a club called Sherry's, which would later feature in Graham Greene's novel, *Brighton Rock*, due to the club's associations with Brighton's criminal underworld. In Esther's day though, the club was packed to the rafters with soldiers, and they would hold tea dances accompanied by a live jazz band playing the hits of the day, such as Glenn Miller.

Amy senior, my grandmother and namesake, who was very much the figurehead of the family, stood at just 5ft 2in tall and had tiny feet, but what she lacked in height she made up for in presence. Her black wavy hair framed a perfectly powdered face, enhanced by red lipstick and painted nails. She also wore 'stays' – old-fashioned corsets – which lent her an upright, authoritative stance. Later in life she lost her sight due to diabetes but was still aware of everything that went on around her. I think she was a tough parent. Later in Esther's life, she would reflect on this period of the war with fond sadness, remembering how she would look up to the sky and count the pilots out and in from their missions – always heartbroken for the ones who didn't make it. The pilots would dip low in their planes to let those watching the skies know that they had returned safely, and that they would join the crowds at Sherry's that night if they could. I think it's easy to forget how much trauma people were exposed to during WW2 and the losses they endured.

Esther felt that what she was doing was helping towards the war effort, supporting the men serving in the forces as much as she could, and trying to bring some joy and lightness to these pilots who were facing such traumatic experiences. Charlie had left for Australia and he and Esther soon divorced, which would have increased her feeling of loneliness. Given all these conflicting feelings, it's no wonder Esther threw herself into a relationship with Harvey – it must have felt so comforting to feel his big arms around her while bombs were dropping on the capital. In her own way, I think she was a casualty of the war; who really knows what lay beneath her tough exterior?

Whatever led her to be that way, it's not hard to see how a rebellious, topless, single-mother mermaid would lay down a blueprint in our family which would be repeated some years later by Kate. I was horrified when Kate came home and told me she was going topless on Page Three, but my mum was one of her biggest supporters and just loved watching her granddaughter's modelling career take off. It was a difficult dynamic, but looking back it's clear to see how the seeds for Kate's complexities had already been sown by the women who preceded her in our family.

As WW2 smouldered to an end, Harvey waved his beloved mermaid farewell and returned to American soil with his platoon, but it wasn't long before a restless Esther set sail to join him on his family's cucumber farm in Green Bay, Wisconsin. Esther longed for the freedom of a new life in America, lured there by the glamorous stories that Harvey had told her. It sounded like a world away from the claustrophobic home that she shared with her parents in Brighton. Alfred Lazereth Cohen, my Jewish grandad, never truly respected his Christian wife. His family had disowned him on religious grounds when they married, and he never got over it. He was cold and unaffectionate, and had the nickname 'The Fox' as he was cunning and kept things to himself. I later found out he was also a gambler and a womanizer. My nan was an unhappy person, desperate for something to fill the void in her life.

Esther, her brothers and her father worked non-stop and Amy would have been left on her own for long periods. She must have felt devastated when Esther set sail for America.

Upon her arrival in America, Esther and Harvey were soon married and began building a life together – but Esther became more and more homesick and anxious to return to England. She wrote frequent letters home to her mother at this time, expressing her disappointment at the reality she found herself in. I think she imagined a life of glitz and glamour in America, but instead, she found herself stuck on a cucumber farm with little in the way of excitement. Her relationships with my dad's family were fraught – whilst they all spoke the same language, they seemed to have been raised in different worlds, and there was very little common ground. The bright lights of Brighton and London, which were all Esther had ever known, felt very far away in rural America, surrounded by nothing but fields. While she was happy to be married to Harvey, the wedding itself felt like a sham without the presence of her family, who she sorely missed. She persuaded Harvey to return to England, and was the one who took the initiative and set about saving up money for their fares, demonstrating the single-minded character that is evident in all the Price family females. She had been given her own cucumber field and sold her harvest alongside wastepaper she collected from the neighbourhood. Esther set sail for America as a single woman on the good ship Mauritania, and returned with a husband on the same boat after two short years. Esther was thrilled to be back on British shores, and the couple soon settled back into life in England. They moved back in with my grandparents and Harvey got a job in the family business, working as a mechanic, whilst Esther returned to waitressing. The pair worked hard, and played hard too, trying to save for the future. They eventually moved out from Esther's parents' home, living all over Brighton in rented properties, before being given a council flat in Hollingdean. Ten years after their return from America, I was born. I was a miracle baby because my mum had just one ovary and my dad had only one testicle. They were told that having a child would be against all the odds but somehow, I defied the norms – an aspect of my character clearly engrained from conception.

My first memories begin around the age of two, when I can still almost feel myself being immersed in warm water. We were poor and my makeshift bath was the kitchen sink. By this time, my grandparents had left London and invested their money in a wastepaper business in Brighton, which proved very successful. My nan always wanted to escape to the countryside, but my grandad didn't, so they settled on the seaside where initially they lived in rented flats around Brighton. I was born in one of these flats, overlooking the blue-faced clock near the King and Queen pub by the Brighton Pavilion. The earliest memory of the kitchen sink bath was in Coombe Road. My grandad and uncles bought land on Brighton's Lewes Road and built two garages on opposite sides of the road – one complete with a car showroom, with two flats above it. My grandfather was very much the head of the family and a very controlling man, so other relatives – even my mum's four brothers – quickly followed him into the business.

Because the garage was such a big concern with the two flats and the showroom, getting planning permission, the finances and the dealership took a while. When the building was complete, my grandfather and nan moved into one flat at the front, while my mum, dad and seven-year-old me moved from a council flat in Hollingdean into the back flat. It was a stark contrast for me to move from the green fields I had always known in Hollingdean to living on a busy main road. My mum had come full-circle, from desperately trying to find independence in America to once again living in close proximity to her parents. My nan was very fond of Harvey, and when she was feeling unwell or needed help, she would often call on him to help her. A&H Motors soon became a very successful enterprise. By the time we moved into the flat, I had already begun to establish my independence. I had been left to walk to school on my own from the age of six and aside from occasional trips out with grandad, I was left to my own devices a lot because my parents were working all hours. I was a latchkey child. From about the age of eight, I used to take myself off to museums on the bus and I used to love the

Brighton library where I would read all the Enid Blyton and fairy tale books I could get my hands on. When I returned home, my little treat after tea was to climb into bed with mum while dad was getting ready for bed. She'd be sitting there doing her nails in bed and she'd let me snuggle up beside her for a while.

Sunday was the day I'd feel closest to my parents, who were big dreamers. Dinner would go in the oven then we would all get in the car and drive around looking at things we couldn't afford – boats, caravans or houses. Mum would do her knitting in the front, and I would be horribly carsick in the back. After two hours, we'd return home for tea and *Sunday Night at the London Palladium*, which I was allowed to watch on TV before bed. This Sunday routine is something I've unconsciously adopted with my own daughters. Sophie, Kate and I love nothing better than getting in the car together and touring around the area near my West Sussex seaside home, looking at lovely houses and buildings. We all take in the beauty of nature in the colours of the trees, the landscape and the old houses and cottages in the villages before having lunch or afternoon tea. We also visit country gardens or historical houses, appreciating their age and beauty. Rarely do we come back without a plant or little item for the home. It's the same when I travel to Devon or Cornwall in my motorhome. I've always had an affinity with the sea, which just feels like home. It reminds me of family holidays in Newquay, where I used to surf on wooden body boards, and trips to Great Yarmouth with nan and grandad, which always featured fish and chips and shows at the Windmill Theatre.

We were really poor, and I remember my dad working all hours as a car mechanic in grandad's garage while my mum helped with the cleaning and some admin. She hadn't lost any of her rebellious 'mermaid' streak, though: as a joke, whenever my mum was in the office working on admin and accounts, any man that entered did so at their own peril. It was usually family members or close friends, but my mum would pretend to pull any man's trousers down, apparently delighting in creating an atmosphere where men were frightened to enter. For some reason, my uncles and cousins would giggle outrageously at this. My mum's side of the family were all outrageous, really, and even as a child I thought, 'This is a right way to be carrying on!' But there are a lot of other really complex things to work out as a child and I just resigned myself to thinking we were a bit peculiar and that's the way it was.

In contrast, my dad was the steady one. He worked hard and yet still found time to help me with my homework. If there was any sewing to be done, he did it. He was a talented carpenter and made us tables and chairs. He was also a skilled welder. I think he tolerated a lot from my mother's family because all of his relations were in America. Reflecting on it all now, I think my mum's behaviour was rooted in attention seeking. Her brothers got all the credit, and she was desperate to be seen as someone who could make people laugh – just desperate to be seen at all really. Can you imagine the path she might have taken if she'd been born in a different era? Perhaps her life would have looked much like Kate's does now. All I really know is that she had a hard life within her own family. And despite her having tried to escape this dynamic twice

– once when she married so young, another when she left for America – when I came along, she had been pulled right back into the centre of it all.

I wouldn't say a concrete garage is the ideal place to raise small children, but I made it my world. The shiny car showroom floor became my roller-skating rink (much to the annoyance of anyone trying to buy a motor, and my uncles who ran the garage) and I began exploring the neighbourhood with my schoolfriends, including my fellow milk monitor Kelvin Robinson, who I adored. He lived in Upper Lewes Road in a house called Kel-Gra, an amalgamation of Kelvin and Graham (his brother) – I've never forgotten it! Another of my best friends was the son of a removal company owner, called Roger Harris. Their lorries were red and green and had 'Harris and Sons' written on them. While other children were playing in parks and going to the seaside, we used to break into his dad's furniture storage unit at the top of Gladstone Place, in Brighton, and play with all the old junk and stored furniture. Another favourite was the local cemetery behind the storage unit, which was a great place to play, despite us having to share it with the dead. Looking back, I'm filled with guilt when I remember how I used to take the flowers from well-tended graves and place them on those that were barren – but it upset me too much to think about people who had been forgotten or unloved. We played there among the dead because it was a green space we could play in. There was also Saunders Park nearby, where we used to play in the bushes, with a huge sandpit where I apparently caught measles (according to my worried mum). Another of our tricks was opening the doors at

11

the back of the local cinema, then called The Gaiety, and just brazenly walking in to watch the films.

But my happiest place of all was Bear Road, a mile-long uphill trek which led to a country lane where horses grazed in a field at the end, opposite Brighton racecourse. I adored those animals and yearned to ride them. Unfortunately, for reasons I've never really understood, my mum and dad were very much the poor relations of the family and so it was an impossible dream. Or was it?

One day, a few months after we had moved into the flat, I was so desperate to make the leap from frustrated bystander to rider, I decided to take fate into my own hands. I resorted to drastic measures, rummaging through my mum's storage cupboard until I found a suitcase full of glamorous clothes she didn't seem to have a use for anymore. I managed to sneak it out of the flat undetected and handed everything over to the local rag and bone man who had a shop under the railway arches. He separated the wool from the cotton and other materials and then everything had to be weighed. He totalled up, then bought it all from me, for the price of five shillings – which is the equivalent of 25p in today's money. It might not sound much but I had enough to realize my dream and feel the cool leather of a saddle on my skin for the first time. Because I had often hung around the stables mucking out, the owners were not too surprised when I turned up with the money for a ride.

My parents went ballistic of course but I didn't care and, if anything, it made me more determined to keep finding ways to gallop away from the confines of garage life and pursue a hobby that made me feel free and happy. So, when things calmed down from the initial shock of my first heist, I took all my mum's pot plants and sold them on a makeshift stall outside the cinema – and off I trotted once more. I could never understand why my wealthy grandad refused to buy me a horse because he told stories about looking after them during WW1 and he knew how much I loved them. He was a gambling man and used to take me with him to Brighton Races, where I would sit mesmerized, watching one beautiful creature after another galloping past. I would keep track of how much money he won or lost, and he always gave me a cut of his spoils (along with some jellied eels) as long as I promised not to tell my nan about his profit margins.

From a very young age, I learned that secrets like these were synonymous with my grandad. In the morning, the *Daily Mirror* would be delivered and, later, the *Evening Argus*. He wasn't interested in the news but used to spend hours studying the racing pages. He had accounts at various betting shops and used to ring in his bets. Whenever the papers were delivered, I used to pick them up off the doormat and take them to him and he showed me how he studied the form of the horses. But nobody really knew how much he was spending; I just sensed he was running up huge debts. And nobody knew what he got up to when he would spend days away from home. I am sure it wasn't business, but rather women that occupied his time. He had a pair of binoculars, supposedly for use at race meetings, which he used to secretly spy on the petrol pump attendants across the road to make sure that they were not skiving. He always dressed in a suit and trilby hat (or 'gangster's hat' as it looked to me). My grandad was a hard taskmaster!

I tolerated him because I had to, but nan was my favourite and I loved her deeply because she had time for me. When we lived in opposite flats above the garage, I used to sit in front of her, leaning back on her legs by the fire, watching TV or pretending to play the piano in the lounge, reading 'music' out of a cookbook. When a telling off from my dad was brewing, I used to run to her for protection from a smacking. She glued the family together, especially on those Sundays when she would summon us all for a Sunday get-together. Absentees would be in big trouble. She loved to cook and when preparing the food, she would sip on her daily bottle of Guinness and chain smoke. When everyone finally congregated, the air was always blue and smoky from all the cigarettes. Looking back, I can't ever remember my nan going out on her own; she was always at home. She had all the material things in life she could wish for – like nice jewellery and clothes – but I think she was treated very badly by my grandad and for that reason she was never truly happy. She never worked, and I think my nan got married to my grandad in the first place because she got pregnant out of wedlock, causing a great rift between my grandfather and his family, who were furious at the prospect of him marrying a woman who wasn't Jewish. I think my nan was determined that my mum would have a better outcome in life than she had had, and as a result, she constantly monitored Esther's behaviour and her actions, as did Esther's brothers.

Looking back on what life was like for women in those days, it's a world away from the freedoms we enjoy today. The contrasts between the things that the boys were allowed to get away with compared to the stringent rules placed upon the girls were shocking.

I remember my mum telling me stories about young women she knew in the fifties and sixties who conducted clandestine affairs with secret boyfriends that their families would never approve of, going so far as to climb out of windows and down drainpipes to meet with them. There was a huge emphasis on money and status in those days, and any man who didn't fit the bill would swiftly be rejected by the family. There was also a huge amount of stigma and shame associated with sex and pregnancy outside of marriage, which took an enormous toll on the mental health of so many women.

This sort of behaviour has travelled down four generations of my family, but I hope that I have broken the cycle in my own life, and for my own children. I believe that compatibility, trust and loyalty are far more important qualities in a relationship than materialistic things, and I know that, while it can make life easier, money cannot buy you happiness or health, something that has been proven time and time again over the years. But I'm getting ahead of myself!

As the years went by, my nan's health declined, and she needed help and support in getting washed and dressed, and getting her insulin injection every day.

Eventually, a housekeeper was employed and she reported that my granddad was sexually harassing her, offering money for 'favours'. Apparently, some improper behaviour had already taken place and my poor nan, who by now had gone blind, could sense it when they were sitting in the same room as her – she could hear them getting up to no good. The family got rid of this employee and found a replacement housekeeper and a rota of nurses to look after my nan. One night, my grandad had trouble sleeping so he took some pills which made him doze off next to the electric fire. His pyjamas caught fire, but he just put them out and climbed into bed to carry on sleeping. In the morning, my mum found him in bed and called an ambulance, which took him to the East Grinstead burns unit where doctors were forced to amputate his leg and give him a prosthetic one. He was in his eighties by then and we thought he would go into decline, but he learned to walk again and occasionally used a wheelchair, so life carried on for him as before.

We soon learned that he was taking a driver to visit his former housekeeper for continuing 'favours'. She lived up three flights of stairs in a block of flats, so this should give you an idea of what he was like. Back at home, my family had employed an additional female companion to sit with him at night three times a week. They were probably wary of him making arrangements without the family knowing what he was up to, and getting injured again, although he did get lonely. I wonder now if they were worried about their inheritance getting taken by someone else. I was only nine and felt very awkward about skulking around the lounge while he sat there opposite this woman in his wheelchair. He didn't like it either and got angry, telling me to leave. That's when my mum had the idea that I should hide behind the sofa to continue my surveillance on conversations and other goings on. I was too young to comprehend the noises they were making but I do remember the lady asking for money to support her son and daughter. In other words, another cash-for-favours arrangement had come to fruition so I told my mum who conspired with her brothers to get the woman sacked.

To me, the sofa expedition was like a game. I didn't know it was wrong – I thought it was like being a detective. But on reflection, what right did my family have to expose me to something so adult and confusing? Sexual harassment was not taken as seriously as it is nowadays and so rather than the moral issues of the situation being important, I think the financial issues and the family's reputation were the reasons for the concern. I was involved in the plot in order to keep close tabs on the family's inheritance, a sum not to be sniffed at because the garage empire was growing – it would eventually be sold off and the money would be used to fund an investment in building Brighton Marina.

My grandad ended up in a detached house with a big garden opposite the Hove garage. I thought my nan would have liked that, but the years of infidelity had taken their toll on her happiness and I don't think she was every truly happy in her marriage wherever it resided. She died at home when I was about 14 years old. I was in the room with her at the time, with my aunts and uncles, and watched my mum faint – something I've never forgotten. Nan lay in an open coffin for three days before they took her away and I remember the eery silence as people came and went, showing their respects. I was also in my grandad's big house when he died five years later, aged 86. I watched in fascination when the Jewish funeral directors came to collect his body in a simple, wooden crate.

He hadn't followed the religion throughout his lifetime and the rest of his family had never embraced the faith, so it was agreed that it was inappropriate to follow the Jewish custom of shiva, which involves a week of mourning as guests come to the home to pay their respects to the deceased. In the end his body was redirected to a Christian funeral director.

I've always been happy with the simplest things in life, which is just as well because my parents never quite managed to get close to purchasing any of the luxury goods they admired. They never spoke about the war either, which is curious considering how profoundly it impacted their lives. What Britain often defines as its greatest generation never talked about feelings much at all in my experience; least of all the unspeakable horrors they witnessed while defending our democracy. I've often wondered about the impact of it all on my dad and us as a family. He lost the top of his index finger on his right hand but when I asked him about it, he would always deflect from the horror with humour. 'I picked my nose too much and it fell off,' he would say; but I sensed there was much more to it than that.

Mum and dad eventually ended up buying transport cafés in Kemp Town, Brighton, Hove and Shoreham, where dad worked as a cook and mum stood front of house serving the customers, who were mainly men. It was almost as if mum's life had gone in a full circle, as waitressing was the job she had given up to become a mermaid. This time, I suppose because she was in charge rather than being ordered about, she loved it and always had a joke with the punters. But money was continuously tight – a fact which I was only too aware of as a small child who was privy to endless conversations about how we would make ends meet. I did get the sense that mum was a woman who wanted more, and never quite made peace with the place where her gender confined her. She always looked after herself, keeping a slim figure which was set off by nice, smart clothes. She strived to keep a clean and tidy house; once, her lawn mower stopped working and she actually got out a pair of scissors and cut the grass by hand. She liked nice things, and was always the life and soul of a party and beamed confidence – at least outwardly. I loved the fact that she could talk to anyone from any station in life and as I got older, we became closer, and I found I could confide in her about most things. She eventually found a way to make money by buying, renovating and selling houses, which she was fiercely proud of – I eventually followed in her footsteps, as a way of ending up with no mortgage.

If Esther was passionate about something, she really meant it. For example, she heard about animals being slaughtered in cramped facilities, so she made placards and stood outside her local Sainsbury's, protesting. She was in her seventies by then, but her spirit was still alive. My mum would never give up on anything and she would strive to get what she wanted by any means. When she was younger and had less opportunity to achieve things for herself, she would channel this energy through me. She wanted me to do well in life, but also pushed me into things as a way of making her family proud of *her*. I knew she loved my dad; they were both working class and seemed happy with their lot most of the time. However, I got a sense very early on that all bets were on *me* to prove their worth. They may not have managed to level up within the family system, but they still had a chance to do it through their daughter. A lot was expected of me and in order to achieve it, I had to dive in at the deep end.

Chapter 2

DIVING IN AT THE DEEP END

I first met Ray Infield, Kate's father, at the Brighton ice rink when I was 15. He was about my height – 5ft 4in – so on the shorter side, but he had lovely dark curly hair, an infectious smile and a great personality. He also seemed manly in a strange way – I wasn't used to that so it intrigued and excited me. At the time, he was an apprentice TV engineer, and I was impressed by the fact he had a maroon and yellow scooter and seemed to be going somewhere in the world. He seemed to like the fact I was a bit quirky. I had crazy curly bleached hair and wore it short, just an inch long. Unlike most other girls my age who were in miniskirts and boots, I used to dress in sports stuff. In fact, I was one of the first of my friends to own a pair of Adidas trainers. Ray and I seemed ideally suited to each other and we tried to spend as many spare moments as we could together. But spare moments were few and far between as I had another commitment that took up much of my time: swimming.

I began swimming simply because I couldn't bear to be second best to a girl called Linda Baker. She was in my class at Fairlight Infant School in Brighton (the last year before senior school), and I was in awe of her pretty brown hair and the fact that – unlike me – she hardly ever got told off by our aptly named teacher Miss Blunt, a bespectacled, grey-haired spinster who seemed devoid of emotion of any kind. Linda lived at the bottom of my road in Hollingdean so I used to play with her after school. I gradually learned about this magical world she would disappear into, called Shiverers Swimming Club. Once she invited me to join her and I was transfixed by her mastery of freestyle – calm legs and breath with arms and head swishing gracefully from side to side. When I had a go, it didn't quite turn out like that and I badly wanted to do better, to swim *properly*, like Linda. So I enrolled with Shiverers and started training. I didn't tell my mum and dad about my new hobby because they weren't particularly interested, and it kept me out of trouble.

Looking back, I suppose my love of swimming wasn't surprising as my mum had started her working life as a mermaid, but it quickly went from what I'd describe as a passion to a calling. At Shiverers, they offered me a modest membership and I made the most of it, acquainting myself with two amazing instructors called Mr Reeves and Mr Franklin, who began to teach me the basics of professional swimming. 'You need to do as much work outside the swimming pool as you do in it,' they used to say while making me practise my technique in front of a mirror.

By the age of 12, I was training every Tuesday and Friday religiously, until I was ready for a very important race at the school swimming gala held at North Road swimming baths. It was a one-length race against other pupils, including Linda and, to everyone's amazement I won. My parents had come to watch and couldn't believe it; they weren't even aware at that stage that I could swim. It just felt fantastic. My parents and I might be considered the poor relations within our family, but I could now prove our worth another way – in the swimming pool. I carried on swimming with a new determination after that and got better and better. Then, as things progressed and started to get more serious, mum and dad became more involved, taking me to training meetings and willing me to go further and faster. I think it became obsessive for them. If things didn't go well, I would dread the dressing down at home. It's very hard for me to reflect on it now, but once or twice my dad even hit me when I did badly out of frustration, because he thought I could have swum better that day, or because he thought I hadn't tried hard enough.

The swimming notched up a gear and it wasn't long before my parents realised that if I was going to reach the top levels, I'd need to be training in London, where the standard of swimmers was higher and there were better coaches. My parents picked out a professional swimming teacher from the *Swimming Times* magazine and they wanted me to meet him at a pool in Bayswater, London. From then on, as well as continuing my training with Shiverers during the week, I would take instruction from a coach called Reginald R. Laxton each Saturday, before spending the remainder of the day exploring the capital by myself. I've always loved visiting museums, so it was a chance to get to know places like the Natural History Museum and the Tate Gallery. One day, while training with Mr Laxton at Crystal Palace, I was spotted by a well-known coach who persuaded me to train with him instead. Training at Crystal Palace made me swim better; it made me feel like a professional. The pool was fifty metres in length and had electric timers at either end, which made it feel like a step up from the public baths I was used to. My time was soon split between Crystal Palace and Shiverers in Hove, as well as Brighton, where the council gave me the sole use of the North Road baths during lunchtimes when it was closed. That's where I first encountered the dark side of swimming.

There was a lifeguard at the North Road swimming baths who made me feel uncomfortable. It was just me and him in the pool area during those lunchtime sessions and, one day, he suddenly jumped into the water and swam towards me. My stomach lurched and I asked myself, *How are you going to get away from him Amy?* I was terrified. Thinking fast, I instinctively told him, 'I'm swimming. I'm not interested.' Luckily, just in the nick of time, a maintenance man appeared to fix the coffee machine and my would-be molester was forced to leave the water to help out. I quickly followed suit, leaping out of the pool, pulling my dress on and running for the bus. I didn't even dry myself. My heart was racing on the journey back to school and my head was pounding with thoughts of what could have happened to me.

Sadly, there was no one at school or at home who I felt comfortable confiding in. Would my mum and dad even believe me, or would they just dismiss it? So much was at stake for my ambitious parents, who were willing me to succeed in the world of swimming and sacrificing a lot to make it a reality

– how could I allude to a fly in the ointment now? The truth is I never felt safe in those swimming baths again. Instead – without causing a fuss – I made some excuse about the London training being more beneficial and continued taking the 3pm train to the Crystal Palace sessions. Little did I know I was walking into yet another trap.

My new coach held a very powerful position in the world of swimming and his 'mentoring' of my career meant my parents no longer had to pay for coaching fees, which was a considerable relief to them – in those days, there was no such thing as sponsorship. They had already spent a fortune on train fares but seemed to think the sacrifices were worth it now I was one of the top swimmers in my age group. Even though I was in love with swimming, there were sacrifices for me too. I didn't really get the chance to have a normal adolescence because the punishing training regime meant no life outside the pool. The only friends I had were in the Crystal Palace swimming world and we all stuck to the same rules: no alcohol and *definitely* no sex – we were told it would ruin our performance. But it seemed that different, darker rules applied to the coaches who wielded a lot of power.

My coach and I had a respectful relationship to begin with, but gradually he began picking on me if I did something subversive like wear make-up. I developed a bad feeling about him and didn't like the way he put his arms around my female team mates when they got out of the water or when he was chatting with them. He tried once or twice to put his arm around me, and I simply said, 'No,' but I sensed he didn't like the knock back.

One day I was entered into a really important qualifier to become a junior international and he said I would need to go to his flat to prepare. I begged my parents not to make me go but they didn't see him in the same light and told me I would be fine. Once we were inside his seedy bachelor pad, he told me I would need a 'massage' to prepare my muscles for the races and he proceeded to climb on top of me. I remember lying there, frozen with fear, thinking, *I can't let this happen.* I felt vulnerable, alone and powerless. My heart seemed to be beating at twice its normal rate. I was panic stricken but somehow, I managed to speak and I told him, 'Just don't bother – I've got a boyfriend; you just don't do anything for me. I'm not interested in you so just get off.' He jerked away from me, telling me never to tell anyone in case he got into trouble.

It was at this time that I met Ray, so our meeting occurred at an opportune moment. Swimming had started out as a fun hobby but was beginning to feel more burdensome, which made romantic possibilities very attractive. He was a cheeky chappie and I looked forward to seeing him on my rare days off from swimming. He was a good-looking boy, but he didn't have a muscly physique like all the swimmers I socialized with. Perhaps that was part of the attraction – I wanted to be with someone different.

Soon after our ice rink encounter, we started going out together once a week, as that's all that I was allowed, and then gradually we would meet up on the train when I was returning from training at Crystal Palace. I soon confided in Ray about the incident with my swimming coach and he wanted to have it out with the coach, but I wouldn't let him. I loved the fact he was so protective of me and, whenever he finished work or college on a Thursday, he would come to collect me at the Crystal Palace pool, and we'd travel home together. Other nights he would catch the train and meet me at the station in Croydon, but he would be sure to get off at Preston Park so that my parents, who were usually waiting for me at Brighton, were none the wiser. In my mind, Ray was my knight in shining armour who was protecting me from a dark force, and it made falling in love with him somewhat inevitable. My parents eventually found out about him after his mum and dad called them to say they had discovered he was spending a fortune on train tickets – all his savings. They went mad but, by then, I had a place in the junior international swimming team and there wasn't much they could do to stop me so they agreed I could occasionally see Ray, as long as I kept to a 9pm curfew.

I maintained the status quo for as long as I could but my coach had cast a dark shadow across the pool. I think I also just came to the point where my dream of living a normal life outweighed my desire to go all the way with swimming. Physically, I was still fit as a fiddle but mentally, I was thinking, *No more.* I was coming up to 18 and preparing for an important race at Crystal Palace to qualify as a junior international, but I just knew it was the end of the road for me in the pool because I had no life of my own and desperately wanted one. So I finally stepped out of the water and onto solid ground – or so I hoped. My only regret is that I did not get the qualifying time to secure my place at the 1968 Mexico City Olympics. I had achieved it in training so I knew I could do it, but I also knew if I had committed myself to all the preparation it entailed, I would have returned home to no friends at all in Brighton, as it was a long acclimatisation in Mexico, and I wasn't prepared to lose the few friends I had made through Ray.

I needed to find something positive to fill the void in my life so I decided to return to the academic studies I had abandoned for swimming and enrolled on a business studies course at Brighton Technical College. Ray also attended the college once a week, so that was very convenient. He would also come to see me at home whenever he could, and we established a regular weekend routine of going to the pub with friends on Saturdays and to the cinema on Sundays. Perhaps our routine became too regular, because I soon realized I missed the thrill of the chase while I was still swimming. As soon as I gave it all up, the dynamic between us subtly shifted and he started spending more time with his mates.

I have to say the situation wasn't helped by my controlling parents. Even at the age of 20, I wasn't allowed to stay out at night and when I returned home from an evening out with Ray, my mum would inspect all my clothes – including my underwear – to see if any hanky panky had taken place. I used to think to myself, *How stupid – do you really think I would keep the same pair of knickers on, knowing the routine inspection was looming?* Of course not. I just made the necessary adjustments to my garments before returning home and I took the pill in Ray's car. I couldn't go to our family doctor for advice as he would undoubtedly have told my mum, so I went to a family planning clinic instead. I wish my parents had been forward-

thinking types who praised me for taking the initiative
and being sensible about birth control, but it was the complete opposite. In their eyes, I needed to be a virgin when I
got married. I remember one night when Ray had got too
drunk to drive me home and I'd stayed the night with him.
The next day, we woke up to find a message on the windscreen of Ray's van, reading 'Thank you for ruining my
daughter's life'. It had been put there by my dad. How dramatic! Perhaps they still needed to project that perfect family
image onto me – whatever the reasons behind the thinking,
I was the one who had to suffer the consequences.

Life at college flourished – after I had gained the business studies qualification, I began a secretarial course, and
then found a job as a secretary for a leasing manager at the
NatWest Bank at Preston Park in Brighton. I was at work
when an awful accident befell our family. One afternoon, I
heard multiple sirens, including ambulances, as they passed
our building. It later transpired that they were hurtling
towards a tragedy which was close to home. My Uncle Alec
had had a heart attack at the wheel of the car, which resulted
in a collision on the main London to Brighton road. He died
on impact, while my Uncle Leslie and Aunt Kate were badly
injured in the crash.

Sadness overcame the family and, looking back, it might
have been the distraction that clouded my judgement. I had
a nagging feeling of doubt about my relationship with Ray.
Before I met him, swimming had completely engulfed my life
and I had had little chance to socialize and build up a group
of friends. Most of the friends Ray and I saw were his mates

and, as I knew so little about the world outside swimming, the prospect of being on my own was too scary to contemplate. So, before we knew it, we were sleepwalking into a mortgage and a marriage.

The house came first. It was a mid-terrace, two-bedroom new build in Hailsham, East Sussex, an affordable area near Eastbourne. We had to leave all our friends and family behind in Brighton to get our feet on the property ladder and we hated it. Until we were married, I could never stay there overnight. My parents' determination for us not to sleep together before we were married meant that we were having to travel back to Brighton every time we visited the house so that I could stay with them. It was no life for youngsters; we really should have rented somewhere closer to home to see if we could get on and live together, and, looking back, it's not surprising that our lives were fraught with argument. But I still wouldn't listen to my parents, who thought Ray was wrong for me.

Not only did my parents control my life before the wedding, my mum took over control of the entire ceremony itself. She had a history of this, having previously arranged my 21st birthday at her friend's house opposite where we lived, only because this woman happened to be throwing a party at the same time. I assume it was because she wanted to avoid the mess. I was told I could invite just two friends. My wedding reception was in the hall next to the church in Hangleton. All our relatives and mum and dad's friends were invited, but I was limited to just one table for *my* friends. The music, food, alcohol and flowers were all my mum's choice. By then,

I had been conditioned to think it was normal for my mum to arrange my life so I didn't think to question it.

My grandad had died and we had our pick of what furniture and carpets were left from his home to decorate our house. A couple of weeks before the wedding, I was looking through some boxes we'd brought back from grandad's. They were next to some boxes Ray had brought from his house and, in one of those, I stumbled across some letters Ray had been writing to another woman about their love affair. I was in shock and felt my heart was breaking, but what could I do? It is easy to forget how different things were for women fifty years ago. Equality was a concept way off in the future. Women were expected to do as they were told and leave the major decisions up to the men! I was hurt, angry, confused – I cried on my own because I couldn't bring myself to tell anyone, least of all my parents, because I felt they would call the wedding off and they would have been so disappointed. All the arrangements had been made and we had a serious, joint financial responsibility in the form of a house. Of course I challenged him, but he simply said, 'There's nothing in it'. So I felt I had no choice but to walk down the aisle in September 1974. I was desperate to believe the love he had shown for me when he defended me from my swimming coach was real, and that things would come good in the end.

For my wedding, I had chosen a white dress from the cover of a magazine and a big floppy hat which hid the mixed emotions etched on my face. The truth was I loved Ray, but I no longer trusted him. There were so many thoughts and feelings coursing through me as I took my dad's arm ready to walk down the aisle. He must have picked up on them because he suddenly looked at me and said, 'It's not too late to turn back'. But as far as I was concerned, it *was* too late. Just like he had done his duty in the war, I felt it was my turn to do my duty at the altar – Keep Calm and Carry On.

Ray and I couldn't afford a honeymoon, so we had dinner at a pub on the way back to our house after the wedding. It was the first time we had slept there together. Suddenly, I had to become a housewife and I was ill-equipped for the job, to say the least. My mum had been so busy trying to turn me into a swimming sensation that she had neglected to teach me how to cook – I didn't even know you had to wash vegetables before eating them. For our first Christmas together, I bought a turkey but I didn't realize it had to be defrosted. Some days, I would just sit and cry, feeling like a total failure, isolated from my community in Brighton. I even started to feel homesick, like a small child who wanted to be helped and looked after. I remember sitting on the bathroom floor crying – I wanted to go back to my mum and dad's.

We were both working hard – Ray was making trips all across Sussex as a TV engineer so he was home late most nights and had to get up at the crack of dawn. It was exhausting for him and, on reflection, I understand the pressures he faced. The area he had to cover for his work had expanded and this meant more travelling and longer hours. We never really settled in our place in Hailsham; soon we'd had enough of commuting so we decided to sell up and move back closer to Brighton. We managed to buy a bungalow in Patcham and that's where our first child, Daniel, was born. He was named after Ray's favourite Elton John song. I'd like to say my pregnancy was a happy one, but sadly that wasn't the reality. I was fit and healthy, but I was under a lot of stress from our marriage. To make up for his long hours, Ray had resorted to letting his hair down in pubs and nightclubs, or by playing snooker, so I spent most of my time with my mum, feeling upset at the way our relationship was turning out. I don't think Ray understood, and consequently was not prepared for, the responsibilities of having a child – he just wanted to do what *he* wanted to do and maintain his social life. I felt so vulnerable and alone. All I wanted was for my husband to be by my side while I was pregnant, but the reality was different – I was very miserable.

There were bills to pay, so I worked at the NatWest bank right up until a fortnight before Dan was born. I used to finish at 5pm and wait for Ray to pick me up if he wasn't working. But he was always late, and the waiting around used to really upset me. Like any first-time expectant mum, I just wanted him to reassure and take care of me. I wanted the old Ray back – the Ray who had been a knight in shining armour, ready to defend me against the lecherous swimming coach. Instead I felt like a discarded after-thought as I paced the pavement, wondering how much longer my aching back would take the strain. I just felt devastated. It was a case of too much, too soon – we were both immature and not at all ready for all the pressure to come.

Dan was eventually born on time on 2nd January 1975 in the middle of the night, weighing a healthy 8lb 10oz at the Sussex County Hospital in Brighton. The 27-hour labour was excruciating; at the time, I didn't know what I'd done to deserve it. Even the doctor refused to stay in the room. He just looked at me through the window and when he did breeze in, he would say the same thing every time, 'Don't worry – it will be over in an hour'. Well it wasn't – in the end, I had an epidural but having a bad back made things complicated. Only half my back went numb, so I could still feel everything else. It all felt barbaric and nothing had prepared me for it, least of all the bloody classes I had diligently attended as an eager first-time mum.

Holding my little baby boy in my arms made it all worthwhile, though, and we formed a close bond from the very beginning, which still exists to this day. It's hardly surprising given it was just me and him in the world together from the word go. To be fair, Ray had been popping in and out during the labour, but he didn't want to see the actual birth – it's not for everybody. For me, despite the pain, it was magical. As soon as they placed Dan on me after he was born, I was instantly in love with him. I was fascinated by how he looked and examined him all over. I couldn't take my eyes off him and thought he was the most beautiful baby I had ever seen – just perfect in every way. I was so proud of him. Even when the nurses placed him back in his see-through cot, I couldn't stop staring at him and all the pain and suffering I had endured instantly went away. Dan had incredibly long fingers and dark hair and he seemed as interested in me as I was in him. He would drink me in with his huge eyes and look at everything around him too. He was definitely a good eater, and I had no trouble feeding him.

My husband was elated to have a baby boy who he could

take fishing with him, but the gift of a Hoover that he presented me with when I got home made me feel as though I was more of a domestic object than a beloved partner. During the pregnancy, Ray had stopped showing me much affection and things didn't improve after Dan was born. When Dan was about six months old, Ray told me, 'I want to do what I want, when I want, with whom I want' and he pretty much did. By that time, he was seeing a doctor for what he told me was depression and we were also having marriage counselling because I desperately wanted a normal family life. Even just the simple pleasures, like eating dinner together as a family, would have changed things so positively for me. I wondered what it was I was doing wrong – was it because I was pregnant or getting fat? Looking back, I can see that I did nothing wrong at all.

The fear of financial disaster was a big theme in our marriage – not knowing if we had enough money to pay the bills and keep a roof over our heads. I was determined to do my bit – after all, I'd seen my mum and dad grafting all their lives – but I wasn't prepared to compromise my son's upbringing to do so. Eventually, I took on cleaning jobs from 6–8am and again from 6–8pm and during those times Ray was at home with Dan. But apart from this, Ray wasn't a very hands-on dad. His job meant that he came home at different hours, and he seemed to be working most of the time. However, it turned out his 'employment' was not just concerned with bringing home a decent wage.

Eventually, I learned from a mutual friend that Ray was having an affair and, with their help, I found out his girlfriend's address and concocted a dramatic Jeremy Kyle-style plan which involved me, my mum, and our 10-month-old son knocking on her door. You can probably deduce that there is a penchant for drama running through our family, and it was in full force that day.

Ray's girlfriend was quite a bit younger than him – in fact, shockingly, she was just 16 going on 17. When we knocked, her parents answered the door. I told them who we were and they invited us in, clearly pleased to have some potential allies to help break up the relationship. Apparently, Ray had untruthfully told them we were separated, and that he only saw Dan at weekends. I could hardly believe what I was hearing when the girl's parents suggested we go through to the garden and wait under the apple trees until they invited Ray in for a cup of tea. That's when the drama really ramped up to box office standard.

Suddenly, the doorbell rang and I heard Ray saying, 'That's nice. Thank you. I'd love a cup of tea'. The next thing he knew, he and his girlfriend were sitting in the lounge with cups of tea in their hands, then we walked in and they looked like they had seen a ghost. His girlfriend was young and pretty with long hair. In the end, we had a conversation rather than a heated argument and I explained that he was still living with me and that we had undergone therapy to try to save our marriage which I thought was being impacted by his depression. I could see she was upset for me and the lies he had told both of us. I didn't hate her because I instinctively knew she understood what I was going through, even though she was so young. She apologized, saying she didn't know and that she would never see him again. All Ray could say was, 'I've been caught, haven't I?' At that moment, I felt strangely relieved – my suspicions that his lack of interest in our family was caused by him having an affair were now confirmed. Now I didn't have to blame myself for our marriage failings. But I was also angry at his deceit and the lies he had told me, her, and the therapist.

I asked for his keys to our house and told him he would need to get his clothes another day. Enough was enough. He handed them over with no questions and my mum and I left with Dan. Ray and I made the joint decision that we should split up and sell the house, but circumstances seemed to conspire to keep us together. I found a flat in Hangleton that I liked but on my earnings alone I couldn't get a mortgage, so Ray agreed that we would apply in joint names. He offered to help with the decorating, and also looked after Dan some mornings while I continued to clean. We'd fallen back into the old arrangement where he would turn up in the early morning and late evening so I could work. And before long, we thought we would try to weather the storm and make another go of it, for Dan's sake. This set up a pattern of unhealthy relationships that I would see repeated time and again in Kate's life. Behind closed doors, despite people seeing us as the ideal couple, nothing had changed for Ray and me.

At this stage, I was emotionally battered. I couldn't help but ask myself why Ray didn't love me. What had I done wrong? Why wasn't I enough for him? I'm sure these are questions that many women in the same position have asked themselves. I could understand Ray's wandering eye if I had done something wrong, but I hadn't. It might seem desperate, but Ray's friends had become mine too, and I was scared of being left out on a limb, just as I had been when I quit swimming. I was scared of having to make new friends and meet someone else. I look back now and think how I should have made a clean break from Ray much sooner because, eventually, I lost respect for him.

However, when Dan was around three years old, I had decided to give Ray another chance.

The arrangement of him popping in and out to look after Dan when I went off cleaning wasn't very satisfactory for any of us, so we agreed to make a proper go of things and buy a semi-detached house with a 300ft garden on top of a hill in Portslade, Brighton. Perhaps unsurprisingly given that we were trying to regrow our relationship, we became obsessed with gardening and spent hours building rockeries, ponds, vegetable patches – the full works. But it wasn't enough to keep us together. Was it Einstein who said the definition of madness is repeating the same thing and expecting a different outcome? Well, he was right because things soon slipped back to their old ways. By now Ray was dealing in antiques and working away a lot. His drinking and gambling habits had worsened and if I challenged him, he could be aggressive, punching doors and throwing things – although thankfully he never hit me.

I always stood my ground with Ray. Once, when he left yet another lovingly made Sunday dinner to go cold and uneaten, I put it on the green of the 18th hole of the local golf course where he could usually be found. There was nothing nourishing left in our relationship but somehow it just rolled on and it was during that turbulent time I fell pregnant with our second child. That's when our story really begins.

Chapter 3

IT'S A GIRL! MEET KATRINA AMY ALEXANDRIA ALEXIS INFIELD

The terrible sickness I endured during the first four months of my pregnancy with Kate was the first sign of the sleepless nights she would cause me later in life. It was so bad I was given medication, which eventually made me drowsy and allowed me to get some rest. I was working from home on secretarial projects for exhibition companies at the time, which allowed me time to recover and really suited my life as a young mum. I could work all the hours I wanted and fit them in around three-year-old Dan's time at the local playgroup, which he loved. It also meant I no longer had to suffer the indignity of waiting for Ray to pick me up after work and I could rest when I felt tired, especially after bouts of terrible morning sickness.

Nothing has ever been straightforward with Kate. Daniel's name had been easy, but up until eight months into my second pregnancy, I still hadn't come to a decision over the baby's name. Then fate stepped in. For some reason, my mind drifted back to the terrible fatal accident involving my uncles and aunt, so I decided then and there that my daughter's

40

names should reflect our family legacy: 'Katrina' after my aunt Kate; 'Amy' after me and my grandmother; 'Alexandria' and 'Alexis' after my Uncle Alec. To me, it felt respectful to preserve the family history in this way and I was disappointed when – 18 years later – Kate formally changed her name to Katie Price. Recently, I asked her why and she said bluntly, 'How would you like to be named after dead people?' I can see her point but if I'm angry or need to get her attention, I still shout, 'K-a-t-r-i-n-a' and it usually works – she has always hated it.

When I went into labour, my waters had to be broken by the doctors, then I had to wait 12 hours for Katrina Amy Alexandria Alexis Infield to emerge on 22nd May 1978. I think it's fair to say she did not enter the world smoothly. Just like with Dan, the pain was excruciating and I kept begging doctors for an epidural, but they refused. They said I was too far gone, and anyway a second baby always comes quicker than the first. So I was left with pethidine, gas, air and pure grit and determination. Apparently, my screams were so loud that people could hear me right down the corridors of the maternity wing at the Sussex County Hospital. I know this because I kept in contact with two mums who were giving birth at the same time, and they told me that my blood-curdling yelps had frightened them half to death. To this day, one of them is still a valued and kind friend to me.

Even when Kate – as she later became known – was finally ready to launch the full force of her personality on Planet Earth, she couldn't resist presenting me with one last little challenge. Her hand was positioned under her chin, which meant she scratched me as she left the birth canal and I had to be painfully stitched up. Looking back, I wonder if Mother Nature was preparing me for the challenges that lay ahead – but at the time, all I could think about as I lay there exhausted, cuddling my 7lb baby girl, was that we had made it through to the other side together. Just like with Dan, I was transfixed by every part of her and to me, she was perfect – smaller than her brother yet content. As she was snuggled in her pink blanket in the cot next to me, I kept looking at her and thinking how lucky I was. I now had the perfect pair, a beautiful boy and a gorgeous girl. Sadly, once again, Ray was not even attempting to play the part of the doting husband and dad. While I had been writhing in pain, he was doing his usual ducking and diving, flogging antiques in the hospital carpark. Doctors, nurses, patients and visitors alike were being treated to the full catalogue of Infield Inc items, including furniture, artwork, china, jewellery (anything he could get his hands on basically), all on display to prospective buyers in the back of his Vauxhall estate car. Talk about a Del Boy moment! God knows where most of it came from. During the time we were together, I got so fed up with coming home to find he had sold our cherished items of furniture – I was forced to buy them all off him with my hard-earned money so he couldn't sell anything on without consulting me first.

To be fair, Ray stayed with me during the labour on and off – as he had done with Dan – but he wasn't actually in the room when Kate was born, and I think that set a precedent for his role as an absent father in both her and Dan's life. By now, we were getting along better but the relationship had changed – he was independent and so was I. It was more like a friendship than a marriage and that's how we rubbed along. We were quite emotionally cut off from one another, so when it became apparent that something was wrong with Kate, I started to feel very alone. Kate wasn't feeding in the same way Dan had; I needed to work really hard to get her to suck the teat of the bottle and she would go blue around the lips. I was really worried about it. Ten days later, when a paediatric heart specialist came to see Kate, the diagnosis was clear: 'She's got a hole in the heart.' I was devastated, but glad I had trusted my instincts and battled for a diagnosis – a determination that Kate would also show after giving birth to her first son 24 years later.

Kate and I remained in the maternity hospital for ten days after her birth because I refused to leave until she had seen a heart specialist. At this point, her medical care was handed over to a children's hospital, which continued to monitor her for a further 18 months. In the end, the hole in her heart healed by itself but she continued to be a really sickly baby. There had never been any health worries with Dan, so it was really daunting for me, trying to care for this poorly little girl alongside a lively toddler. I used to check in on Kate all the time when she was sleeping to make sure she was still breathing – and for good reason. When Kate was three months old, she caught whooping cough. Sometimes she would turn blue while trying to catch her breath and was often sick while coughing, bringing up all her food in the process. Her coughing was so bad she developed a hernia in her belly button and looked so miserable and lifeless. I just wanted to wrap her up in cotton wool to protect her from everything and everyone – a feeling which has never really gone away.

By this point, Ray was working as a fully fledged antiques dealer, which required him to go away a lot, so my mum and dad stayed to help me in the night with Kate, who had whooping cough. I had become so much better at being on my own, but Kate's health concerns meant I was just too frightened to sleep at night. The relationship with my parents hadn't always been easy, as I've explained, but they were there for me when I needed them most and I will always be grateful for that. Looking after Kate together, we developed a closer bond, and I knew that they supported me – now, without judgement. They had long ago accepted I wasn't going to elevate our family into wealth by marriage and I no longer felt any pressure to 'perform' for them. We all used to go to bed at night with an ear open, waiting for Kate's coughing to alert us to her distress. I'll never forget the night when she was about three months old and she stopped breathing. My dad instinctively grabbed her by the feet, turned her upside down and slapped her back. Lots of phlegm came up and we just stood there, terrified, waiting for her to breathe. My dad was a tower of strength and could operate in this way without any fuss or panic – his army training enabled him to become a lifeline for his little granddaughter.

I think watching my mum and dad care for Dan and Kate taught me the importance of a grandparent's role, and it's certainly something I've tried to live up to for all my children and their children – but especially for Kate. She has spent so much of her life as a single mum, and I can empathize with that struggle because that's how I felt a lot of the time with Ray. My dad used to play games with both Kate and Dan when they were young. My mum used to come with me and watch them swimming, or taking part in sports days and school plays. My dad would make them sandwiches and cups of tea. He used to talk to them about everything and Kate used to love brushing his hair. As the children got older, they used to pop in and see my mum and dad just for a chat.

By this stage, I didn't fancy Ray anymore and the feeling was no doubt mutual. I began to wonder what it would be like to be with someone I was really attracted to and – most importantly – someone who would love and care for me and my children. Was I content to go through life settling for second best? No, I wasn't but I did have to keep a roof over our heads, and for that, I needed Ray. What's more, I'd lost all confidence in myself, resigning myself to believing I was unattractive. It was a genuine surprise on the occasions I went to the pub and men paid me compliments. I'm sure Ray was feeling equally bored and rejected at the time, too.

Part of the reason I kept my distance from Ray at this time could have been because he was beginning to lose his hair in his twenties, which brought back difficult memories of my abusive swimming coach. So severe was my trauma, that I even found a clinic and arranged for its sales rep to come and visit us at home to see if he would consider a hair transplant. When the guy arrived and explained why he had called, Ray simply said, 'No!' and shut the door in his face. He then turned to me, exasperated, asking why. I said matter-of-factly that I simply thought he would like to have hair again, concealing the real reasons behind my madcap scheme. I just didn't feel safe enough in the relationship to communicate these feelings or know where to start. With hindsight, I would have been better off seeing a therapist than a hair transplant clinic. Looking back, I think how hurtful this must have been for Ray.

By the time Kate was three, her health problems had finally subsided and she began to develop like any other child. She loved cuddles but, despite everything she'd been through, she wasn't a clingy baby and I was able to drop her off at playschool groups when I needed a break or had work to do. Dan used to go to clubs too and I think having an older brother meant Kate was – developmentally – quite advanced because she had someone to look up to and play with. When she got a bit older, she had a favourite game she would beg Dan to play. She used to make him go down on all fours and would get on his back, pretending to ride a horse around the living room. When it was Dan's turn, he preferred turning Kate into a typewriter, tapping away on her back. They were quite close, and she probably enjoyed having a ready-made playmate because she was quite shy and loved nothing more than playing in the garden with her favourite toys – her Tender Heart Care Bear, My Little Pony and Rainbow Bright Doll.

Kate also loved all our animals, which included dogs, cats, a rabbit, a budgie and even a lizard which belonged to Dan. One day, to my horror, I found locusts jumping all round his bedroom after he had tried feeding them to his reptile roommate. It sounded like we were living in a jungle. On another occasion, when Kate was a little older, I received a phone call from our local pet shop to say they had rabbits for sale. Kate asked if she could have one, but I refused because we already had enough pets. A few days later, I had another call from the shopkeeper who said he had my cheque for the cost of a hutch, straw, food and a rabbit and he wondered when it would be convenient to deliver them. I couldn't believe it – Kate had taken a cheque out of my cheque book, signed it and then posted it to the pet shop. I confronted her about this and she confessed. I told her it was wrong, but at the same time I couldn't help but admire her entrepreneurial spirit – it reminded me of when I sold my mum's clothes and her plants to go horse riding. A few weeks later, I relented and bought her the rabbit and hutch.

Despite all the challenges I faced in my marriage with Ray and looking after Kate and Dan, I loved being in our house. It needed a lot of work, but it was worth it to be in the countryside surrounded by fields. It was during this period I finally realized my dream of owning my own horse – a 14.3 hands part Arab called Raffles. I kept him at the farm just along the road, so it was easy for me to look after him. Subject to my mum helping me out with the children, I used to feed him and clean out his stable in the mornings and evenings, and ride him whenever I got the chance. It was such a wonderful feeling to leave behind my role as wife and mother for an hour or two and gallop out across the fields with the wind in my hair. Sadly, it just wasn't feasible to juggle everything long term, and I had to sell him after a year, but it helped to instil a passion for riding in Kate, who is at her happiest when she is in the saddle. Kate had riding lessons at Ditchling Stud for years, and now she does the same thing with her own children at another livery yard.

The only thing that was missing from my life was someone who cared for me. Ray and I enjoyed going to our local pub at weekends and it wasn't long before everyone got to know each other. Everyone thought we were the ideal couple, full of fun and laughter. One day, I spotted a guy who my mum had previously introduced to me as 'The Greengrocer'. I had first met him when I was picking her up from the shops and he was helping mum to carry her bags to my car. We got talking and mum told him I was looking for somewhere to live because we were thinking of selling the house in Patcham and splitting up. He turned and pointed to the flat above the shop and said I could live there if I was stuck. I didn't take him up on his offer, but every time mum returned to the shop he asked her if I'd found anywhere. So when I spotted him in the pub, we got talking and he told me he visited our pub because it was his football team's local, and he was there every weekend. He seemed to have a reputation as a womanizer and a Jack the Lad who would get cheered on by his team each time he left to go on a date with a woman. He must have had a huge ego because there were always women fawning over him.

Before long, I started to feel flattered when he spoke to me or said hello while other women looked on enviously. Ray didn't seem to mind or – perhaps more accurately – notice. We would catch each other's eye even if we weren't in the same group and we enjoyed chatting to each other. One thing led to another and what started as cheeky chitchat ended up in what youngsters these days would probably call a 'friends with benefits' relationship. He lived with his brother and, once in a while, when my parents or a close friend were looking after the kids, I would go back to his place. Each time, I felt a heady mixture of nerves and excitement because it had been such a long time since another man had seen me as feminine and sexual, rather than a mum or housewife – I truly felt like a woman again. I can remember physically shaking and muddling up my words when we talked, and I was really clumsy around him. In some ways, the affair was inevitable given how far apart Ray and I had grown, but I knew it allowed me to avoid facing up to the problems in my marriage. I started to like this guy a lot, but I also knew it would go nowhere. Perhaps that was part of the reason why I let it continue. In the end, it was short-lived because we were once again struggling to pay our bills and had to move to a smaller place in Hove to settle our debts. My relationship with the greengrocer came to an end after just three months, but we are still good friends with him and his wife after all these years.

Despite all the emotional ups and downs, I relished my role as a mother and loved watching the kids grow up together. Being a mum to two small children came with its accidents, though. I remember Kate using Dan's skateboard – she would get down on her knees and push herself off over the pavement. One day, she crashed and landed face down. She came running into me crying with blood coming out of her mouth – I panicked when I saw that she had badly chipped her front tooth. I took her to the dentist after putting the broken piece of tooth in milk (I don't know where I got that from!), only to be told that the remains of the tooth in Kate's mouth could change colour and die. We didn't want to risk it, so Kate eventually had a veneer put on it – the first in a long line of dental procedures she would have done as she got older. I often wonder if she would have left her teeth alone had this broken tooth been repaired more successfully.

Kate had a close friend called Claire at primary school, but otherwise she was quite a solitary child who seemed content to focus on her sports. As she got older, they included swimming, horse riding and cross-country running. Dan was very sporty too and excelled at cross-country running, long jump, football and swimming. But Kate wasn't an extrovert in any sense of the word. In fact, she just blended in, which is extraordinary when you think of everything that would unfold in her adult life. She used to come with me when I did my aerobic workouts, and she was very close to my mum who used to spend hours brushing her hair when it eventually grew (for the first two years of her life, she had none at all and then a mass of curls just appeared from nowhere!). My mum definitely formed a close bond with Kate after helping to look after her in her critical early years; I think Kate would probably agree that some of her happiest times were spent going shopping with her nan and me when she was young, ending up in Woolworths with a comforting cup of tea and a delicious piece of cake while eyeing up the toy counter. She has always been most content with the simplest of family pleasures. Their closeness meant that my mum told Kate all about the torment and bullying she'd endured at school, coming from a Jewish background. Little did my mum know how Kate would one day tread this path herself, experiencing the same sort of demonization and bullying, initially for nothing more than a failed marriage.

I tried to make our family life as solid as possible for Dan and Kate, but the reality was that by the time Dan was seven and Kate was four, my marriage to Ray was under ever-increasing pressure. His work was still not going well (not least because he continued to gamble) and we were in a lot of trouble financially and had to move. I didn't want to go out to work full time and leave my children, but equally I didn't want to be in a position where I was reliant on Ray for money – so I decided to take in some of the overseas students who flocked to Brighton to learn English by the sea.

Fortunately, I found a five-bedroom house right in the middle of the student district in Hove. It was a bit cheaper than a lot of other properties on the market because it backed onto a railway line and it needed work. Somehow, Ray and I managed to sell our house in Portslade, pay the bank back what we owed and retain £250 for a deposit on a new mortgage. I had a fantastic mortgage broker back then who managed to secure us a new contract. I also decided it was time for me to have my own bank account and even managed to persuade the bank manager to lend me some extra money for new curtains, carpets and bedding. Before long, I had done the place up and was offering lodgings to 13 students throughout the summer. During the winter months, four Middle Eastern students joined us, who understandably thought the English winter was atrocious. Some of them were from countries at war with one another but there was harmony in my house and I was proud of that. Some of the young men from more conservative cultures found it strange that a female was in charge, but they soon realized they had to respect me. The students may have learned the English language in their classes, but they learned about the culture at their lodgings. I had to teach them to clean the bathroom after they had finished using it and to put dirty washing in the laundry basket, rather than back into drawers with their clean clothes. It was all done in a friendly way and we ended up having great laughs and learning a lot from each other

It was a really lively, interesting time for me and the kids, and I finally had to learn to cook. I was constantly doing housework and cleaning, but I enjoyed having a full house and the company of others – plus it relieved the financial pressure on me. I could finally take a break from wondering when the money was coming in to pay the bills; in other words, I could pay for our keep. It was quite expensive paying for all the food, electricity and heating, but I still managed to make a little profit from the start. I look back and know they were happy times. Dan still fondly remembers Khalid, one of the Arabic students who stayed with us for two years; he was a huge lad and couldn't speak a word of English when he arrived. He was 18 but still very homesick, so I used to cuddle him!

Before long, my investment really started to pay off: I was making a decent living in a job which meant I could continue to be there for Dan and Kate pretty much all the time. However, the constant washing, cooking and mothering of the students as well as my own children was really exhausting – that's why my best friend's plan seemed so enticing. Her husband was also an antiques dealer and he and Ray used to go away working together. She also took in students and we often met to swap stories. One day, she suggested we go for a holiday during the week when our husbands wouldn't miss us. At first I just laughed, but then I realized she was deadly serious. After years of raising the kids pretty much single-handedly, why shouldn't we have a holiday? We decided to go skiing and I think the travel agent might have thought we worked for MI6 because we instructed him never to contact us on our home phones.

My mum was on board with the plan and agreed to move in to look after Dan, Kate and the students while we were away. My friend's parents had offered to do the same. We had briefed everyone to tell our husbands we had gone to a spa for a couple of days if they returned unexpectedly. Neither of us had ever been skiing, so we took some lessons at a local dry ski centre. We were terrible at skiing, so we never got further than the nursery slopes but we loved every minute of freedom amid the pure white snow. We loved sledging and we found a little cable car to take us up the mountain, where we sipped glühwein and felt on top of the world – a million miles from our lacklustre marriages and domestic drudgery. The only thing we missed was our kids. We were away for seven days and had to face the music when we returned. Ray had got his own back by selling all the bedroom furniture and my friend's husband had spent the money she had saved in the building society to refurbish her kitchen. Our husbands conspired to ban us from ever seeing each other again, but petty rules could not separate us, and together we planned our next great escape on a bench in the local park: DIVORCE.

Chapter 4

MR PAUL PRICE

I'm not sure that I'd have ever been able to make the leap to get a divorce if it wasn't for Paul Price. Paul – or 'Price' as I have always affectionately called him – didn't so much sweep me off my feet as *arrive* at my feet and stay there. When I met him, I had spent so many (*too* many!) years feeling uncertain and unhappy as Ray's wife and I knew divorce was the path I was heading for. Both Ray and I knew we were living different lives; he was 'working away' more and more, but I needed to continue working hard as a student landlady to support my kids so I stayed focussed on earning a living while making plans to end my marriage. That's how Price arrived on the scene. Not with flowers and Champagne, but with a sturdy hammer and a chisel – he came to do the kitchen floor at the student house. When he finished, I thought I'd never see him again but – on the contrary – he never really left my side.

When I first met Price, through Ray, I thought he must have been in his thirties at least. He was quite manly and had a strong physique for his age and had what I thought was a worn face with wrinkles around his brown eyes and a mop of black curly hair. So I was gobsmacked when he told me he was actually 19, a whole nine years my junior, and living above his dad's butcher's shop. After he finished doing our floor, he started working with Ray in the antiques trade. They worked away a lot and when Ray returned to sell the wares he had gathered up, Paul was usually with him. To start with, I wasn't interested in him at all and – if anything – I thought he was a bloody nuisance. He used to listen in to conversations I had with my friends and if I went out, he would occasionally turn up at the same pubs. He used to pop up all over the place like a friendly stalker. He also knew that I was a landlady and one day he asked me if he could pay me to cook him a hot dinner each night, which he said he would eat alongside the students. So – over time – me and the kids got used to seeing him around and before long, it was like he'd always been a part of our household.

I soon learned that Price's dad was an abusive gambler, and that Price would try to protect his mum from the ferocious tornadoes of anger that would tear through the household when he lost. Surviving a difficult childhood was something we had in common and the more I got to know Paul, the more I started to admire the fact that he had made his own way in life after leaving home when he was just 14. A friendship started to grow between us and we used to chat about all sorts of things. Occasionally, Ray would give Price money to take me out for a meal or a drink while he was away or socializing. The idea was that he would keep me company, but it also meant I didn't interrupt Ray's agenda which I already knew involved other women or meeting with his mates.

Price probably felt sorry for me seeing how hard I was

working in the student accommodation, while presumably also knowing what Ray was up to behind my back with his womanizing and gambling. It got to the stage where if I told Price where I was going with my friends, he would usually turn up uninvited. They used to wonder why he was there and I genuinely couldn't give them an answer because I didn't have any inkling that he fancied me. I thought he was attracted to one of my friends. Sometimes, I would be sitting on the beach with the kids and he'd turn up there too, telling me all about his girlfriends. 'Great,' I would say, while privately wondering why on earth he thought I might be interested. He wasn't my type, and he was so much younger than me. Then, one day about a year after I had first met him, I was serving up dinner and realized he wasn't there as usual. I rang him up and said, 'You never told me you weren't coming'. Afterwards, I reflected, wondering why I would miss him when he wasn't there and it dawned on me for the first time that I might be falling in love with him.

I think the final test was a little trip to Ibiza with my girl-friends, which I had planned and saved up for. We all arrived at the hotel reception and there, behind a pillar, was none other than Paul Price. My friends hit the roof because it was supposed to be a girls' holiday, but the truth is I wanted to spend most of my time with him and our relationship blossomed from there. When we got home, he said, 'So what are we going to do about this?' It was the trigger that fired the final shot through my relationship with Ray. I felt sick to my stomach with nerves as I finally went to him and told him we were definitely over and needed to make it official. He couldn't believe I had fallen for Price and had the nerve to say he was disappointed with my choice, warning me that Price was no good. It was a great weight off my shoulders when I'd finally had the courage to confront Ray and I wasn't turning back – his criticism of Price had the effect of a recommendation! Ray accepted this new relationship, and then he didn't. He was really angry and hurt, so he came with me to see my mum, and she persuaded him that we couldn't carry on as we had been, and he agreed. That was the end of our marriage, from my point of view.

Price and I went to see if we could get a mortgage together, but I still needed to get Ray to agree to a divorce. He was in denial and thought we still had a chance of reconciliation. But the kids were used to seeing Price around and loved being with him because he's a very gentle, loving person. Beach, sports, family days out – you name it, Price was alongside us. In his youth, Price had been a brilliant footballer so when Dan played, Price encouraged him from the side lines and gave him tips. He also used to come and watch Kate ride and support the children at their swimming club. To be honest, he was always there for me and the children at these events and it was one of the reasons I loved him. The family unit I had always craved finally seemed possible with him in our lives. The future was certainly looking clearer and more hopeful – until one summer's day when Kate was six.

I was still good friends with some of the mums I had met while pregnant with Kate and we had arranged to go for a picnic together at a popular park called St Ann's Well Gardens in Hove. It was a balmy summer's day and life felt good as we shared our parenting stories and gossiped about relationships. While we sat back and relaxed, our children joined hands and excitedly ran in and out of a small clump of bushes on the periphery of the park, playing hide and seek in their fresh summer dresses. We were watching them closely in between bites of ham sandwich and felt happy to see them skipping around without a care in the world. Then, all of a sudden, the mood changed when the three girls, including Kate, came running towards us looking terrified. The girls said a strange man had been lurking in the scrubland and had coerced one of them to perform oral sex on him. Kate also confessed that he had touched her intimately. I felt frozen with shock and saw my horror reflected in the other mothers' eyes. How could our happy world have descended into such a dark place in an instant? We called the police and they came quite quickly and started to investigate, but were unable to find anyone at the scene. They took statements from the girls but not surprisingly, considering what they had been through, their statements were muddled and didn't seem to match up. There was nothing else we could do so we took our children home and gave them hot baths and cuddles. I remember the police coming round later and taking a statement from me, before gently coaxing more information from Kate. In those days, children's trauma was not taken so seriously and so there were no offers of therapy or aftercare.

I was devastated. The park had always seemed such a safe and tranquil place and the children were always within earshot. It was inconceivable that it could have happened and even more unbelievable that the man was never caught because he must have done something like this before. We never heard from the police again after the girls gave their statements, except to learn that the descriptions they had given were all different, which is hardly surprising given their ages and the trauma they had experienced.

Kate never really spoke to me about the assault again and I presumed she had forgotten it, but before long I started to notice some unusual patterns in her behaviour. Once, she went on a school trip and when she returned, her teacher excitedly approached me and said, 'I'll be sure to tune into the TV tonight'. Somewhat confused, I replied, 'Pardon?' She explained that Kate had told her she would be doing a dance on TV in a white ballet costume. It was complete fiction. I now wonder if Kate was throwing herself into a world of fantasy in order to escape the horror of the park incident.

Kate had taken after me and was a really good swimmer. One day, several years later in her early teens, I dropped her off for a lesson at my old club Shiverers. When I returned to collect her, the staff told me that Kate had suffered a panic attack in the water. Apparently, she just froze and couldn't continue with the strokes, so the lifeguards had to pull her out. Unfortunately, she immediately developed a phobia of swimming which lasts to this day. We hoped this was a one-off incident linked only to the water, but it happened again when Kate was staying with her cousin Esther, and then again on the school bus. She completely froze and had to be helped by the driver who alerted her school. She later visited a doctor who diagnosed panic attacks. At the time we did not understand why these were happening, but now it is clearer to me that this may well have been an early indication of how Kate's body was trying to process some very difficult feelings linked to the sexual trauma in the park.

I felt Kate's behaviour made a stable and supportive home life a priority, and this added some urgency to trying to sort things out between Ray and me. Although I had already told Ray about Price, he hadn't seemed to take it seriously. In the end, we decided to be grown ups and Ray, Price and I agreed to meet up in my lounge. Price told Ray straight, 'I want to be with Amy. I know that you two have not been getting on so please will you relinquish your stake in the property so she can sell it and move on.' They both agreed a sum of money that Price would pay Ray, and Price wrote a cheque out there and then. Looking back, it seems odd that my fate was decided by two men and a chequebook, but in those days working-class women like me had less financial freedom, especially when we had children to look after and a home to keep. Anyway, after that I went straight to a firm of solicitors to start divorce proceedings. This was the point that it became real for Ray. I used to get phone calls from him asking if we could stay together. Worse still, he used to sit outside the house and wait for Price to pull up before attacking him. Once he smashed his windscreen with a hammer. They would actually arrange to meet up down the seafront and have proper fights with one another, like some sort of ridiculous medieval dual. After they'd finished, Ray would ring me to tell me he was sending Price back home to me, and I would thank him! You couldn't make it up! One thing Price and I did have to get straight was his role in relation to Dan and Kate. I told him, 'Their dad will always be their dad' and he was very respectful of that. In the beginning, after we split for good, Ray came to take them out quite regularly but over time it became less and less and sometimes he didn't turn up at all, which left me feeling furious and hurt on their behalf. Eventually, he would go on to remarry twice so it felt like we were all moving on.

After the divorce, Price and I bought a Victorian house in Hove, which we all moved into. Money was still tight so we still needed student lodgers, but instead of looking after them for 12 months of the year, I reduced my workload to the April to September season. This supplemented the income from my job and meant that we could afford to have the occasional holiday and pay for house repairs. I was able to work full time because my mum picked Kate and Daniel up from school and they stayed with her until I could collect them. I was very conscious that because of Kate's awful experience in the park, she needed a stable routine in her life and needed to feel loved. At the time, Kate gave the outward impression of being happy. Price decided he wanted to get married and I happily said yes – so he did the gentlemanly thing and asked my mum and dad, who also readily agreed. They said they liked him because he was a worker. Interestingly, Kate is also attracted to this quality in men but, sadly, any semblance of a job her partners have is soon relinquished in pursuit of shared fame.

A couple of years later, we moved from Hove to Patcham. Price went down to the registry office in Brighton and booked our wedding – *three times*. I didn't turn up on the first two occasions because I was so wary after how things had unfolded with Ray; I just lost my nerve. Eventually, I decided

I had to trust again – as Price couldn't have done much more to demonstrate his determination and his loyalty, I wanted to spare him any more embarrassment in front of the guy at the registry office who told him he wasn't going to take any more bookings from him if I didn't show up this time round. The celebrations finally took place on 17th December 1988. Price and I were both so happy and the kids – by then aged 10 and 13 – were both fully involved in the wedding as a bridesmaid and page boy. I had been to a shop in Rottingdean where I found a dress I fell in love with, so I felt comfortable and happy as we performed our wedding dance to George Michael's 'Careless Whisper'. People used to say to me, 'Weren't you lucky that Price took on you and your children?' and I used to reply, 'Wasn't he lucky to have a ready-made family?' I always felt we were equal in that way. Price shared this view and our marriage has been equal. There has never been an 'I'm a man and you're a woman' situation; he has always supported me to pursue whatever I have wanted in life and has actively encouraged me too. There have been so many times when he's thought I was crazy, but he's never stopped encouraging me, saying he would never prevent me doing anything I wanted to do. I love him for that. Three days before we got married, we moved into a house in Patcham which would be our family home for 12 years.

We didn't have a honeymoon because I felt the kids needed this marriage as much as I did to make them feel secure and I didn't want to be away from them. In the end, we had a disco in our local pub and then stayed the night in a themed room at a hotel overlooking the West Pier. It had black silk walls which we thought were hilarious and we fell sleep amidst a fit of giggles. The next morning, we went back home to the children and then returned to work as usual the following Monday.

Kate loved and was incredibly loyal to Price, which was no doubt why she decided to drop the double-barrelled surname Price and I had given the children when we married and took Price's name only when she was 18. However, she'd undoubtedly been affected by the events in her life so far, as well as my divorce from Ray, so I was delighted when Kate started to find a healing pathway in horses, which has lasted a lifetime.

It all started with Saturday lessons at Ditchling Stud when she was six. The wonderful staff taught her to ride and look after horses – and from the word go, Kate just loved being with these majestic creatures. They seemed to transport her to another world where she could just be in the moment. She used to ride with her tongue between her teeth because she was concentrating so hard. Obviously, she was gently reprimanded for doing this as it was too dangerous to adopt as a long-term habit.

Just like me as a youngster, Kate used to ride the same horse every week and became very attached to it. In the summer holidays, when she got a bit older, she would spend every waking hour at the stables, and we would save up to send her to summer camps too. From the word go, Kate was so caring with horses and took pleasure in seeing them trotting towards her when she called their names – she loved the fact that they recognized and relied on her. She was meticulous about the way she cleaned the stables and would diligently brush the horses and clean their hooves, all the while listening to her transistor radio. She would spoil them too with Polos, carrots and apples. In some ways, Kate seemed to take more pleasure in caring for the horses than she did riding them – especially the way she meticulously cleaned out the stable every day, banking up the straw to make a comfortable bed for every animal she was tasked with caring for. Everything was spotlessly clean and tidy. I used to think, 'Why can't you be like that at home in your bedroom?' I began to wonder if, after the awful, abusive episodes she had endured, she was unconsciously making a safe, peaceful space for herself as well as the horse.

The horse world can be a bit snobby, though, and we have come across the more difficult side of it too. The staff at one stable, perhaps sensing Kate was not from a typical Pony Club background, made her do so much mucking out, sending her out to pick up poo from the fields all day long, that she cut one of their horses' tails short in a pique of temper and stormed off. I found her walking home along a country lane and told her off, but she turned to me and said, 'Mum, they are charging you a lot of money for me to go there and all I do is work and hardly ride the horses. This is child labour!' She never went back there. I think it was an early sign of a very independent streak in her character.

As someone who loved horses myself, I supported Kate in her hobby wholeheartedly and bought her all the horse magazines and books I could afford. She was always grateful and would read them from cover to cover, diligently taking in all the information. Her favourite was – and still is to this day

– *Horse & Hound*. I think once horses are in your blood, they never leave you and even now they remain her quiet, stable place – her sanctuary. Sadly, as with many aspects of her life, this great love has sometimes become mixed up with more ill-suited human loves and interestingly, she has bought most of her partners a horse in what appears to be a test of their shared devotion. Yet even horses haven't been able to fix Kate's relationship woes, but more of that later.

We were on more stable ground, both emotionally and financially, so we discussed how we could get Kate her first horse on loan, something we managed to do by the time she was ten. We paid for his keep but didn't actually own Star, who was a New Forest gelding aged around 18 and deemed safe to ride. He was about 14 hands and Kate adored him. He was stabled on a farm at the top of Ditchling Beacon and the farmer would let him out in the mornings, while Kate would take care of him in the afternoons and evenings. She seized every opportunity to ride her bike there after school and in the holidays, balancing a small radio on the handlebars.

Kate took the task of looking after Star incredibly seriously and seemed to get as much satisfaction from caring for him as she did riding him. She meticulously organized all the food bins and his grooming kit and buckets. She loved the smell of the sugar beet that she soaked overnight. At home, we religiously watched all the jumping championships on TV, from Hickstead to the Horse of the Year Show, and we were both mesmerized by it all – the horses, the riders, the whole atmosphere. Kate got to know the names of all the riders and horses by heart. I remember our pulses racing as we watched the famous Puissance at the London International Horse Show just before Christmas, where horses jumped over a large wall, which was built higher and higher with each round, until only one horse remained.

Kate and I were both mad about horses, but we certainly weren't born into a world of privilege like many of the other riders we encountered. Some horsey people think they know everything about horses but are not particularly good riders, so I think Kate often exceeded their expectations of a working-class girl from Brighton. Everyone knew that Star was on loan and all her equipment was very basic, but Kate was grateful for what she had and never complained to me about anything. However, as she got older it became more apparent that there was an element of competition and comparison, in terms of who had the bigger and better trailers and horse boxes. As a youngster, Kate always knew these things were out of our reach so I'm pretty sure there must be a great sense of satisfaction in being able to buy them for herself and even maintain her own stables as her wealth has grown.

When Kate was 16, she had saved up enough money to buy her own horse but of course – Kate being Kate – it wasn't a straightforward process. She heard about a retired race-horse which was being sold cheaply because it was on its way to the knacker's yard. It had been unsuccessful and was no longer wanted so of course Kate was attracted to it. It had ended up on the scrapheap with worn-out feet and a weary look in its eye, but the more vulnerable the animal, the more compelled Kate was – and still is – to come to its rescue. In fact, its feet were so damaged it couldn't tolerate normal horseshoes and had to have leather ones made to go over its hooves. It was also completely uncontrollable, but the most important thing for Kate was that it had been saved from death. This theme would be repeated again and again and she would later go on a mission to rescue a group of New Forest ponies who came complete with lice and worms. There was part of Kate that clearly needed to be taken care of, but I imagine that if she dwelled on her vulnerabilities, it would draw painful memories to the surface, which she no longer wanted to confront. So instead, she started to pour that care and attention into animals. Perhaps it feels safer to locate the most vulnerable parts of herself in animals and deal with the difficult feelings there? We noticed a similar, almost fanatical compulsion to care for others when Kate's sister Sophia Hannah Price was born.

Kate was 10 and Dan was 13 when Sophia was born. I hadn't been sure if I could have another child, but I knew Price wanted one and I did too, so I felt very lucky to discover I had managed to get pregnant again at the ripe old age of 36. Price was ecstatic and so was Kate, who loved the prospect of having a little baby to play with – just like a doll. Dan was pleased too and I began to feel hopeful of achieving my dream of a complete and happy family at last. I had the usual tests for older mums to make sure there were no problems, and all was good. I had no morning sickness and spent the majority of my pregnancy thinking that Sophie would be a boy, after the dreadful morning sickness I had had with Kate.

Overall, the pregnancy was good and I worked full time. But towards the last month or so I had to be monitored every few days as the nurses at the hospital couldn't always find movement or a heartbeat. I could definitely feel my baby moving and was told it might just be sleeping a lot, but it was still a worry – especially after what I'd been through with Kate. I was also advised that this baby was on the small side so when the due date came and went, the midwife decided to leave her to 'bake' a little longer. Everything was ready at home and Kate and Dan were excited to find out if they were going to meet a brother or sister. I thought it would be more exciting for everyone if we waited until the birth to find out. Price used to say 'he' would be a footballer or 'she' would be a tennis player – and it became a bit of a joke in the family.

Price and I were happy together, but economically we were living through a recession and things were stressful because interest rates kept going up and up. I was resigned to the fact I would have to go back to work pretty quickly after the birth, but I tried to put that to the back of my mind as I waited for my child to arrive. I was knitting baby clothes, a hobby I love and one that both Kate and Sophie have picked up from me. (Kate has even taken this further and also sews – she can create almost anything without a pattern.) I knitted cardigans with matching hats and booties for the new baby, which I had done for both Kate and Dan before.

In the end, Sophia Hannah's birth on 29th November 1989 was different from the others in one major way – Price was by my side throughout at the Sussex County Hospital in Brighton. The nurses suggested I had a pessary to try to get labour started, so I agreed and waited and waited, but nothing happened. Hours later, they inserted another one and Price

– who assumed it would take some time – said he would go and check on Dan and Kate, who were with my mum. No sooner had I walked him to the lift and got back on the bed, I started having pains, and by the time Price returned an hour or so later, I was in full labour.

My waters broke, but there was a problem – I had been doing yoga and gardening all through my pregnancy and my cervix had slipped to the back of the baby's neck, so they had to put it back on the crown of the head and that really hurt. Price kept holding the gas and air mask over my mouth, telling me to breathe in and out deeply, but I had to keep taking it off as it was just too much. He was trying to help so much. I told the midwife I wanted to push and when she examined me, Sophie was already well on her way. Price stayed with me the whole time and was very supportive, even cutting the umbilical cord when she was finally born, something he would do years later for Kate when she gave birth for the first time. Price cried when he set eyes on his daughter; he was so happy and proud and I was shocked because I had never seen him so emotional. He was a hands-on dad from the start, whisking her off for a bath while I was being stitched up. I definitely wasn't used to help like this and it was further proof of his integrity as a husband and a father. Our family was now complete – just in time for Christmas.

We managed to have a lovely festive season with all the trimmings, despite a dark cloud looming in the background. The recession meant we were behind with our mortgage payments and there was a repossession order on our house. We had agreed a payment plan, with all the added fees for solicitors' letters from the building society (which added up to more than our monthly payments each month) – we just didn't have the money to pay it back. So, when Sophie was just two weeks old, we went to court to save our house. My mum and dad paid the arrears for us until we were more financially secure and able to pay them back and I contacted one of the building society's board members to tell them about the impact the solicitors' fees had had on us. He agreed with me that the charges were preposterous – particularly as we had not missed any of the actual mortgage payments – so he refunded us the full amount we had paid out to lawyers. I learned a valuable lesson that day – never be afraid to question anything and everything. Never take no for an answer. I would need to demonstrate that kind of feistiness in my future life time and time again.

I did eventually go back to work when Sophie was six weeks old and she went to a childminder. Things improved with work for Price too and we gradually got back on track. Meanwhile, at home Kate and Dan were adjusting to their new sibling. From the word go, Kate saw herself as a little mother rather than a rival. She fed and changed Sophie constantly, even sometimes waking her up to make her cry, just so she could look after her.

It was extraordinary to watch Kate care for her sister; she absolutely adored her. To this day, Kate still reminisces about the blue Maclaren buggy she used to push Sophie around in. As they grew older, Sophie looked up to Kate and loved being in her company. They were inseparable. Years later, Kate would confess to me that on a few occasions she waited for me to drop Sophie off at school before immediately picking her up again, aiding and abetting the odd day of truancy. She took Sophie to the stables and encouraged her to ride, treated her to trips to the hairdressers. Later, when she began earning decent money of her own, she even bought Sophie her first car: a brand new Mitsubishi Colt convertible. It was amazing to see Sophie's face when Kate presented it to her, complete with a big red bow around it.

As Kate's career progressed, Sophie went everywhere with her as a trusted companion, including a memorable stay at the Beverley Hills Hotel in Los Angeles, where they shopped on Rodeo Drive feeling just like Julia Roberts in *Pretty Woman*. Sophie has always been spoiled by Kate, but they still argued over normal things like borrowing clothes. Dan also did his bit to look after Sophie and once played his part in saving her life when he rushed her to hospital with a burst appendix. We all got on really well as a family and the children were very close, despite the age gap. But I did sense tensions in the relationship between Dan and Kate as they entered adolescence. He refused to introduce Kate to his friends at school or let her go to the youth club because he didn't like the fact that his friends might want to go out with his attractive sister. Occasionally, Kate used to feel upset about this, but she needn't have worried. One day they would all know her name – the whole nation would.

Chapter 5

FROM BODY-CONSCIOUS TOMBOY
TO TEENAGE TEMPTRESS

I can trace my daughter's transformation from body-conscious tomboy to teenage temptress to a moment which is still razor sharp in my mind. We were preparing for a surprise party I was throwing for Price's 30th birthday and I gave Kate, who was 14 at the time, some money and freedom to choose her own outfit.

Moments before we were due to leave, Kate stepped out of her bedroom in her chosen attire. I couldn't believe that the girl standing in front of me was Kate. She was wearing high heels and a tight black leather skirt and top from Topshop, with a silver zip down the front. She had applied a full face of make-up and elaborately combed her curly hair over to one side to create the image of a sex siren far beyond her years. My sister-in-law and I were getting ready together and when Kate appeared in front of us, our eyes popped out of our heads. We were dumbfounded, absolutely stunned. It reminded me of the moment in *Grease* when Olivia Newton John shakes off her conservative girly dresses and woos John Travolta in a black Lycra catsuit and high heels.

This was a transformation for Kate. For years she had thought she was too thin and always covered her body up with leggings and baggy tops. She was more interested in horse riding than clothes and never went out anywhere to warrant dressing up. Believe it or not, she had shown no interest in boys either – or at least if she had, I was unaware of it.

Kate's discomfort with her body began when she was 13 years old. She had come home and excitedly told me that a school friend had invited her to model for a clothing brand called Joe Bloggs, which specialized in baggy trousers and tops. The initial photo shoot took place in Churchill Square in Brighton; there were seven children involved. The photographer was called Kees Quant. He was bald, average height, in his thirties and there was nothing distinguishing about him except the fact he was well spoken and seemed very gentle. It all seemed above board and we were excited when he contacted me and asked if Kate could visit his studio to pose for some more photos, because he believed he could get her some catalogue work. I remember driving her to his detached, chalet-style house in an upmarket area called Kingston, near Lewes, and being invited to sit in the kitchen with his elderly mum while he took pictures of Kate in an adjacent room. He had shown me his portfolio which seemed impressive, and it had convinced me that he was a real professional. Because he had suggested catalogue work, we didn't suspect anything when he wanted to photograph Kate in her school uniform. I wasn't allowed to accompany her because he said it might be a distraction if other people were in the room while they worked. Kate loved modelling. She was a pretty girl and looked very trendy in the Joe Bloggs clothes. I felt proud of her because she took to it like a duck to water.

Things seemed to be taking off for Kate. We were invited back for another shoot and, this time, Quant had a female stylist with him. Everything seemed normal, so much so that I had taken the dogs with me and took them for a walk while Kate was in the studio. However, just as I got back, Quant came storming out with sweat pouring down his face, telling me, 'Your daughter has been so rude to me. She's dreadful. She simply won't do what she is told.' I was stopped short of reminding Kate of her manners when she emerged from his studio with chocolate around her mouth. What was this man's real agenda? What was the point of this photograph, which had nothing to do with modelling clothes? Kate told me in front of him that she would not see him again. On the way home, she described how he'd asked her to stick her tongue out provocatively and wear a bikini in some of the shots. But things had come to a head when he and the stylist had asked Kate to pose in a T-shirt with nothing else on underneath. Kate realized that this was wrong and refused to do it.

I had experienced similar abuse at the hands of swimming coaches as a young girl desperate to get ahead in the sport, and somehow history was repeating itself. I felt sick. How could this have happened? An event like that is not something you can easily brush aside but we did try to move on. However, a few months later we were visited by the police. We discovered the photographer was in fact a paedophile who had been luring other young girls on the promise of modelling portfolios and drugging them with milkshakes. It was only at this stage that Kate revealed that she had been offered one of his milkshakes but, thankfully, she had refused to drink it. She was interviewed by police and Quant was eventually convicted and jailed for child sex offences.

Kate had wanted to visit him in prison and tell him how much damage he had done. But thank goodness she didn't because, some years later, we learned that Quant was about to be released after serving his time in jail and that photos of Kate and other girls had been found on the walls of his cell. We supported Kate as she tried to put it all behind her. It was only later that I read the influential book *The Body Keeps the Score*, by the brilliant American psychiatrist Dr Bessel van der Kolk. He describes how traumatic events such as these have a lasting effect on the body, in particular the immune system, the muscular system and the brain. It is not simply the traumatic event itself that haunts you; its effects play out again and again in the years that follow. The trauma determines your behaviour, becomes part of who you are physiologically as well as emotionally. I now believe this incident, and the incident in the park when she was younger, played a part in shaping the person my daughter would later become.

Kate gradually became more uncertain of her appearance. If I asked her to buy something new, she would always come back with tracksuits, trousers and jumpers – never anything feminine. She didn't wear make-up either, and often refused to brush her hair. Going to school, she would insist on pulling on two pairs of thick tights to cover up what she perceived to be her too thin legs. She had established herself as an outstanding cross-country runner at school but no longer wanted me to watch her race because she said running made her face look funny. I told her she was being silly and didn't look odd at all, but the feeling was clearly real to her.

By giving her some independence to dress for Price's party, I hoped it might encourage her to take more pride in her appearance and feel confident enough to socialize at the event. None of us was prepared for how she interpreted this gesture. As Price first glimpsed her, he just raised his eyebrows at me as we both acknowledged the fact of Kate's curvaceous figure, and realized that we were likely to have trouble with her from this point onwards.

At the party, she turned heads. Unsurprisingly, there was a lot of male and female interest and disbelief among many that she was only 14. I honestly think that this was the moment when Kate understood that she could have an impact on men and control them with her body. It was like she had suddenly reclaimed it and made the decision to put it out there in a provocative way. This was the moment she began to realize that the male gaze was a weapon that could be used as a means of control. This was a pattern which would repeat itself many times in her career and I have found myself wondering about the origins of her compulsion to expose her body and feel those early traumatic experiences may provide the answers.

There was a definite shift in her appearance after that party. She went from wearing non-descript leggings to green or red jeans or jodhpurs, and she started to put padding in her bras. I used to tell her that all the women in our family had ample bosoms and she should give herself time to blossom and stop worrying. One thing was certain, though – she was developing into a young woman who was doing fashion *her* way. For instance, she would buy high shoes that looked like boots and customize them with drawing pins, or drape a matching mini-skirt over a ladybird- or strawberry-embossed bikini. As she grew older, she began turning heads on Brighton beach with her tiny figure and long curly hair, a warning of the challenges to come.

Chapter 6

SPIN CYCLE

A friend of mine once warned me that parenting teenagers would be like watching the spin cycle on a washing machine – it could get fast, bumpy and out of control in the blink of an eye. Well, she was right. Kate started that cycle at the age of 14 and, at times, it feels like she has never reset the dial. While the first warning I noticed of Kate's turbulent adolescence ahead was her jaw-dropping 'Olivia Newton John moment' at Price's party, if I look back, there were subtle warning signs even before that.

There was no doubt she was becoming less shy of her body and more aware of how she could use it to get attention. For instance, she took it upon herself to wear a tie to school, even though it wasn't a mandatory part of the uniform, and she suddenly started blackening her eyebrows and wearing red lipstick. I received a letter from her school expressing concerns that other pupils could be influenced by Kate. The tie was worn loosely with her top button undone and the headteacher said it could cause all sorts of problems if her style was adopted. I just put her behaviour down to the fact that my daughter was coming out of herself and wanted to be noticed, but on reflection I think the incident in the photography studio had triggered more trauma than we realized. She must have felt powerless, trapped and very frightened in that situation but now it seemed that she was calling the shots with her appearance, reclaiming some power in the way she presented herself. I wasn't aware of these dynamics at the time, so I just told her to calm it down. Of course, Kate being Kate, she would leave for school with no make-up on, then apply it on the school bus. She did lose the tie though.

It was also around this time that Kate began voicing ideas about becoming a professional model. Ever since primary school, Kate had told me she wanted to be famous. Although the Kees Quant episode had been traumatic, Kate had actually enjoyed modelling for the camera before things turned sour. She began to contact London modelling agencies but because of her previous experience, I insisted on accompanying her to meetings, including one with the famous Storm agency. However, they rightly told her she was too young and suggested she get on with her studies and return in her late teens. They also told her she was too short to make it as a fashion model at 5ft 4in but thought she might be able to get work focussing on her hands, feet and face.

So instead, she started writing to TV programmes in the hope of being invited to take part. She wrote to the ITV talent show *Stars in Their Eyes* when she was 15 and asked to appear as Mariah Carey singing 'Hero'. Perhaps this was a form of escapism – if she could stop being Kate Price and morph into someone else, albeit briefly, she could find some respite from the difficult feelings she was experiencing. Sadly, she never heard back from that programme, but her disappointment soon became the least of my concerns.

Kate was just 15 when she met a 25-year-old second-hand car dealer at the small, three-stable yard where she kept her horse. Despite the fact that he kept his own horse there, Kate never mentioned him to us. It was only by chance I saw them together when I went to collect her one winter's evening. I was often late to pick her up, as I would have to drive to get her after working in London all day. I remember how he struck me as being a really big guy. In the beginning, he was offering Kate lifts to and from the stables and I tried to stay calm, hoping it would all fizzle out after a few weeks. But Kate started arriving home later and later, neglecting her schoolwork. When I confronted her, she reassured me that she and this man were just friends, but I instinctively knew different. Her character had changed; she had started answering me back and lying. Even the school began expressing concerns about the change in her personality, but Kate wouldn't listen to anyone.

One night she got her friend to tell me she was staying at her house after she had been to an East 17 concert to celebrate her 16th birthday. Years later, I would read in one of her books that she had in fact spent the night with the man from the stable yard, and that was when she had lost her virginity. I still feel excruciatingly sad that I had to discover this in a book, and wasn't told about it at the time. I never had the chance to be open about these things with my mum, and I wanted things to be different with Kate. We'd spoken about birth control, and I had mistakenly thought that Kate would have come to tell me about her first time.

For the first but not the last time, Kate had been drawn to a man she thought was big and strong, someone she felt would take care of her. Sometimes he would bring Kate home when she had finished at the stables and he would just walk past us without speaking or looking at us and barge straight up to Kate's bedroom. Unsurprisingly, we banned him from the house. I was beginning to get the gist of this man, and understood him to be weak and flawed. He drank a lot and it emerged that he had an ongoing court case coming up. He was in trouble with the police for non-payment of fines, which eventually led to a jail sentence of several weeks at Lewes Prison. Kate had gone to court with him to support him, and you can imagine my surprise when she turned up at home after driving his car back from the court without a licence or insurance, when he wasn't released. Somehow, my 16-year-old daughter had miraculously learned how to drive without my knowledge. I was at my wits' end and called social services for help, but they said that she was too old for them to be able to do anything.

At the time, I simply couldn't understand Kate's attraction to a man like that. Now I know about a psychological phenomenon called repetition compulsion and I'm beginning to realize that it might not have been a conscious choice of hers. Freud was the first great thinker to identify this phenomenon, whereby a person repeats an event or its circumstances over and over again as a way of trying to come to terms with it. This includes re-enacting the event or putting themselves in situations where the event is likely to happen again. I truly believe that this describes Kate to a tee, and that the tragedy

81

of the sexual predators she encountered as a very young girl had a profound effect on all her subsequent relationships. At times, it has felt as though she is magnetically drawn to these men, some of whom have experienced trauma themselves. They exploit her vulnerabilities and ultimately position her as a victim. Then, as a couple, the two of them become trapped by a mutually tragic forcefield.

The trouble with my eldest daughter is that when she likes someone, she dives headfirst into a relationship and thinks – *hopes* – they are going to build a life together. She seems to be striving for an ideal, but it blinds her to the reality of what is in front of her. In many ways, it was the same with me and Ray. For years, I wanted to believe we could be a happy family and I put up with so much in the futile pursuit of it. I'm sure Ray feels he put up with a lot too.

I tried to talk to Kate about how her schoolwork was suffering and about the inappropriateness of the age gap, but she wouldn't listen and would constantly fire back that there was a significant age gap between Price and I, so why should it be any different for her. Because we had banned him from the house, I wondered if my antagonism towards him was making him a more exciting and interesting proposition and whether I should back off with my criticisms. I wish I'd had the benefit of age and wisdom when Kate was in her teens but, like all parents, I was learning as I went along and didn't really understand what she needed most – which I'm certain now was someone who could help her *think* about these dynamics and prevent her from acting them out. Instead, she received my anxiety-laden wrath, which only thrust her further into the clutches of this relationship. At the time, I was also unaware that I was repeating the behaviours that I had experienced at the hands of my own parents, who kept an unbearably tight rein on me as a child and unwittingly drove me into finding Ray a more attractive prospect than I might otherwise have done.

On the day that Kate's boyfriend was released from prison, I was devastated to come home from work to find that she had packed up her stuff and left home to move into a flat with him. She had messed up her GCSEs because she had not studied hard enough and had become rebellious and rude to her teachers. Now I felt as though Kate was being completely isolated from us as well. Dan, and particularly Sophie, who shared her bedroom, missed her desperately.

In despair, I went to see the boyfriend's mum to try to come up with a plan of getting my daughter back, but she wasn't any help. For a couple of weeks or so, Kate cut herself off completely from the family and there wasn't even any phone contact. But then a call came inviting us to a horse event. We all went to watch Kate, but she spent most of the time with her boyfriend's family and we didn't really get much chance to talk. However, we had broken the ice and after a while, Kate did begin calling me more regularly again and I could tell she missed living at home. She wanted us to accept her choices and I said we would try, but it was all so uncomfortable and wrong. In Kate's eyes, she was in a proper relationship that had the potential to make her happy ever after. In our eyes, it was the worst scenario possible.

Kate and her boyfriend's combined vulnerabilities soon

proved to be a recipe for disaster. He was insanely jealous of any man who looked at her. He lost his temper at the slightest provocation and would shout at and hit Kate. But despite all of this, she stuck with him and after a month or so they moved into a tiny cottage in Hurstpierpoint, a picturesque village on the edge of the Sussex Downs. She got a carer's job at a nursing home where she had to feed, wash and take old people to the toilet. She even had to lay out dead bodies – a lot of responsibility for someone so young. She seemed happy in her job, but the money wasn't great, and she still wanted to ride horses.

In an attempt to boost her income, Kate began to show the first signs of her entrepreneurial streak. She had seen her boyfriend dealing in second-hand cars and, despite not yet having passed her driving test, she recognized that she could also make a profit doing the same. She started off with a yellow Volvo, which she sold on to another dealer for a good price. She then bought an old-fashioned dormobile van, which she initially had the idea of living in if ever she had to travel to horse shows, but eventually she flogged it and made money on that too. She also bought herself a motorbike. Perhaps this phase was not quite as bizarre as it initially seems, considering my family's car business and her dad's trade in antiques.

Kate had drifted away from us. We didn't see her for weeks on end and it was painful for all of us. One day, I received an invite to visit the cottage the couple shared, but my heart sank when Kate opened the door to reveal the dark, filthy interior. There were no carpets, very little furniture and only a few lightbulbs without any lightshades. I didn't comment on

the shabbiness of the place because I didn't want to be con-
frontational. Of course, the house wasn't the only darkness in
her life. The stage had already been set for the first controlling
relationship of Kate's life.

Soon she started calling me more regularly, initially just to
let me know she was okay, then asking what we were all doing
at home. At the time Kate didn't reveal the horrors that were
going on behind closed doors; I don't know whether that was
to prevent me interfering, or if she genuinely thought that
her boyfriend cared for her and that things would get better.
Eventually, we began meeting up for coffee here and there
and she confided in me more and more, revealing that he was
incredibly controlling and was telling her what clothes to
wear and to refrain from applying make-up in case other men
looked at her.

Once, I got a desperate call and she told me she couldn't go
to work because she didn't have any clothes. I asked what she
meant but she sounded shocked and started pleading, 'Please
mum, believe me. I just can't go anywhere.' I told her I was
coming right away and – sensing something was desperately
wrong – set off for the cottage at speed. I couldn't believe
my eyes when I saw my daughter standing on the corner of
the road with just a towel wrapped round her in the freezing
cold. In a fit of jealous rage sparked when Kate tried to leave
the cottage without his permission, he had had cut up all
her clothes with scissors and even slashed her leather boots
to pieces with a knife. This so-called fairy tale romance had
descended into a dark narrative of drudgery and domestic
violence.

It certainly didn't seem to me as though this was the first time something like this had happened, as Kate seemed to have become numb to it all. All she said was, 'Let's go. I just want to go home.' She didn't cry on the way home. I told her I hoped she was now putting an end to the relationship and tried to make her see sense – 'Kate, this is not normal. You cannot have a relationship like this. It's ridiculous.' As a family, we had never experienced anything like this before.

It's funny what you recall during stressful times. Dan remembers Kate returning home that day wearing nothing more than a pair of the boyfriend's prison socks – apparently, they were grey with red rims around the toes. To our horror, she only stayed a few nights before returning to the relationship. From that point onwards, of course, things went from bad to worse. The phone calls asking me to pick her up became more and more frequent. A couple of weeks later, they had a huge row. Before I was able to drive off with her on this occasion, Kate's boyfriend came over to the car and asked Kate if she had told me the 'good news' about the pregnancy. She burst into tears and pleaded with me to drive off, before confirming she was in fact three months pregnant. I asked her why she hadn't taken the pill as we had discussed, and she shrugged and said she'd run out.

I couldn't comprehend why she had been so irresponsible, but she was clearly under a lot of stress, and I knew that we had to focus on the here and now. Kate didn't think that she wanted to continue with the pregnancy because of the violent behaviour she was enduring. I told her it was her choice but reassured her I would have thought the same in her position.

It was clear she was having major problems, but I was powerless to do anything other than come to her rescue when she needed me. A few days later, when she was once again back with her boyfriend, she called me because she had started bleeding. We never did get to the bottom of what had happened. Price and I took her to hospital, where doctors confirmed she had lost the baby. Kate was simultaneously upset and relieved that the final decision regarding an abortion had been taken out of her hands. Nowadays, I would hope that women who find themselves in a position like Kate's would have greater access to support from those who have the expertise to help them.

Thankfully, Kate finally quit the relationship for good after six months and returned home to us once more, but her ex called our house repeatedly. After a while, the phone calls and visits stopped, and we were relieved that the relationship was finally over.

By the time Kate reached the age of 17, she had begun to pick up the pieces of her life. She passed her driving test first time and casually told us, 'Don't worry – I've got a car lined up already,' before appearing in a silver Mini she had acquired for £280 through her own dealership. You can see how Kate's fascination with cars started years ago – although she didn't insist on them being pink back then.

Dan and Sophie were pleased to have their sister home. Dan had already passed his driving test and we managed to buy him a Ford Sierra. He later traded it in for an old yellow VW Beetle and his friend graffitied VW in flames on the bonnet. Dan was a very different teenager to Kate. He studied hard at school and from the age of 17, worked weekends and holidays on the pizza counter at Asda where he met a check-out girl of the same age called Louise Osborne. She became the love of his life. Unbelievably, it turned out that I already knew her mum – we had worked alongside one another at an insurance company. I was pregnant with Dan and she with her daughter Louise at the time. We even shared the same maternity dressmaker and stayed in touch for a while after our children were born. But because she lived in Peacehaven and I lived in Patcham, the contact had fizzled out. I couldn't believe it when Dan revealed who he was dating, and I felt so pleased he was involved with such a lovely family. He was really smitten with Lou – as we all call her. Then, as now, she was beautiful with her long brunette hair, slim figure and modest, shy personality.

Dan found it hard when it was time to pack his bags to study Business and Marketing at the University of Greenwich. Price and I knew it was serious with Lou when he called to say he wanted to move back home and transfer to the University of Brighton because he was missing her too much. He went ahead and never looked back, eventually marrying Lou when they were both aged 28. They have produced beautiful twins, Amalie and Betsy. At least Dan was forging a steady path in life, which holds firm to this day. He and Kate are like chalk and cheese in that respect.

Kate eventually got a job working as a receptionist at a business centre in Hove, where she would dress very professionally in suits with scarves round her neck. After just a few weeks on the job, she told us that she had been chatting to a colleague (an older lady) and Kate had mentioned her ambition to be a model. By a stroke of luck this colleague had a friend who was a photographer who suggested she get some photographs taken of herself in a bikini on Hove beach. The photographer had contacts in the modelling business and sent the pictures to the Samantha Bond agency and to *The Sun* newspaper for possible Page Three selection. We were aware of *The Sun* – Dan and Price both read it, because what man didn't back then – and I desperately didn't want to have my daughter appearing topless in it. I wanted her to have a career and didn't think appearing in this way in a mass-market tabloid constituted one. In the end, I didn't have to worry because the bikini shots she sent to *The Sun* were turned down, with the editor stating that they weren't what they were looking for. Kate was adamant she wanted to keep trying and – still aged just 17 – she went to chase up the Samantha Bond agency.

At around the same time, Kate met a local electrician called Gary at a Brighton club. Sadly, he turned out to be jealous and unfaithful. He wasn't tall like her last boyfriend, but was quite good looking. He had dark curly hair and a good sense of humour. He was an electrician, popular with his friends, played football and was very sociable. Interestingly, his ex-girlfriend was a topless glamour model, and I got the sense that Kate felt some pressure to fill her shoes in order to keep Gary happy. She told him about her plans with the agency and, cruelly, he made her feel insecure by telling her that she wouldn't make it because her boobs weren't big enough. He also said that she was 'not good enough'.

I used to tell her Gary was talking rubbish and reassured her once again that she was beautiful. But Kate constantly

AMY PRICE

worried that she wasn't going to be enough for Gary, physically or emotionally. One thing's for sure, if he clicked his fingers, Kate would nervously go running and over time we noticed that she became increasingly insecure. Once, my dad's brother and sister came over from America to visit and Kate drove us all to Hampton Court, near London, for a day out. Towards the end of our trip, Gary called her so she raced us all back down the motorway at 100mph. I've never forgotten the look of terror on everyone's faces in the back of her car as we risked our lives to fall in line with his schedule. Kate clearly felt so insecure in this relationship and always seemed worried that another woman would take her place if she didn't please Gary enough and do exactly as he said.

Kate's body insecurities were then made worse by an unfortunate incident when she was 17 on Brighton beach, where we often went together. She had chosen to wear an eye-catching white bikini and matching skirt covered in red cherries. Granted, it wasn't the most low-key of outfits and it did seem to spark envy among some of the other females on the beach. But Kate was a teenager who enjoyed experimenting with fashion and often wore daring outfits. In my opinion, if you've got it flaunt it! We were used to people staring at Kate – she was beautiful after all – and we usually ignored it. However that day, the lifeguards – who we often chatted to – came over and alerted Kate to the fact that someone on the promenade was taking photos of women, including her. One of them said he felt uneasy about it and decided to call the police. They eventually arrived and quizzed this man who – as it turned out – had reels of film in his bag with pictures of scantily clad young girls. He was taken away by the officers. I felt sick to my stomach and couldn't believe history was repeating itself in this way. Unwittingly, Kate had ended up causing quite a stir and a woman and her son who were sitting near us on the beach started sniggering and making rude comments. Kate overheard them making a comment about her chest being flat. It felt so cruel because they were openly, loudly, laughing at her. I tried reassuring Kate and told her not to listen, but these people had found her weak spot. I remember Kate looking down at her bust and telling me, 'I've just got to get them done'. The need for surgery had been unleashed.

Meanwhile, the pictures Kate had sent to the Samantha Bond agency were received with enthusiastic interest and she was called up to London for a meeting in June 1996. After what had happened to Kate in the photo studio as a young girl, I was scared and wanted to protect her from further exploitation, but I knew it meant so much to her to be accepted and have her beauty validated rather than denigrated by awful boyfriends. We agreed that I would go with her to make sure everything was above board. It certainly seemed that way – there were models in the office waiting to be selected for a calendar shoot and they all seemed happy. I had felt really unsure about the direction Kate was heading in because I knew the modelling world could be seedy, but from the moment we walked into the agency offices, I sensed that things were safe and trustworthy and that Samantha Bond took care of her girls. Also, this agency wasn't asking the girls for money to make a portfolio like some others. At last an agency was finally interested in ALL of her, but she was told she would need to take her top off. 'Don't you dare,' I told her. 'Modelling – yes. Topless – no.'

Because of her height, though, catwalk modelling was always going to be a 'no go' so she was desperate to go ahead with glamour. On the way home, she was very excited about it all and couldn't wait to go to castings and get work. The agency explained it would be very competitive, but Kate was determined to make a go of it. Aside from the possibility of Page Three, there was also the possibility of catalogue work, swimwear, underwear and shoe modelling – plus promotional opportunities which she could get involved in. Kate met other models through hairdressers and make-up artists. From the outset, she knew that she would have to raise her profile, so she began going out with them to nightclubs, dressing in outrageous outfits to get photographed. Meanwhile, she worked hard by day and we would give her the petrol money to go to castings, which she said were like a conveyer belt. Girls would turn up, go into the studio and pose for a Polaroid before stepping aside for the next girl. Then they would just have to wait for a call to see if they were successful in getting the job.

Kate had only been with her agency for two weeks when the bosses told her that one of the other models had failed to show up for a Page Three trial and wondered if Kate wanted to go for it. She agreed and was advised to choose a 'topless name'. They were worried that Page Three work would damage her chances of securing more upmarket work, and they wanted to protect us as a family. After some brainstorming, Samantha's assistant, Paul, came up with the name Jordan. Quite why he thought of this name I do not know.

This time, *The Sun* instantly fell in love with Kate and decided to feature her in a five-day series to coincide with the release of the Demi Moore film *Striptease*. She would begin the week in a corset and stockings, before gradually removing an item of clothing each day until she was naked with only her arms and legs covering her dignity. The pictures would be taken by a famous Page Three photographer called Beverley Goodway, who Kate really came to respect.

Beverley was a gentleman who looked after his models with caring gestures like making them jacket potatoes for lunch. Kate was so excited about the series, but we were horrified at the prospect of our daughter baring her breasts to the nation. I was working in London as a PA for a payroll company when the photos came out, and almost fainted when I saw a colleague had 'Jordan' as his screensaver when I entered the office. There was also a quiz doing the rounds, where readers were asked to match the models' boobs to their faces – including my daughter's. It was so embarrassing – I hated it.

Dan loathed his sister's new career path. He was still at university when she began glamour modelling and when he visited friends' rooms, there were often pictures of Kate on the walls, but he was too embarrassed to reveal their connection. Similarly, when he played football, he found pictures dotted around the changing rooms and he was occasionally goaded on the pitch. Once he took Kate to a student evening in Brighton and he said it was like a swarm of bees around a honeypot. He felt that she was bringing shame on the family.

Of course, Kate's pseudonym didn't protect her family from those who already knew who she was. Sophie was still quite young and remembers a lot of fuss, but she wasn't directly affected until she got to secondary school and was bullied over Kate's career choice. There was one incident when two boys got a picture of Sophie's face and stuck it on a picture of Kate's body before circulating it round the school. Kate was really concerned and decided the solution was for Sophie to avoid school altogether, so from time to time, she would pick her up from school and take her out for the day. Sophie really suffered at the expense of Kate's fame. She was so young to have to deal with the level of abuse that she received from both girls and boys at school, and it really did affect her. We moved her to a different school to see if it would help, but things only became worse there, so eventually we moved her back to her old school, and things seemed to settle down.

Overall, it felt strange for all of us to be looking at Kate's boobs in the paper while she was so shy at home. Unbelievably we had never seen her nude around the house because she was very private. It was a shock to know we were seeing her naked body for the first time alongside the entire world. My mum and dad were the only family members who took a different view. They bought *The Sun* and were so proud, showing the pictures to all their friends and neighbours. They also started keeping all the articles on Kate, just like they'd done with me and my swimming.

Kate and my mum shared an exhibitionist streak and naughty personality, which meant they became especially close. Nothing was off limits. They could talk about anything – even sex. Shockingly, given how conservative he had been when I was a child, my dad was open about it too. I can remember Kate asking them if they still had sex when they were in their late seventies and my mum casually replied, 'Oh no dear, your grandad is too ill now – but we still have a cuddle.' Nothing phased them and every week Kate would go around and talk about what she had been up to while they sipped their cups of tea. Incredibly, my mum used to say, 'Do what you want Kate', and my dad would back it up with the mantra, 'You only live once.' They watched every show and bought every magazine Kate appeared in. My dad would even send clippings back to his family in the USA. They used to praise Kate and were very proud and protective of both her personal and professional life. If she brought a new boyfriend to meet them and they didn't like the look of him, they would give him a negative review, but if Kate herself received any negative publicity they would say, 'Kate is just acting so why don't they leave her alone?' If only it was that simple. Kate was always a loving granddaughter and made my parents laugh while cuddling them.

The rest of us weren't finding Kate's chosen career path so funny but despite our reservations, she was merrily forging ahead trying to navigate an industry which we soon learned was cut throat. When she was still just 18, she decided to leave the Samantha Bond agency and transfer to a lady called Helen Smith, who she thought would be able to raise her profile faster. Helen quickly delivered, arranging for Kate to go on a date with a Manchester United footballer who she really fancied, called Teddy Sheringham. But the date ended up being splashed on the front page of *The Sun* with the accompanying headline 'On My Bed Ted!'. This left Kate feeling understandably confused, but she was beginning to demonstrate just how business savvy she was when she thought there might be a problem and returned to Samantha Bond, knowing that she was a safer bet. We were all so naive and too trusting back then. This was our first wake-up call.

Back at her old agency, Kate was introduced to a female photographer called Jeannie Savage who worked freelance for *The Daily Star*. She told Kate she didn't like her curly hair and added, in no uncertain terms, 'You've got to have big boobs otherwise you won't get on.' When Kate was 16, she had wanted to get a boob job, but I had forbidden it because I felt she was far too young to take such a step. She was now nearly 19 and had booked herself an appointment – I still managed to talk her out of it, but only for a month or two. She was more determined when she booked an appointment the second time. I was livid, furious, and asked for the surgeon's number so I could call him and get the appointment cancelled. Around this time, *The Sun* commissioned a survey asking its readers if they liked natural or fake boobs, specifically posing the question: should Kate have them enhanced? The readers categorically answered no (they liked natural), but Kate was adamant she wanted the op to go ahead so on the third occasion she did not tell me of her plans.

The first I knew of her boob job in 1998 was when Kate called me as she was going down to the operating theatre, saying, 'In case I don't wake up – you know I love you'. Imagine hearing that as a mother. I was worried and angry, but I couldn't do anything about it because by this time she had turned 20. If you were to ask Kate about that now, I'm certain that she would tell you that 20 is too young for surgery. I think she found it scary and afterwards she was in a lot of pain and used to walk doubled over in agony. When she eventually had the bandages taken off, she loved the look of her new breasts, which had increased from 32B to 32C – but we thought they resembled two stuck-on balloons. It also marked the end of her Page Three career.

The whole family was in shock. We had only just got used to the fact we had a topless model in the family, let alone one who was going to have her boobs operated on. Dan was disgusted and said she was letting us down and Price thought it was embarrassing because he was constantly having to put up with jibes from his mates. Meanwhile, I used to lie awake at night wondering where my little girl had gone. Kate's body insecurities had been bubbling for some time, so perhaps I shouldn't have been so surprised. In no time she seemed to have developed two personas. There was my tracksuit- and slipper-clad daughter Kate who would come and cuddle up to me on the sofa at home, and Jordan the model who was brash, loud and already strutting her surgically enhanced body on the London nightclub scene.

Jordan was like a celebrity second skin, covering up the more vulnerable Kate. I didn't recognize this mouthy, exhibitionist woman who stared back at me from the newspapers with her tongue sticking out while winking at the camera. Every time I asked her about Jordan, she would dismiss her as a character who helped her get work and press coverage. But from the outset, the creation of Jordan seemed to set Kate up for a fall. I saw Jordan as an imposing suit of armour put in place to protect Kate from further harm – but many believed this lairy loudmouth was the real Kate. The negative, intrusive headlines began to roll off the presses, something that would last a lifetime.

Chapter 7

NO MAN IS WORTH THIS

While much of Kate's adolescence had been stormy, her boob job seemed to move her towards a more even keel. She was very focused on carving out a glamour modelling career and photo shoot offers were in abundance. Her relationship with Gary had fizzled out. She also had her sights set on a pop profile, so the world was her oyster. Initially I'd been sceptical, but there was no denying my pride as I saw how she was increasingly in demand, appearing in all the leading lad mags like *Esquire*, *Maxim*, *Loaded* and *FHM*.

While we, as a family, were struggling with Kate's choice to bare her body in public, I could see that there were different attitudes to mine in the female population. And interestingly, part of my daughter's unique appeal was that she was popular with men AND women. Unlike top shelf magazines, which were considered tacky and perverted and exploited women in a covert and furtive way, Page Three was open and unconcealed. Some women saw Page Three as a liberating vehicle through which normal women could show off their bodies with pride to mainstream audiences in a more natural, celebratory way – just like they did on the beach in Spain and France. The stigma associated with bare breasts in conservative Britain seemed to be passing and Page Three was becoming increasingly popular. It was also launching the careers of women in different directions; for some, particularly working-class women who identified with Kate, there was a sense of empowerment. I think they could see that she was from a similar background and believed that if Kate could make it, they could too. Her personal trials and tribulations made her more real in their eyes, even though she was still so young. In retrospect, Page Three was a tame phenomenon compared to the porn which was later made available on the internet.

I learned a lot about modelling through watching Kate, and was surprised to find early on that it isn't as easy as it looks. There are lots of pretty girls in the world, so you've got to be savvy in front of a camera and know how to work it. Kate knew how to control the camera rather than be controlled by it. I think you either have it or you don't, and Kate definitely had it. In this way, her personality showed through and leapt from the page. Kate also had an independent streak and the ambition to succeed. She soon realized that she had to be the brand and could build on her success, hence the emergence of brand Katie Price, rather than her merely being an advertising tool for someone else. Then you need the additional gumption to drive your brand. Kate was brilliant at this and there was a sense that things were finally on the up for her, professionally and personally. One day she called me feeling elated because she had been selected for a ten-day calendar shoot in Arizona. She was so young and naive and really missed home, so she sent me a postcard every single day. I remember one of them saying, 'Mum, you were right. There are cactuses everywhere here.' It was so touching in its innocence. Kate's career would eventually take her all over the world, but back then she was just a wide-eyed young woman taking her first tentative steps away from home. It must have been like a dream come true – she'd had so many knock-backs from people saying she would never make it as a model, but now here she was travelling America with other models.

Kate seemed happier in her private life, too. For some time, she had been chasing after cruel men who fuelled her sense of self-loathing. Now she discovered she was in the driving seat and could get the attention of pretty much any man she wanted. She met her first celebrity boyfriend in 1997 – Warren Furman, who was a regular on the hit British TV show *Gladiators* under his Gladiator name Ace. Kate was acting in the pantomime *Robinson Crusoe* at the time, and was introduced to Warren by her co-star Mark Smith – another participant on the show, who was known as Rhino. The pantomime was the first time Kate had done any acting and my mum, Esther, and I went along to see her at The Pavilion in Worthing. I remember Kate being so shy and nervous. The other cast members would tease her, saying she would have to sing at the end of the show, and she was petrified. Esther was so proud of her granddaughter strutting across the stage in the guise of the exotic Princess Atlanta that she cried. Perhaps it brought back memories of her showgirl side, when she'd entertained a different kind of audience during the war. I felt extraordinarily proud too, thinking of how brave Kate was to get up on that stage in front of a packed crowd, something she'd never done before.

I liked Warren. He was gentle and kind to us as a family, but Kate moved in with him in Sawbridgeworth, Hertfordshire, after just a few weeks, which was far too quick. She was so young and just starting out in her career so the last thing she should have been thinking about was settling down. In the end, it didn't last. Kate often gives her all to men, and finds it hard to put boundaries up to separate her personal and professional life. Before long, she either meets a new man on the job, or involves her man with her job, and her partners often try to control her. So she falls out of love and begins to retreat. Sometimes she finds it hard to leave, and sometimes she falls for someone else – either way she can never be on her own. In the end, Kate fell out of love with Warren and moved back home with us because her own house was being rented out. Warren sold stories to the tabloids about Kate, but in later years, he contacted Price to apologize. He told him that he had fallen into the celebrity circus where everything has a price, and we really appreciated his honesty and self-reflection.

Kate was, at this stage, getting promotional work as a grid girl with the Formula One racing team with the same name as her, owned by Eddie Jordan. She used to go to all the grand prix events and pose next to the cars and drivers in yellow and black team colours, which resulted in a brief romantic encounter with the racing driver Ralph Schumacher. Her profile was on the rise. Dan had returned home from Greenwich to resume his business studies in Brighton, and was shocked at the amount of fan mail Kate was receiving, passed on to her by the local newspaper. He thought it would be better for fans to have a direct link to her, so he suggested she should have a website and her own fan club, which he offered to manage for her. She didn't believe it would be successful at first, but Dan was confident. He took out a bank loan, built a website and purchased merchandise for Kate. For a monthly or yearly fee, Kate's fans could now chat on forums or take part in live webchats with her. It was a very forward-thinking idea at a time when the internet was brand new, and was also a huge relief to the posties who had been having to move around sacks of fan mail.

Dan had gone from being very much against his sister's choice of career to getting positively involved in it – from condemning it to actively promoting it. Over time he helped with everything, from attending shoots to managing her financial affairs – a job he still assists with to this day. Sadly, he could not manage her personal life in the same way – that side of Kate is too stressful for anyone to manage. More about this later.

Instinctively, I knew we would have to wise up to the celebrity machine fast if we were going to stay intact as a family. Kate was beginning to socialize in very different circles. To begin with we were fascinated by her encounters, but we didn't like the publicity that came with them – most of it was negative or 'kiss and tell' stories. Kate used to say, 'I'm building my career, so all publicity is good publicity.' But it's not as simple as that, and in Kate's case, we've seen the damage that can be caused by bad publicity. Over the years, the relentless blurring of boundaries between her professional and personal life has caused untold mental stress as so-called friends, exes and various other 'sources' have sold stories about her. Kate has a kind heart and wears it on her sleeve, but her vulnerability is sometimes exploited by others who pretend to lend her a trusting ear when she needs them most, then go on to sell this information to the press. At times, she has been her own worst enemy, but every human being deserves to be treated with kindness, especially when they are at their lowest ebb and Kate has been to dark places more times than anyone might imagine. Unfortunately, Kate is not good at finding loyal friends and only has a handful that she can trust. We've lost count of the number of people who have made money out of people she has confided in. We tell her time and time again, 'Stop talking about your life to everyone who wants to listen – save it for your dearest and closest friends if you need to talk. That said, I had no patience with most of Kate's friends, and the same remains true today. I could see through them and thought many of them were simply using Kate. Sadly, I don't think that Kate has many true friends.

In 1998, Kate met the DJ and band member Dane Bowers at the *Wild Wild West* film première, where they got chatting and exchanged numbers. He later asked her to meet him at a club in Croydon where he was performing as a DJ. As usual, Kate was all in from the word go. He was in a band called Another Level and Kate already liked his music, but now she started playing it all the time. I was surprised that Kate had met one of her idols and she seemed infatuated.

My take on Dane was that he was good looking and straight talking, but arrogant. We got on well with him initially, and he and Kate seemed in love. He would come to family barbecues and even occasionally met me with Kate for lunch when I was working. It seemed as if Kate wanted approval on the person she was dating. I would say he made an effort to get to know us, which we appreciated. He was also different to her previous boyfriends – he was more romantic and would write Kate letters and buy her presents. For the first time, she seemed to be with a man who had comparable ambitions, so in that sense it was a good match. He knew his own mind and he made her laugh. Sometimes, though, I felt awkward knowing the intimate details of her relationship. She was very open with me after her disastrous first relationship as a teenager, and from then on, we had no-holds-barred conversations about everything in her relationships, from sex to the day-to-day stuff, and we still do to this day.

Dane was originally attracted to Kate's glamour girl status, but the reality of being with a woman who was constantly on the covers of lad mags perhaps proved to be challenging for him and he became jealous of her and her career. This seems to be a trend in all of Kate's relationships. I expect it must be difficult to accept that other people are looking at your girlfriend's body all the time. Dane left Another Level to pursue a solo career at the same time as Kate's profile was in ascendence. He seemed to resent this and started belittling her, calling her a 'two-bit model'. Although he teamed up with Victoria Beckham to produce the single 'Out of Your Mind', his solo career hadn't really taken off. Perhaps it was jealousy, but in my opinion, he became ultra-critical of Kate, which seemed to increase her paranoia and exacerbate her feelings of low self-esteem. Whenever I met up with Kate, I could tell how unhappy she was, and she seemed to be drinking too much in an attempt to blot out her misery.

I was made aware of her first suicide attempt one afternoon in 1998 when she was 20. I was at home when I received a call from her make-up artist and flat-mate Sally Cairns, who told me that Kate had been taken to hospital after taking an overdose of sleeping pills. I could feel my pulse racing as I tried to make sense of what I was hearing. According to Sally, Kate was at Dane's flat when she swallowed the pills, but became very frightened when her heart started racing. Thankfully she made the decision to telephone Sally, who initially engaged her in conversation but then found her unresponsive. Sally called Dane who in turn called an ambulance. When the paramedics arrived, Kate was drifting in and out of consciousness but she managed by some miracle to open the door. They found Kate clutching a photograph of Dane. I knew that they were having problems, but I started to feel angry, as well as scared, that she was acting out her feelings in such an extreme way rather than talking them through with someone she trusted. My initial thought was, 'No man is worth this'.

I frantically called Price and asked him to come home from work as quickly as he could. Panic stricken, we dashed to Croydon hospital. The journey seemed never ending. We had no idea what state Kate would be in when we got there. Price was concentrating hard on the driving so we didn't talk much. My mind drifted back to my own suicide attempt at the age of 15 – mine had been over swimming as one day the pressure and stress had just got too much and I'd had an argument with my mum. She told me to wait until my dad got home but I felt

I couldn't keep going like that; I'd had enough. I took some paracetamol, not many, but when my lips started to feel numb, I realized what I'd done and ran to tell my mum and they took me to the hospital where I had to drink charcoal to make me sick and soak up the pills.

I was roused from my reverie when we finally arrived at the hospital. We rushed inside and at last, breathless, Price and I found Kate on a bed in a private room. Sally was holding one hand, while the other was still clutching the picture of Dane, who was on a chair seated in the corner. Kate, now awake, was clearly distraught and crying non-stop, saying – between sobs – that Dane didn't want her anymore. I was so angry. I didn't care if he was in the room or not. I kept saying to Kate, 'Good riddance to him. If this is what your relationship is doing to you then you are better off without him.' I could hardly face Dane, but I knew the relationship had run its course, even if Kate didn't know it yet. This is when we began to worry about Kate and her mental health, and the impulsiveness and unpredictability of her behaviour, even back then.

Later that evening, the doctors said it would be alright to release her, so I told Kate she was coming home with us. Once again, Price and I drove her back to safety. It wasn't the first time we had rescued her from a broken relationship, but we had never seen her react in such a dangerous, risky way before and I was shocked and concerned about her mental health.

Sophie was only 11 at the time. She was overjoyed to see Kate back home in one piece but, of course, being so young she didn't understand what was happening to her sister under the surface. We told her that Kate had been ill. Kate would still take her riding and shopping like nothing had happened, so Sophie just saw an occasionally troubled soul who stayed at home with us. Dan understood more and tried to sympathize with Kate, knowing that all the clubbing and drinking was a cover up for how she really felt. But there were times when he felt mad at her too and couldn't comprehend why she was so different to him and causing the family so much grief. He was also trying to help her to manage the business side of her career and found the continual blurring of her personal and professional life hard to handle.

I used to ask Kate about her feelings and encourage her to talk to us, but she just used to say she was sorry and she was fine – even though we knew she wasn't. We would see her flamboyant antics in the newspapers. She would dress outrageously to get noticed. She would stick out her tongue and wink at the camera. She would kiss other girls, show her knickers or lift her top up to show her boobs in a bra, or push them together for the camera. All this was to get noticed for the publicity. When photos of her emerged drunk and being carried out of clubs, that was different and we knew she wasn't doing that for publicity. We knew she was drinking to excess to hide her hurt and feelings because she didn't know how to cope with another rejection. Kate had endured a lot in her previous abusive relationships, but Dane's rejection was playing out on a public stage, which came with its own humiliation and shame. Silly things, like the fact that she was banned from the guest lists and promotional events that Dane was attending, constituted a form of open rejection that Kate just wasn't strong enough to endure.

The trouble with Kate is she doesn't like to upset me, so she often withholds the whole truth while she tries to manage situations by herself. Now, whenever Kate stops answering our calls or texts, we know she needs help. She has coping mechanisms – one that she developed very early on involved going out partying and it was being splashed across the tabloids. A second, more concerning, coping mechanism was (and still is) cosmetic surgery.

After the suicide attempt, to me the situation with Dane still seemed very unsatisfactory. Dane was openly dating other girls, which he was entitled to do, as he was single, and yet Kate would pop around to his flat just for sex. Was this a 'friends with benefits' situation? The on-off relationship finally ended after nearly two years and two months in November 2000, and Kate decided on a second boob job as part of her self-prescribed recuperative therapy. Kate would have done anything to get back with him, but it wasn't to be, so she tried to put herself back together – both literally and metaphorically – with a boob job, taking her from 32C to 32D.

At this point, I started to realize how vulnerable she was to surgery when relationships weren't going well. I read something recently which said that the decision to pursue cosmetic surgery is often associated with the contemplation of relationship difficulties – this rings true with Kate. To me, Kate's need for surgery seems to be rooted in feelings of low self-worth, which materialize whenever a relationship ends. Kate has always been terrified of needles, so why else would she be so desperate to go through painful operations to change her body? Back in the year 2000, I knew she needed help, but there was no obvious person or place for a working-class family to go to find it. Therapy was still something that was only associated with rich people and Americans, and we were neither of those, so we just had to try to work it out as a family by ourselves. We were just there to listen to her and talk to her. It was hard for all of us. This was new territory for us, just as it was for Kate, and we had no-one giving us advice – we had to find out for ourselves how to help.

When people see Kate get surgery, I assume many think that she's silly. That she's so vain. That she's so selfish. What they don't see is the anguish and pain that drives it. In some ways I think Kate has pursued surgery as a way of holding herself together when things feel like they are falling apart. It's easier to stitch a body back together than a mind. At times, the procedures haven't gone to plan, causing her a lot of pain. Sometimes, a surgeon might perform an operation on her and it's a total mess, so she has to go to another surgeon to correct it. They're not always good surgeons – in my eyes, surgery can almost become a form of self-harm. I've noticed that, once you start, plastic surgery can become so addictive. In my opinion, it's Kate's worst form of self-harm.

When I ask her why she's doing it, Kate's answer is always, 'It's my body. I can do what I like with it'. But when I press further, she doesn't have an answer. Inevitably, she gets infections and says she'll never do it again. But then, as soon as it's all cleared up and something challenging happens in her life or she thinks she perceives an imperfection, she starts again. I think she probably can't give a straight answer because so much of this behaviour is acted out unconsciously; it's like she's being driven towards something that even she can't really put into words. It's probably quite a strong feeling of unease deep inside her that drives her to do it. She doesn't understand the damage she is doing to herself and can't comprehend that she is unconsciously trying to fix her head by fixing her body.

These days, Kate has her favourite surgeon who often tells her off and says she doesn't need anything else done. But when she is really determined for something to be carried out, he will sometimes agree to it, thinking it is better if he performs the surgery safely rather than exposing her to risks from other, publicity-seeking surgeons, some with less experience. These are usually the ones that comment on her surgery in the press. In their eyes, Kate's surgery might be bad, but they want to portray the fact that the services they offer are good, and to seek new business from other women looking to change how they feel on the inside by changing the outside. Kate's drive to have the surgery overrides any of the risks. Her favourite part of the operation is the anaesthetic, which she always says enables her to have a 'lovely sleep'. She doesn't think about what the chemicals are doing to her body. I tell her I think it's dangerous, but my view just doesn't register. Before she goes under for an operation in any country, she'll text and say, 'In case I don't wake up – you know I love you', just like she did when she had her first boob job. I feel scared and cross, thinking, 'Oh, you stupid girl'. I cross my fingers and wait for her to call me when she wakes up. Kate doesn't tell me in advance anymore because she knows how much I disapprove, so the texts are often the first I hear about any impending surgery. When it is over, I get a call or a text but it's usually a day or two before we FaceTime because Kate doesn't want me to see the immediate aftermath as it can sometimes be messy, and it upsets me.

Of course, Kate's surgery obsession has been one of the main reasons for the intense press interest in her life. At the beginning of her career, we were living in a no-holds-barred era of press intrusion; one of the mechanisms newspapers seemed to employ to create good news stories was creating heroes and villains. Someone always had to be worshipped, while someone else was the scapegoat. For some reason, Kate's vulnerabilities, which she wore so openly, made her a perfect candidate for the latter role. We, her family, knew instinctively that her first suicide attempt was a complex and worrying cry for help, one that culminated in more surgery, which led to her being vilified in the media. But did she have the right to complain about her portrayal? After all, these were the same platforms she was earning big sums of money from. If someone asked me, 'Who was to blame: Kate or the media?', I think my answer would be, 'Both', but I question where the awareness was of mental health back then? Kate is still vilified for everything she does, but I think that people need to question what it is that lies behind her actions, and why the media still targets her so relentlessly.

Chapter 8

MY HERO HARVEY

I had breathed a sigh of relief when Kate's relationship with Dane Bowers ended, but my sense of peace was short lived. It was only a matter of weeks before an even more complex chapter in our lives began. As usual, once she was separated from Dane, Kate found it impossible to be alone. She had barely been single for five minutes when the Manchester United footballer Dwight Yorke offered to buy her a drink in London's Attica nightclub in November 2000. He had a reputation in the media as a womanizer, so a few months after their first meeting when Kate told me they had started dating, my heart sank. I knew we would all need to be prepared for more heartache and negative headlines. What I could never have imagined was that this brief, year-long relationship would produce my first, special, complex, courageous grandson – Harvey.

Of all the men Kate has dated in her life, Dwight Yorke will – perhaps surprisingly – always be my favourite because he gifted us this incredible child. Despite my initial reservations, I got to know him well over the short time they were together – I thought he was a funny man who was quite down to earth. He and Price clicked and played golf together. Yes, he was a typical playboy footballer and behaved very disrespect-fully at times, but I genuinely believe there was a period when he loved Kate and had good intentions to care for her. Sadly, it never came to fruition because he clearly wasn't ready for any kind of commitment. I remember Kate telling me that she was constantly finding other women's toothbrushes and hair-brushes at his house, and I think it really hurt her even though she would dismiss it with her usual bravado. However, he was in the North playing for Manchester United and she was in the South East building a modelling career, so it was always going to be a challenge to make their relationship work. And so, it was a huge surprise when, just a few months into their relationship, Kate fell pregnant with their child.

She initially thought about having an abortion and visited a clinic three times, but simply couldn't go through with it. She came home and just blurted out to me and Price that she was pregnant. Our initial reaction was one of shock, but she was 24 and we knew that she had made her decision and we would be there to help her deal with it. She had already told Dwight over the telephone, and he made it clear he didn't think they had a future so any decision would be hers alone.

To further complicate matters, Kate's manicurist noticed a lump on her finger and advised her to seek medical advice. The doctors identified it as leiomyosarcoma, a form of cancer. She was operated on and the lump was removed, but she still has to have check-ups every five years.

Kate has always had a very strong maternal instinct so we knew she would be a great mum when she told us she was committed to seeing it through. Once or twice, Dwight did agree to attend scans and classes with her, only then to not show up. Kate was left feeling very vulnerable, so I started accompanying her instead. She also sent Dwight a baby book so he could see the various developmental stages of his child but he seemed more concerned with what his personal agents were saying about the pregnancy and their desire to keep Kate and Dwight apart. He told her his mates thought she was keeping the baby just to get his money. She has certainly proved them all wrong on that count. On and off Dwight did pay some maintenance money, but over time the payments dwindled.

At this point, Kate was still sharing a house with her friend Sally, but they had recently been burgled and Kate was petrified by this, so it seemed like the safest option was for her to move back in with us. Kate was adamant that she could juggle her career with her pregnancy, and later with raising a child, and continued to do tabloid shoots right up until she was six months pregnant. After that – in 2001 – she decided to leave the Samantha Bond agency because she wanted to enter the music industry. She signed up with a new manager called Dave Read who promised to take her career in a new direction, getting her more personal appearances and dealing more proactively with negative press. Samantha Bond was a modelling agency which had served Kate well, but they did not deal with the press, so Kate felt she needed a manager. Regardless of how things worked out with her career, now that she was due to be a mother, Kate knew that we – her family – would help her as much as we could. She got more excited as her belly grew and loved choosing clothes and customizing her own with her sewing machine, as well as picking out furniture for the room the baby was going to share with her in our Brighton home.

While she was pregnant, Kate refused to give up on Dwight and the dream that he might eventually settle down with her and their baby. One night she heard he was in London and went searching for him, but he didn't want to know – I felt so sorry for her when she returned home, deflated. It was extremely painful for me to watch my pregnant daughter running around after a man who, by this point, clearly didn't love her. Deep down I think she hoped things would be different when the baby was born, so she stayed in touch with him throughout the pregnancy. She couldn't understand why he wasn't interested in his baby. She seemed to be going round in circles; once again she was stuck in the trap of trying desperately to get someone unsuitable to settle down with her. But all this paled into insignificance when she gave birth to a beautiful baby boy, who she named Harvey Daniel Price after her grandad and brother. I was overwhelmed by this lovely gesture which showed how deeply she loved them.

Kate had planned her birth meticulously. She asked me and Sally to be her birthing partners and she also invited Price, Dan and his wife Lou to be present at the start of the labour. She wanted us all around her. Sophie was at school. Kate picked the music she wanted to play and told us all before going into labour, 'We're going to play cards and it's going to feel really relaxed'. Fat chance! When it came down to it, she wanted complete silence in the room and we weren't allowed to talk.

Kate called Dwight to inform him of the impending birth, and he made it to the Royal Sussex County Hospital just in time to see her in the final stages of labour. In the end, Sally was rubbing Kate's back and I was holding her hand when a beautiful baby boy finally appeared at 1:15pm on 27 May 2002. Kate asked Price to cut the umbilical cord.

I'd never seen so much blood in my life – I had to call the nurse to ask if it was normal and, apparently, it was. After Harvey had been cleaned up, Dwight, Kate and their beautiful baby boy spent over an hour together, looking like a happy family. As a family, we had welcomed Dwight with open arms, and he seemed over the moon and was clearly delighted as he came out of the room with Harvey in his arms. The proud new dad showed Harvey off to everyone and he really did seem ecstatically happy with his son, but sadly their opportunity to bond was short lived because there was pressure for him to return to his Manchester United training schedule. Price and I were left to take the new mum and baby home the next day, and we returned to find the most enormous bouquet of flowers from Dwight, which Kate was so happy about. They must have had very mixed feelings about one another at this stage.

Harvey appeared to pass all the standard health checks and was discharged as a 'normal' baby, but warning bells soon sounded in our heads. He was such a good baby – too good. He slept most of the time and was feeding well, but he just wasn't that active. Kate noticed too; she kept saying, 'Mum – he isn't following anything with his eyes or squinting at the light'. I didn't know what to say except, 'Wait until we see the health visitor'.

When the health visitor finally came to examine Harvey for his six-week check-up, she agreed that there was a problem with Harvey's eyes. He wasn't following light as he should, and she suggested we make an appointment with our doctor to explore the possibility that he could be blind. Kate and I just looked at one another. I think we both knew instinctively in that moment that our lives had changed forever. She kept saying to me, 'He's blind, mum'. Straight away I could feel Kate's fear and devastation, hardly believing what we were being told, even though we'd been presented with the evidence ourselves. My reaction was to try to reassure her, so I said, 'He will be able to see something, I'm sure, so let's just wait until we get professional ophthalmologists to look at his eyes.' Kate and I didn't cry together as we were both trying to be strong for one another, but I know we did separately – a lot. The whole family was devastated. We just couldn't understand why nothing had been picked up in any of Kate's pregnancy scans concerning his health.

In many ways, Kate had invested so much hope that this little boy would make her happy and complete. She felt to me as though she was destined to be a mother, having demonstrated her caring nature in the way she looked after her little sister, her horses and the elderly at her first job. Now, in the cruellest twist of nature, she had been given a baby with complex needs, when she was still so young. We used to take Harvey out in his pram and people would say, 'What a lovely baby'. But rather than accept the compliment, she would reply, 'But he's blind.' I think saying it out loud was her way of trying to process the harsh reality of the situation. Meanwhile,

I went into 'fixing' mode because I just wanted to be able to make things better for my daughter and grandson. I asked our trusted family doctor – Dr Khan – to help us and he immediately advised getting Harvey's eyes checked at the local ear, nose and throat hospital.

The hospital doctors conducted an examination, before confirming that Harvey was blind and telling us that nothing more could be done for him. Kate and I, utterly overwhelmed, returned to Dr Khan saying we couldn't accept this diagnosis without seeking a second opinion from the world-famous Moorfields Eye Hospital in London. We looked up various doctors and eventually got a referral to Professor Tony Moore, who told us Harvey was not in fact totally blind. With the right work, Professor Moore believed his eyes could be trained to function in some way. It's impossible to put into words what that news meant to us – but one word is close to doing it: hope.

This kind and skilful doctor explained the reason Harvey couldn't see was because his optic nerve was underdeveloped, and he also had a condition called nystagmus – which was causing involuntary movements in his eyes. Stress also played a part, making his eyes wobble. Seeing with this condition is extremely hard; Harvey was having to move his head to one side to find the best angle to see through the wobble. We were referred to the regular Moorfields clinic and worked extensively with Professor Moore and his team, who taught us techniques to help stimulate Harvey's eyes. He helped us for years, making sure Harvey had the right help and guidance, including referring us to Dr Alison Salt, a consultant paediatrician, who helped us to understand how Harvey's brain functioned, and how best to support him. One simple strategy involved dangling CDs on a string over his cot so he could see the light reflecting off them. Another was to shine a torch under his blanket in the darkness to train his eyes to follow the light.

Although Dwight had continued to see his son, right from the beginning the signs were there that Kate was likely to be a single parent. Dwight was certainly trying hard to do the right thing and I genuinely think that he and Kate might have had a chance to build a solid friendship, at the very least, for the sake of their son, if it weren't for the pressures on them, which included their demanding jobs, which were in different locations, and Harvey's challenges. However, they did agree to go and register Harvey's birth together, but on the way there, Dwight took a call from his agent telling him not to register the birth because they wanted Harvey to take a DNA test to make sure that Dwight was the father, because Harvey was so pale. What should have been a lovely memory was spoiled by this cynicism. Kate and I were both upset and angry, particularly as Dwight had acknowledged Harvey as his son. It seemed that Dwight was having his life run by other people, and I suspect that this has been the case for years. Despite this, Dwight did visit Kate and Harvey once a week at our house to get to know his little boy, and Kate kept him informed of Harvey's medical appointments in case he wanted to attend. To begin with, Dwight paid her maintenance, but over time, the payments dwindled before stopping altogether, and Kate was left to support Harvey alone.

Before he parted ways with Kate, Dwight and I spent time

together and had many conversations about life in general. I remember one time when he was round at my house and watching me like a hawk as I made him a sandwich, ensuring that I spread only the tiniest amount of butter on his bread, because he was so health conscious! He spoke to me about his ambitions to represent his country of Trinidad and Tobago in the World Cup in 2006 and I told him it would be an incredible opportunity for him. Sadly, they didn't win, but to my amazement, he called me after the match to tell me how proud he was. He was awarded a Chaconia Medal, the second highest honour in Trinidad and Tobago, and named sports ambassador for his country. I know that if Harvey could have understood, he would have been so proud of his dad.

Kate went back to work modelling for *OK* magazine just ten days after the birth. When Kate was back in the full swing of work and doing personal appearances, she would slip out of her comfy 'Kate' tracksuit and trainers and pull on some outrageous 'Jordan' outfit. She used to tell me, 'I'm dressed for work now mum' before kissing me and Harvey goodbye and heading for the bright lights of London. To me it seemed just like an actress putting on a costume before going to perform on stage. Harvey and I went everywhere with her because she never wanted to be apart from her little boy.

Kate and I had always been close, but now we had to work as an even tighter team in order to look after Harvey. While we waited for further instructions from Moorfields, we joined a charity called Look Sussex which supported visually impaired children. We met other parents whose children had visual impairments and were encouraged to attend Dorton House

School for the Blind, where specialists helped us to stimulate Harvey's eyes and engage him in play. He joined when he was three months old and ended up staying for ten years, until it sadly closed due to lack of funding. After that he moved on to Linden Lodge School in Wimbledon, South West London, and now he is in a college.

Harvey was very slow developmentally, but physically he was growing at such a pace. His appetite was insatiable, and he wanted milk all night long. Kate wanted to do the majority of the feeding herself but at one point, when he was about six weeks old, he was drinking 13 bottles a night and she became very tired, so I helped out. Before long, we both sensed there was more to Harvey's challenges than blindness. He could be triggered into a meltdown by the most ordinary noise – like a door closing or cutlery rattling in a drawer. At the time, we didn't know his ears were so sensitive to sound. When Harvey was about two and old enough to go for a meal, we were concerned by how much sweet stuff he consumed – he wanted to eat packet after packet of raisins, believe it or not! At the time, we had no idea his brain simply wasn't able to give him the normal signals that he was full, because he had Prader-Willi syndrome, as well as diabetes incipitus that left him constantly thirsty, though this hadn't yet been diagnosed. We also didn't yet know that he had autism, which meant it was hard for him to have a varied diet, because sensitivities to different food textures is a trait of autism. The mums at Look Sussex kept on at us to take Harvey to a consultant called Dr Dattani at Great Ormond Street because they recognized that he had similar symptoms to their children, who were also blind or partially sighted. This doctor had been particularly brilliant at diagnosing the reasons behind this. They supported Kate and me during dark and difficult times and Kate and I will never forget mums Jeanette, Helen, Jude and Wendy who started Look Sussex, and all the other remarkable parents of disabled kids we have met along the way.

We needed a referral to Great Ormond Street, but we had to battle to get the consultants at our local hospital in Brighton to accept the idea that there were further complications which hadn't been picked up by the health visitor or the doctors in the early weeks following Harvey's birth. Eventually, we met with Dr Dattani, who diagnosed Harvey with a rare condition called septo-optic dysplasia – a disorder of early brain development which, amongst other things, affects how our body's hormones are produced, and can lead to serious side effects. We were told that it was imperative that Harvey now accessed the right medication to prevent further brain damage. If he had had an MRI in the first year of his life, it would have detected his underactive thyroid, but the rules at the MRI clinic in Brighton at that time stated that children under the age of one could not have a scan. Because the thyroid problem had not been detected at an earlier stage, Harvey had not had the relevant medication and this had affected his brain even further.

Kate and I were dealing with one bombshell after another – first seeing the signs in Harvey, then battling for diagnosis and support. And as he got older, his needs became more complex. First it was his eyesight, then his hearing, his moods, his eating habits, his lack of speech and lack of emotions. Despite falling out with Kate, Dwight was still in touch with me and realized that Harvey needed more support. One day when I was with Harvey, he called to say he thought it would be a good idea if I left my job at a payroll company to help Kate with Harvey full time, and he offered to pay my wages. Price and I needed two incomes to support our household, so I agreed and this arrangement stayed in place until Harvey was four years old. I was grateful for this time spent with Harvey, as it meant that I could support Kate with him at appointments and at home, and establish a proper routine, which is essential for an autistic child.

With me not at work, Kate and I became an even closer-knit team and I agreed to accompany her on a pivotal career trip to Los Angeles in the autumn of 2002 when Harvey was only around three months old. It was the first time I experienced the worrying blurring of boundaries between my daughter's personal and professional life. I couldn't understand it and I found it disturbing. As if it wasn't hard enough being an ordinary, working-class family plunged into the limelight with no rule book to follow, now we were learning to care for a demanding child with special needs at the same time. Deep down, Kate was devastated by Harvey's diagnosis – absolutely heartbroken – but she adored him and rather than hide him away, she set out on a mission to persuade the entire world to love him as much as she did. However, I felt deeply uncomfortable with the process. I did not disagree with the idea of Harvey having a public profile when he got older, but at that time we hadn't even had a chance to process his difficulties in private, and it felt way too soon to parade him in front of the world.

As far as I was concerned, the main reason for taking Harvey on this trip to Los Angeles was so that he could see an endocrine specialist we had heard about to get a second opinion on Dr Dattani's diagnosis. We wanted to see if American doctors were of the same opinion, as it was all new to us. As usual, Kate was doing it her way, though, so she invited Richard Macer and his camera on the trip. He was one of the first ever reality TV producers – a one-man band who had seen potential in Kate and ended up shooting 200 hours of footage with her for three BBC documentaries which aired from 2001 to 2003. Kate explained to me that she needed to make money to support Harvey and saw the trip as an opportunity. Despite my scepticism about the media, Richard was a familiar face and I liked him. He was not intrusive like the film crews who would come later, and I could be honest with him.

Kate had been invited to meet Hugh Hefner, which was a big deal for her career; in fact, she would say that it was the pinnacle of it. So, we agreed that I would check into The Standard hotel in Downtown LA, with Harvey, while she accepted Hefner's invitation to stay at the Playboy Mansion. I remember Richard questioning me about the Playboy visit as we were walking down the road in LA one day. I told him that although I had thought that Hugh Hefner had been kind and courteous in inviting Kate to his mansion, I was sad and angry that Harvey had become a focus for the media and I didn't want to talk about that. I can still recall Richard filming the wheels of the pushchair as we walked along.

The American doctors confirmed the septo-optic dysplasia diagnosis but also suspected Prader-Willi Syndrome, which explained Harvey's insatiable appetite. It was just one thing after another, and another and another. In America, it felt like another bombshell had hit us, having yet another complication to consider. Kate dealt with it – as she so often did – by throwing herself into work.

The Standard is a really trendy hotel and there were a couple of nights when Harvey needed extra milk and I found myself pushing his buggy outside the hotel and past the Viper Club thinking, 'How on earth did a normal grandmother from Brighton end up here?' But that wasn't the most surreal part of the trip. One morning, I was woken up at 1am to a knock on my hotel door. When I opened it, I found Hugh Hefner with eight of his bunnies – including my daughter – standing on the other side. Kate wanted to see Harvey and, in my naivety and half-awake state, I agreed they could come in. Hefner told me, 'You know, your daughter is a very naughty girl, don't you?' and before I knew it, Kate was snapping a photo of me and Harvey with Hugh and the other bunny girls while I stood there in my nightie. That – on reflection – was when I sensed the boundaries around her and our family's private life were collapsing, and I didn't like it. Of course, Kate was in the mansion in pursuit of wealth and celebrity – no one is denying that. But I know my daughter and at this particular moment she was a proud mum wanting to show off her child. She had been talking to Hugh about Harvey's condition and Hugh had expressed a desire to meet Harvey. When he did, he seemed genuinely interested and asked some thoughtful questions. Hugh was very gentle – he held Harvey in his arms like a kind old grandad and we talked about Harvey in the most natural way.

Unbeknown to me, her manager had set up an interview about the trip with the *News of the World* which also involved a photo shoot. The piece would combine the glamour of the Hefner meeting with the more sombre storyline of Harvey's hospital visit, which was supposed to be a very separate thing. It was against my principles and I felt totally sad that Kate was mixing something so personal to us and her son with something so frivolous and public. I was horrified and thought, 'How can you do this?'

I had believed our hospital visit to be a private event. I felt this part of our lives should be for us as a family only, not shared with the nation and mixed up with someone's Sunday morning titillation. Harvey was a child and – to my mind – his personal life should be kept sacred because he couldn't make the choice about sharing it; it was up to responsible adults to decide that for him. I couldn't get my head around it and felt quite angry, a state of mind which was not helped by a photographer in Kate's entourage who wanted to use my bedroom balcony to take pictures of famous models who happened to be using the pool down below. These models wanted their shots taken by the paparazzi and that's when I realised the truth behind the fame game. I found this request by the photographer to be absolutely grotesque and intrusive. It left me feeling very worried indeed about the world my daughter, now a mother, was inhabiting. I was angry with her and it took me a long time to understand her rationale in involving Harvey in that newspaper article. My anger was made even worse when we received the doctor's diagnosis and she confirmed the septo-optic dysplasia diagnosis.

Kate had the opposite attitude to her son's visibility in the media, no doubt with the best intentions. Her attitude was, why hide him away because he is disabled? On reflection, I think Kate's determination to tell the world about Harvey's complications was motivated by the same thing that caused her to tell people he was blind when they looked in the pram. If she announced his conditions before people asked questions and took control of the talking, perhaps it felt less painful for her. Her comeback was always, 'If I don't say anything, it will get out and then we'll have to explain it anyway so it's better if I do the talking.'

At the end of the day, Kate's lack of understanding of boundaries was making things increasingly difficult. From the beginnings of her foray into the world of fame, she seemed to struggle with identifying which parts of herself should be off limits, and which parts could be offered up. We were just an ordinary family with no one advising us. Her managers seemed to want her to offer up all aspects of her body and life on a platter, which they could sell to the highest bidder. We were learning as we went along so, before we knew it, there were no boundaries left at all. In LA, Kate's manager was partying alongside her – where was the professionalism in that?

Since her turbulent, teenage years, my daughter had needed a great deal of support but now my life had become even more dedicated to her. We were faced with this amazing yet challenging baby who had so many complications. These would later be compounded with a diagnosis from Dr Ahmed and Dr Santosh at the Maudsley Hospital of autistic spectrum disorder (ASD), attention deficit hyperactivity disorder (ADHD) and pathological demand avoidance (PDA). Almost overnight, we had to adapt our whole lives to him. But despite our differences in opinion around Harvey's public image, I couldn't deny that Kate was absolutely marvellous with her son. With my help, she began fighting for Harvey from day one and has been doing so ever since. One of the worst parts of his condition is the fact he is cortisol deficient. This means that he could just die at any time if he doesn't have an injection at the right time – if he hurts himself or gets a high temperature, or even a simple cold, he has to be monitored in case he needs an emergency injection and sugar gel to prevent him from going into a coma, after which an ambulance has to be called so that he can be monitored in hospital. He also needs a hormone injection every night. I'll never forget the feeling of panic when Kate and I were told by one of the Great Ormond Street nurses that we would have to give Harvey these injections for the rest of his life. We had to begin practising on an orange to get the feel for it. This was initially difficult for Kate, given her fear of needles, but it's just one of the many things she has had to deal with as part of the huge responsibility that comes with keeping her son alive.

To Kate, Harvey is and always has been a 'normal' child. Looking after him has been challenging but rewarding and she is so patient with him, even when his meltdowns trigger him to smash TVs, iPads, car windscreens and windows. He also punches holes in walls and headbutts them, but nothing phases his mum. Interestingly, he will hit out at everything and everyone except her. She knows he loves her unconditionally and she loves him back with all her heart. After an outburst, Harvey always says sorry and gets very upset because he can't help himself. It makes your heart melt. We love him regardless of his challenges. He joins Price and Dan as part of the triumvirate of men who love her unconditionally, regardless of her flaws.

In the early days, when Harvey was being diagnosed, I think it was hugely stressful for Kate, but she knew she had to be strong for him even though she had no partner herself to lean on. She also had to deal with cruel headlines which insinuated that her party lifestyle had somehow caused Harvey's disabilities. The truth is that nothing that Kate did could have caused these conditions – they are genetic. Imagine how you'd feel if you had to read articles in the tabloids about your beloved child or grandchild that talked about his private health conditions and were filled with things that you knew to be untrue?

Thankfully, Kate and Harvey had a loving family to anchor them during these turbulent times. For me, giving them the intensive support they needed meant there was less time for Dan and Sophie, but they have always been incredibly understanding of this dynamic. Dan had been working alongside Kate, building her website and fan club, so he understood how much help she needed with Harvey and he was particularly angry with Dwight for not supporting her. Sophie was at school at the time and used to get upset watching Harvey struggle, but at home we kept everything as normal as possible, eating meals together and watching TV – just trying to carry on with normal life. I hope I'm right in saying that no one else felt neglected because of the situation with Harvey. Sophie was busy socializing with her school friends, Dan was living with his girlfriend Lou, and Price was always there supporting everyone. He's very good at listening and he was brilliant at saying the right things at the right time. He was amazing with Harvey too and, along with Sophie, fed and looked after him if Kate and I needed a break. Overall, the family came together and it was a simple unspoken fact that this was how it had to be.

Another thing that drew the family together in 2003 was a sad event. My dad died. For the last few years of his life he had suffered severely with bad health. He had been diagnosed with diabetes in his fifties. Initially this had been controlled by his diet, but eventually he had to inject himself with insulin. He also had heart problems which led to a triple bypass. As the diabetes worsened it affected his kidneys to such an extent that he was hooked up to a dialysis machine for three days a week. As anyone with diabetes knows, the feet and toenails must be looked after but unfortunately he caught an infection that turned to gangrene in one of his feet. This meant another hospital stay. We knew the end was near so we stayed around his bed. He opened his eyes, looked at us, then closed them for the last time. He was a lovely man who had mellowed with age. Kate made a recording of the song 'Show Me Heaven' which was played at the funeral. Half of his ashes were sent to his family in America and scattered over his mum and dad's grave, which had been draped with the American flag, as he had been in the U.S. armed forces. The other half were kept to be buried with my mother when she died.

We were sad to lose my dad and Kate had been especially close to him. Despite all these challenges, Kate remained determined that Harvey would enjoy life as much as any other individual and she is not ashamed of him. She continues to show the world he can have a good life and do what other people his age do – go on holiday, go swimming, dancing, listen to music, make music, go on scary rides, go flying, go to the cinema and hold a conversation. Kate and I haven't always seen eye-to-eye on Harvey, but she is and always has been an amazing mother to him. She only has to look in his eyes to know what he's feeling and her deep understanding of his disabilities has opened up conversations which have reduced stigma and shame. She has never hidden him away. That's why, when Harvey was one and a half, the three of us ended up in the Australian jungle on an adventure which would, ultimately, produce another father for Harvey – although not one who would stick around forever.

Chapter 9

INTO THE JUNGLE

With its Roman marble columns and vaulted gold ceilings, Australia's Palazzo Versace Gold Coast Hotel was a far cry from the flat above the Brighton garage where I grew up, but I'd come to expect anything as Katie Price's mum and constant companion. Despite all the challenges she had faced, my 26-year-old daughter was now courting considerable fame and some fortune as a feisty glamour model and single mum. For some reason, the public couldn't get enough of her. I'll never forget her then-manager Dave Read telling me somewhat gleefully in 2004, 'She's a licence to print money you know'. For the best part of eight years, Kate's fame had remained a mystery to us, her closest family, but we had come to accept it. And so it wasn't surprising that year when the producers of the survival reality TV show *I'm a Celebrity* came calling. Kate accepted and, before long, I was on the 22-hour flight to Brisbane with her and Harvey. None of us was prepared for the fact that she would return captivated by a fading Harrow-born Greek Cypriot singer, who had been brought up by strict Jehovah's Witnesses.

One-hit wonder Peter Andre had achieved brief fame as

the singer of 'Mysterious Girl', but later worked in a gym to make ends meet. To the public, Kate and Peter's relationship would be the ultimate reality TV love affair, but behind closed doors it would turn Kate's world upside down in the worst possible way.

My first main contact with 'Pete' came via a phone call the night before the contestants were due to enter the jungle. He and his parents had relocated to Australia's Gold Coast when he was six; he was living with his parents nearby and he was hosting a barbecue for contestants and invited Kate to attend. We had planned a cosy family night in together before her foray into the Springbrook National Park in Queensland, so Kate politely declined. Pete called again trying to persuade her, but she wanted to give Harvey the 'mum time' he desperately needed before her absence. Plus, she was intent on consuming 12 boiled eggs in an attempt to stave off hunger in the jungle. For some reason, when I woke up the next morning, Peter Andre was still on my mind. Before Kate left to be helicoptered into the jungle, I remember saying, 'Whatever you do, do not end up with him'.

From the word go, something didn't feel right about Peter; I had an inkling that he wasn't who he claimed to be. He came across as gushing and gentlemanly, but I sensed a manipulative side to his character; a man who spoke from the mouth rather than the heart. His career was in decline and I think he saw an opportunity in my daughter, an opportunity he was quick to seize.

When she was younger, Kate had had pictures of Pete on her wall and I told her not to fall for him partially because

I had never really taken to him. Thankfully, when she arrived in the jungle the next day, Kate didn't appear overly impressed with him and instead focussed on jumping into the experience with gusto. Harvey and I felt immensely proud watching his make-up free mum charming the public with her dry sense of humour and feisty courage. The way she tackled the trials was typical of her too – she's always been up for something that's different and daring. Some of the challenges Kate had to undertake to win stars to gain food for the fellow contestants still make me shiver. She had a fishbowl placed over her head filled with huntsman spiders, cockroaches, beetles and snakes. Kate was particularly brave when she swam out of her depth in a pond full of snakes and eels, despite her history of having panic attacks in water. She ate live bugs, witchetty grubs and fish eyes. The show was a real ratings topper, and I found it surreal that my daughter was on one of the most popular shows on TV. I've never thought of her as famous because to me she is just Kate, my daughter, and has never acted any differently towards me or others in the family.

Each day, the contestants' family and friends were shuttled to the TV set where we were shown a live stream of the programme, waiting for the next celebrity to be eliminated. Spending so much time behind the scenes made me realize how much of reality TV is down to the edit – things are never really as they seem, and these shows have the capacity to make or break someone's career. It gave us the chance to mingle and meet some of the other supporters, including Pete's agent Claire Powell, who seemed nice and approachable. We had lunch together and she expressed an interest in managing Kate alongside Pete if they ever became an item. I thought it was an unusual thing to say and, whilst I thought a relationship between them could potentially work, I thought that it was highly unlikely that they would get together. Kate needed an agent who could take her career to the next level, not just doing photoshoots and public appearances, and it felt as though Claire would have been able to provide this, but before long I began sussing things out. I was getting to know the camera crew well, and started to ask them what they made of Claire. One of them looked me straight in the eye and said, 'You need to research Martine McCutcheon'. The internet was not quite so easy to access in those days, but I went back to my hotel and a Google search showed me that Martine had won libel damages from Powell over an article in a tabloid newspaper, which wrongly suggested she had tried to avoid paying Powell a debt. The story, which appeared in the *Mirror* in April 2001 under the headline 'Martine's Cash Tiff', suggested that the singer and actress, who rose to fame as Tiffany in EastEnders, was 'locked in dispute' with her former manager. Clearly, the court deemed it was not true. I was being alerted to Claire not being as popular with her clients as I had thought, but I couldn't do much more than bear it in mind. The same friendly camera crew also alerted me to the fact that Pete was rapidly coming on to my daughter in the jungle – a piece of information that left me with a nagging feeling of dread I couldn't quite put my finger on. In the jungle, Pete suggested to Kate that they play along for the cameras to prevent them from being voted out, and I didn't feel comfortable seeing Kate being drawn into that sort of gameplay.

By the time Kate emerged from *I'm a Celebrity* in early December 2004, she had fallen hook, line and sinker for Pete. I remember seeing him for the first time at a post-filming photo shoot and saying a bit brusquely, 'What have you done to my daughter?' He didn't answer. It was like he had hypnotized her. Kate was head over heels in love with him and all she could talk about was wanting to be with him. She was smitten and conceded that she would have to talk to his agent Powell about how things might pan out with their schedules. I think the love was genuine on Kate's part, but it felt more business-like in the Pete camp. A friend of mine had come out to help me look after Harvey and Pete's brothers told her that they didn't think that Kate was Pete's type, and that they shouldn't be together. After they emerged from the jungle, Pete did not seem too keen on linking up with Kate at first. He was more occupied with his management and doing interviews. At that stage I got the impression that any affection he had shown in the jungle was staged for the camera and the publicity it generated. The jungle was an unreal environment, and it was difficult to tell someone's true character while they were inside it.

Things got even more surreal when Kate's boyfriend of the time – a garage owner's son called Scott Sullivan – called to tell me he was on his way to Australia to meet Kate. Their relationship had not been making either of them happy, but he had been watching the show back home and had seen Pete coming onto her in the jungle and was having none of it. I wasn't allowed any contact with Kate once she was in the jungle, but the film crew passed me a note from her one day, in which she asked me to tell Scott to hand back her car and house keys. I was put in a terrible position and had the awful task of telling him over the phone that she didn't want to see him. The lovesick boy boarded a flight regardless but when he arrived, he realized he had no hope of seeing Kate, so he returned to the airport and went home. She was now totally besotted with Pete and any sense of reality had been lost.

Things may have been slow to start but before we knew it, we were all back in England and Pete was moving into Kate's beautiful house in Maresfield, near Uckfield. I was surprised to hear he had brought his brother Mike with him from Cyprus – hardly the actions of a besotted suitor, and I found myself questioning Pete's motivations for wanting to date Kate. Whatever they were, any previous reservations his family had had seemed to dissipate once he was able to take up residence with her, and we assumed that they had accepted her. From the word go, both Price and I thought the relationship was problematic, not least because Kate and Pete appeared to be very different characters from different cultures. From here on in, we witnessed Kate's mental health challenges escalating to a new level.

As Kate's fame increased, I think Pete was struggling with not being in the spotlight as much as my daughter. Meanwhile, his management seemed to want total control over Kate, who was a big money earner, and a PA who worked for Claire and her partner, Neville Hendricks, began accompanying Kate everywhere. Kate couldn't say anything without this team of people vetting it first, or go anywhere without telling them. I truly believe that this is when Kate's serious mental health problems began. It seemed as if they wanted a puppet who would do whatever they asked of her. When she asked Pete what he thought, his standard reply would be, 'If I were you, I would do it, but of course, it's up to you.' The feelings of low self-esteem that had first surfaced in her childhood were re-triggered and she began to lose any real sense of herself. I noticed cracks quickly appearing in their relationship. They had different ideas about how to manage their careers and the directions they were taking with so much public attention, and gradually and subtly it made Kate doubt her own ability to make a decision. How could a person be expected to live under this kind of scrutiny every day?

Pete and Kate were only weeks into their relationship and their PR machine was making the outside world believe it was a match made in heaven, but behind closed doors neither of them seemed happy to me. I quickly learned that my opinions on the matter weren't particularly welcomed, as well as realising that it was best not to speak to Pete before he'd had his morning coffee! Pete and I never argued, but I think we both knew that there were certain topics that were off-limits, so we never crossed that line. They had not had time to get to know one another privately before the cameras started to roll. The public wanted to see more of Kate and Pete together as a couple so CAN Associates (Claire and Neville Associates) had the idea of starting a reality TV show, and brokered a lucrative deal with ITV2. A relationship in front of the cameras inevitably involves a level of pretence. Kate had us, her family, living nearby. Pete's family were on the other side of the world in Australia so he invited his brother Mike to live with him and Kate. Understandable, but awkward. Then there was also Harvey to factor in. It was a difficult situation for Pete because he had never lived with a child, let alone one with such profound disabilities. Kate and Pete had also been brought up differently culturally and religiously – Pete was a Jehovah's Witness, but Kate had never been christened, as I wanted her to find her own religion, like Sophie and Dan. They had moved into Kate's home, which she was in the process of renovating, so she had a body of friends nearby – whereas Pete had been out of the UK for a long time and many of his mates were back in Australia. This was probably why it seemed that Claire was his best friend as well as being an agent for both of them. This didn't go down too well, as it seemed to me that Kate wasn't expected to have much of a voice of her own, or to express opinions.

Kate and Pete were told more or less when and where they could go and what they could do when they got there. There was no 5pm cut off time – they were essentially working 24/7. These were clearly not conditions that would enable a fledgling romance to flourish.

Pete seemed at such a loss professionally – he tried to revive his music career by re-releasing old material. It was then decided that he would record an album with Kate called *A Whole New World*. In contrast, things were really taking off for Kate; she was getting opportunities to create all kinds of things – children's and adults' books which became bestsellers, a bed linen range for Matalan, affordable jewellery sold in Argos, a keep-fit video, lingerie, and equestrian clothing and boot ranges. Her fan base started to include women, single mums and also people in the horse world. When Kate mentioned these ideas to her management company, Neville and Claire dismissed most of them, preferring to concentrate on producing shows, so she found her own people to action them.

This was the point of no return, where all boundaries between Kate's private and public life broke down. Soon, no aspect of Kate's private life was off limits. *When Jordan Met Peter* was the first six-episode series, which aired in November 2004. It was narrated by the veteran BBC presenter Terry Wogan and followed the first six weeks of Kate and Pete's relationship after their jungle romance. People had been so engrossed with watching the romance develop in the jungle, they wanted more. They wanted intimate conversations, disagreements then making up, Pete making coffee or Kate eating breakfast, Pete going to the shops or Kate choosing what clothes to wear or putting her make-up on. For some reason, the public couldn't get enough of it and more than 1 million viewers tuned in. A further series was commissioned for broadcast in 2005, and then another, and another, and another.

Up until then, we had been used to Richard Macer with his single camera and unscripted style of recording, where nothing was put on. In contrast, this new set up was taking things to a whole new level. Every day of Kate's life was a full-on production which involved cameras, sound, hair and make-up, and wardrobe – everywhere you turned there was a lens trained on your face. Kate had been used to filming reality shows with Richard Macer, so it was nothing new to Kate – but it was to Pete. It began about two months after they had started living together and included footage of them at work, at home, on holiday, and introduced the Price and Andre families.

It seemed that filming took over Kate's life completely. I was used to accompanying her with Harvey to his medical appointments and to school, but when the filming started it was difficult for Kate to keep coming along. I was furious when the crew wanted to film Harvey's hospital visits. I thought this was going too far. However, Kate felt it important to show Dr Dattani talking with us about Harvey's condition. She also felt it would show other families with disabled children that they were not alone. I felt frustrated because I wasn't able to sit down and have a heart-to-heart chat with Kate about having Harvey in the public eye, as the cameras were ever-present, and they seemed to want to record all of our conversations.

When I watched them filming together, I would say Kate was herself, but Pete liked to play act. He could switch it on and off as required. At this time the filming was not edited very much. I remember one evening when we had Kate and Pete round to our house for a murder mystery supper. It was meant to be a simple gathering with just a handful of our close friends who were shocked when a full production team turned up with lights and cameras. It seemed as if they were planning to film an episode of *Poirot* rather than our informal meal. At the end, we were all left speechless when Pete stood up and thanked everyone for taking part. Nobody had realized that they were supposed to be in a show to begin with – Price and I were hosting the evening, but it felt as if it had been taken over and I felt embarrassed for him. It felt as if nothing was sacred or private anymore. As the series progressed it started to be scripted with a storyline – and this was edited by CAN. Towards the end of their relationship particularly, the editing seemed to make Kate look moody and uncooperative and Pete look the good guy. Kate and Pete were drifting towards separation and after the split, CAN were intending to continue to represent Pete.

My main priority was making sure that Harvey's medical needs were being met. The heavy filming schedule meant that Kate was forced to miss more and more of his appointments and it bothered me until I got so annoyed, I insisted on her management team putting them into the diary. To my horror, they tried sending cameras with us to Great Ormond Street and Moorfields Eye Hospital – in no time at all, reality TV had taken over all our lives and any sense of normality was lost. I do have one happy memory of this time, which was an extraordinary moment when we had the opportunity to meet the Queen, as she was there for the opening of the new children's section of Moorfields Eye Hospital. I'll never forget that day.

There is no question that Kate had signed up for the cameras in order to earn money and enhance her profile, but I don't think she truly understood what kind of beast she had unleashed. There was no aspect of her life the cameras didn't want to intrude on. On reflection, I think it set a dangerous precedent for her mental health. At times, she didn't want to show her true feelings on camera, so she'd bottle them up until they culminated in depression. There was never any end to the filming – sometimes Kate would put her foot down and say,

'You've got enough'. But enough was never enough. And if she took a bit of downtime, like going to a spa, her management were constantly on the phone asking when she would be coming back and how much longer she would be.

Kate wasn't as clever as Pete at playing the cameras. Sometimes she couldn't hold back her upset, but her anxieties were met by him with, 'What's wrong with you now?' or 'Why are you going on?' – he used to turn a subtle cry for help into an argument for the TV which would make Kate look bad. These documentaries were filmed more or less every day and could involve a lot of travelling and being away from home. I remember a trip not so far from home where we went to Harrods to look around. Kate was told she had to buy something for the filming. I remember it was a Versace dinner set and an eiderdown for her bed. Usually, she would have bought them from M&S, but this was what she had been told to do. Pete found it easy to play up to the cameras, whereas Kate struggled with that level of sophistication. It felt so false, and that's because it was. In contrast, I remember a wonderful evening where Primark very kindly gave me and Kate the opportunity to shop to our heart's content after-hours – we had both always loved their pyjamas and slippers, and in all honesty, I think we both enjoyed that experience far more than the shopping spree in Harrods.

A cruise was organized for the Price and Andre families. The intention was for us all to get to know each other. It turned out to be a disaster. We were meant to do activities together or go on excursions; that didn't happen. We were meant to have dinner together each night; that didn't happen either.

It was probably the age and cultural differences that caused the problems, but things weren't helped by the fact that it was like being in a goldfish bowl with people constantly taking photos of us. The atmosphere changed when Kate announced that she was pregnant. Fortunately, Pete was very happy with the news and proved to be a very supportive father, so Kate's second pregnancy was a happier time than her first. Junior's birth in June 2005 was, without a doubt, one of the lowest points – it was terrible. I'll never forget standing by the hospital lift waiting for my daughter to return from the operating theatre, when a camera was thrust in my face and someone clearly wanting to manipulate a script began asking me questions like, 'What do you think of this? They've been a while. Do you think there's something wrong?' In reality, nothing out of the ordinary was happening. Nothing was wrong, but they needed a storyline. It was bad enough for me, so I can hardly imagine what it must have been like for my daughter having a camera shoved in her face minutes after giving birth. You need time to get yourself together, but she had no privacy at all. And, of course, Junior wasn't able to make that choice about his privacy because he was just a baby. On reflection, the strangest thing of all is that we all just did what we were told by the film crew and Kate's management. It was like we had been sucked into a cult and no one except me was questioning it – but even I wasn't doing it loudly enough.

Kate was exhausted and depressed after Junior's birth. The bond between her and her second-born son didn't develop in the same way as it had with Harvey – probably because she wasn't able to have the same quality time alone with him.

Pete's parents had come over for the birth and they stayed on much longer than anticipated. They wanted to move into Kate's house, but she felt it wasn't big enough and she wanted to spend time alone with her son, so they stayed in a hotel. In the end, they were welcomed, but the whole atmosphere was still very claustrophobic, and, as if that wasn't hard enough, the cameras were constantly whirring in the background. It seemed to me that Kate had no privacy at all, and this made being a new mum very challenging. Meanwhile, Pete is from a culture where family is everything and I am all for that, but it seemed to me that once Junior came along, and his family stayed, Kate always came second to her mother- and father-in-law. She sensed this very early on in their relationship and it hurt her. She used to cry a lot and drive over to my house to escape the pressure-cooker atmosphere of her own home. Kate learned that when they argued, Pete would never give way. It was up to her to back down, then he would come out of his mood. As if having one mum wasn't enough, Pete would often ring Claire telling tales about Kate, then Claire would ring Kate to quiz her. This kind of interference made me feel cross, and all of this created the perfect storm for a diagnosis of post-natal depression in the first few weeks of Junior's life.

I tried to support my daughter as best as I could. From Pete's point of view, he was probably equally fed up with me being around five days a week, taking Harvey to and from school, but with so much change going on, I knew how important it was for Harvey to have a consistent routine. Initially Pete tried hard to form a relationship with Harvey, and even wanted Harvey to call him dad, but this wasn't made easy because Dwight kept popping in and out of Harvey's life and he too wanted to be called dad. Harvey did not have the capacity to understand the situation. At one stage, Pete was looking into adopting Harvey, but unfortunately, this never happened. Pete's presence in the house did have a stabilizing effect for a while, but over time things got too difficult to handle with Harvey's behaviour, so I found a special needs nanny for my grandson to help them.

One day when I was at the house, Kate just broke down and confessed, 'Mum, I can't cope with everyone here all the time and the cameras everywhere'. I wanted to make everything better, but I didn't have a magic wand. My daughter's relationship with Pete was beginning to bring back memories of my time with her father. We were in love at the beginning but refused to acknowledge the negatives in our relationship before we were in too deep and walking down the aisle. I always sensed that Kate had far stronger feelings for Pete than he did for her. Their union seemed to be a money-making opportunity for all concerned and there was far too much interference from their management for it to ever have a chance of surviving. Perhaps it was never meant to last.

Despite all the alarm bells, Kate seemed excited when she told me that she and Pete had decided to get married just a few weeks after Junior's birth. She was going to be able to realize all the big wedding dreams she'd had as a little girl playing with her Barbies – especially the pink dress and Cinderella carriage. I think weddings give Kate a chance to reset the dial on her relationships. Whatever has gone before, it can all be whisked away, and she can erase it from her mind.

She imagines that a wedding will act like a magic wand, allowing her to have the happy ever after she has always craved. But from the outset, I could see that it wasn't going to be that straightforward. A normal couple might have expected to arrange their own wedding, but Kate and Pete's management had negotiated a deal with *OK!* magazine, and there was an expectation of spectacular, exclusive photos to justify the pay-out.

Kate was insistent about wanting a particular wedding dress designed by Isabell Kristensen. It boasted a seven-metre train and had pink crystals all over it which took a team of 12 people to sew on. No wonder she kept its appearance, and the fact that it cost £20,000, a secret from me until just before she walked down the aisle. She knew I would have considered it over the top and too much money. In the end, this was a drop in the ocean of the wedding budget. This was the era of the Big Celebrity Wedding. The Beckhams had already set the ball rolling in 1999 with their £750,000 bash, complete with gold thrones and a world exclusive *OK!* magazine deal, when they married at Luttrellstown Castle, near Dublin. A year later, Madonna's wedding to Guy Ritchie at Skibo Castle in Scotland had cost an estimated £1.5 million. Both nuptials resulted in a tabloid feeding frenzy, which increased circulation figures and enhanced the profile of the couples concerned. In light of this, Kate and Pete's management were quick to jump on the bandwagon five years later, securing a £1.7m deal with *OK!*, leaving them with a handsome 20 per cent cut and the remaining budget to organize the ceremony on the agreed date of 10 September 2005.

A wedding planner was enlisted by CAN Associates and it was agreed that I would be filmed alongside Kate and Pete on their quest to find a venue. However, I quickly realized that my opinion as a mum wasn't really wanted or valued. I was just an addition to the storyboard for *Jordan & Peter: Marriage and Mayhem*, the next six-part ITV2 series on the reality TV conveyor belt, which launched on 23 September 2005 and averaged more than 750,000 viewers. In the end, Kate and Pete settled on Highclere Castle in Hampshire for the venue. They were won over by the library, which felt warm and offered just the right atmosphere for 150 guests. It would later become famous as the setting for *Downton Abbey*, but in 2005 it was about to take centre stage in a reality TV series which was taking over my daughter's life.

I was asked to keep an eye on costs but, in reality, it was all being done by a wedding company chosen by Claire Powell. The cameras gave the impression I was arranging things with the planner, but the only real impact I had was on choosing some flowers and bay trees for the dining area. I thought they were a sensible option because Kate would be able to put them on her driveway afterwards. Everything about the build-up to the wedding suggested it was being organized with a 'show' in mind rather than two people who were going to exchange serious vows and live happily ever after, but both Kate and Pete seemed excited.

Kate was the mother of a three-year-old child with special needs and a three-month-old baby, but the weekend before her wedding, her management asked her to film a keep-fit video and then fly to Monaco for her final dress fitting.

I would have liked to have gone with her, but I was resigned to the fact that I had to accept the disappointment and continue to take a back seat in the wedding preparations.

Meanwhile, a week before the wedding, Pete took Junior to Cyprus to celebrate his parents' 50th wedding anniversary; Kate cried over the fact that she'd be away from her new son, and she was still experiencing the symptoms of post-natal depression. It seemed to me that Kate's mental health was not being fully understood by everyone.

There was no doubt that Kate and Pete's management was incredibly successful at building a brand for the two of them, but it came at a high price. The pursuit of money and fame was taking precedence over everything – there was no longer anything sacred in Kate's life. I think most mums imagine sharing intimate, happy moments planning a wedding with their daughter, but nothing about the build-up to this event was joyful. Even the hen do, which was hosted at a health farm, was filmed for the reality show and photographed for *OK!* magazine. Kate had only agreed to allow the cameras in for a while, but in the end the whole day was taken over by them and we all got very fed up. After that, Kate and Pete had to record their single 'A Whole New World' in time for the wedding dance and the day before the wedding, she had to wear her wedding dress and have her hair and make-up done as it would be on the actual wedding day to fit in with the magazine's schedule.

On the day of the wedding, Kate was excited but emotional and she kept crying. But she wasn't even allowed to go near a window for a breath of fresh air in case a rogue paparazzi got a shot of her. She wasn't on medication for post-natal depression – her doctor had instead prescribed relaxation and rest from filming which, of course, never happened. The security crew employed by *OK!* magazine took their jobs very seriously and Kate was like a prisoner in her hotel room, surrounded by her bridesmaids and the camera crew. It wasn't until she stepped inside the pumpkin-style coach to take her to the castle ceremony that she got some time alone with her stepdad Price, who she had chosen to give her away. He posed the same question to Kate that my dad had once asked me before marrying Ray: 'This is your last chance. Is it definitely what you want?' Price thought the whole thing was a big mistake and a farce, so he wanted to give her the opportunity of backing out, but Kate said it was what she wanted and they trotted onwards.

I never really saw Kate on her wedding day; she was constantly filming and posing for *OK!* magazine photographs. It didn't feel like she was getting married at all and it was really sad to see what should have been such a special day become just another work event. Everything was staged for the magazine and the reality show. Nothing felt authentic or real.

One of the few things I liked about the wedding was being shown around the castle before the ceremony by its owner, Fiona the 8th Countess of Carnarvon. I'd worked as a volunteer at Arundel Castle in Sussex and love history so I felt so privileged to have been shown some of the artefacts of Tutankhamun, discovered in 1922 by Howard Carter in excavations funded by Lord Carnarvon. As we walked around the grounds chatting, I was so engrossed that I actually missed everyone else getting ready. I had to get changed quickly and couldn't even do my dress up because there was no one around to help me. I went out into the corridor and luckily I met Nick and Royston, Kate's hairdressers. They had finished helping Kate and the bridesmaids and saw my dishevelled state and said, 'You can't leave your hair like that. You look like you've just put your finger in a socket'. They quickly put my hair up and helped me to get dressed. They were great fun and I think this was the part of the wedding that I enjoyed most. I rushed down to the central gallery, hoping I hadn't missed the start of the proceedings.

I felt like I'd stumbled upon a circus. I saw Pete and his brothers getting ready to go into the library, then Kate appeared in this huge pink jewel-encrusted dress, and I thought, 'Wow. Is this really what you want to get married in?' Pete was in his element, but to me he looked like a sweaty marshmallow. His cream suit included a waistcoat with crystals all over it and he and Kate had commissioned a matching pair of bling rings which were so over the top. Everything was so big and gaudy – to me, it seemed like a grotesque display of money. The number of diamonds in their rings shocked me. Pete's ring had 20 princess-cut diamonds mounted in platinum – yes, this is for a man! Kate's ring had 35 princess-cut diamonds, elevated on a bridge of pink gold encrusted with pink diamonds. It was grotesque. It was so big it didn't look real – it was more like a toy ring out of a jamboree bag. They didn't want to be outdone by each other and this streak of jealousy continued throughout the marriage. They were both as bad as one another. I hate people who show their wealth and boast about it. It's classless and embarrassing. It's not the way I was raised and I couldn't bear all this sense of showing off. To cap it all, Pete even had hair extensions put in before the wedding.

Nobody was really thinking about or taking care of the people that really mattered. I felt that we – Kate's family – were side lined because all the management and magazine were interested in was getting celebrities on the cover. Harvey was with me after he walked down the aisle, and there were meant to be seats reserved for us in the front row, but by the time we got there with my mum, Esther, they had been taken. People had to move back to allow us in, and we sat squashed together, practically in each other's laps. Harvey was dying to see his mum after the ceremony, but she and Pete had to pretend to sign the register all over again for the cameras so it was another two hours before they appeared at the reception. Photos of us as a family were only taken right at the end of the day as an afterthought, and I didn't receive any of them in the end as they were the property of the magazine.

I could see that Kate was overworked, tired, emotional and still suffering from post-natal depression. The relentless filming schedules meant that she never had the time to recover from giving birth to Junior, but no one cared. It was all about money and magazine sales. This meant that family and friends were side lined by celebrities who were given more prominent places in the seating plan. My mum was one such casualty. She was moved from the front of the room to the back, and never forgot it until her dying day.

I think the image that best sums up the wedding was at the wedding breakfast the next morning. I came down, expecting to finally have a lovely chat with family about the previous day.

But our version of events was eclipsed by the newspapers laid out on the tables in front of us. The idea was that we could analyse coverage of the wedding for the cameras. Someone in Kate's management team thought that was important, and it really sums up the world she was living in.

No sooner had the camera batteries been recharged from the wedding, they were being fired up again during the honeymoon to the Maldives. I went along to take care of Harvey and Junior, and could see the toll that the constant filming was taking on both Kate and Pete. What should have been the most romantic moment of their relationship to date was reduced to a series of wardrobe changes and hasty meals shared with the crew.

In 2006, I had to go into hospital. While I had been in Australia during the jungle filming, I had been taken ill and was admitted to hospital on my return to the UK to have a hysterectomy. I was now in hospital again because I'd had a prolapse and had to be operated on. By a bizarre coincidence, my mum was in the same hospital with emphysema – she had in the past been a heavy smoker. When I awoke from the anaesthetic, the nurses told me mum was dying. My bed was wheeled near to my mum's and we shared the same stat machines. I was cuddling mum and telling her that I loved her. I don't know if she could hear me, but my stats went down so I was taken back to my ward. A few hours later, I stabilized and was taken to be with her for a few hours in the evening. When I was returned to my ward, I was under the influence of so many drugs I couldn't do much more than just lay there thinking of my mum ... and then I was told she had died.

I cannot tell you how much I miss my mum. Losing my dad was devastating, but it took me years to come to terms with my mum's death. You only get one mum.

After this sadness, I had to find the strength to keep supporting Kate and overseeing Harvey's welfare. To begin with, the reality TV editing process made Kate and Pete's post-wedding relationship look all lovey-dovey and nice, but in reality they had never had the chance to get to know one another alone, away from Pete's family, us, and his management company. Pete's brother Mike was still living with them months into their relationship and one by one, the entire Andre family came to stay, including Pete's mother and father. Kate thought moving to a bigger house might give their relationship the space it needed, but his family just decamped to the annexe. Of course, it's natural for a son to want his parents to come and stay from time to time, but it seemed Pete's family were on constant rotation and Kate found this reality overbearing. As a family, we have always given each other space and Kate no longer had this in her personal or professional life.

By the time Princess came along in June 2007, it seemed to me that Kate and Pete's marriage was in trouble and they didn't stand a chance of repairing it with so much outside interference. Kate was terrified of re-living the post-natal depression she had suffered with Junior and was adamant she wanted to be left alone to bond with Princess. In the end, Pete's parents returned to England, and stayed in the annexe of the house. Moreover, Claire Powell was always hovering in the background, keeping a watchful eye on her reality TV assets. Whenever Kate and Pete had a disagreement, he would be straight on the phone to Claire for advice. Kate would follow suit, separately, asking for her opinion too. It was a 'management marriage' which included Claire at every turn and it never stood a chance. I found it strange and unhealthy that a manager was so intrusively mixed up in their private life. I'll never forget the worst example of this, at Kate's so-called 'surprise' 30th birthday party held in 2008 at the Luton Hoo Hotel. Of course, it wasn't a surprise at all because it was yet another precious life event being staged for the reality TV cameras. But all elements of privacy were well and truly thrown out of the window when I was invited into Kate's bedroom by a personal assistant to find Claire placing sex toys and condoms all over the bed. I knew that, due to the post-natal depression Kate was still suffering with, sex was the last thing on her mind, but no one else seemed to understand that. Claire thought it would be 'creative and fun' to try spicing it up for the storyline. How low can you get? And how bizarre for a manager to involve herself in a couple's relationship in this way? I actually felt sick to my stomach. The birthday party, unsurprisingly, turned out to be a sombre affair.

The only outlet Kate ever really had outside of it all was riding. She would often invite me to come and watch her, just like in the old days when I used to take her to riding lessons at Ditchling Stud on a Saturday morning. But she was interrupted with constant phone calls from the PR machine, 'Where are you exactly?' 'How long are you going to be?' Sometimes they would even call me asking how long she was going to be. Kate invited Pete along to watch her train and participate in competitions, but it never seemed to me that he took much interest in something that meant so much to her.

There were moments when I saw how happy Kate could be. She had been selected to perform dressage at the Horse of the Year Show in Birmingham in 2008. We were both so excited about it, having watched it on TV for years. The fact she was actually going to be taking part was like a dream come true for the whole family and we all received tickets. It was a rare time when she was doing something for herself, supported by her loved ones. Unfortunately, towards the end of the evening, things got tetchy, and Pete told us that he was feeling unwell and needed to leave. This meant that Price needed to drive Pete the 150 miles home to Woldingham, Surrey, leaving Kate and I to make our own way back. I felt that the evening things got tetchy, and had been ruined and that joy was ebbing away from my daughter's life.

She just wanted the freedom to do what she loved, but the PR machine around her chipped away at her until she literally gave them carte blanche to edit her life in the way they wanted. I am not denying that my daughter wanted to be famous – although the reasons for it are complex – but by the time she capitulated to cameras filming the birth of her first child she had a set of values I no longer recognized, and I was rightly fearful for her future.

Throughout all this turbulence, I tried to keep a close eye on Harvey, who I had a very special bond with. From the outset, although Pete had said he wanted Harvey to call him dad and he might have had good intentions at the start, it was clear that Pete just didn't know how to cope with him and his behaviour. In many ways, I can understand that because Harvey could be so unpredictable and hard work. Recently, I was shown a deeply disturbing video which has been circulating on Twitter, which I can't get out of my mind. It's an excerpt from one of the old reality shows featuring Kate, Pete and Harvey. To begin with, Kate is outside the room and Pete is alone with Harvey in his wheelchair, then around the age of seven. Pete tells Harvey to impersonate Matt Lucas's disabled character from *Little Britain* by saying, 'I want that one'. Harvey obeys his instruction. Then, as Kate returns to the room, Pete says, 'He looks a bit Matt Lucasy – eh?' Kate replies, 'No he doesn't. He's my Harvey.' When I saw the video, I felt that Harvey's face indicated that he was aware of being mocked, and it shocked and saddened me because he was so vulnerable.

After he split from Kate, Pete said he would continue to see Harvey at weekends, and I was tasked with finding a suitable nanny with special needs experience to help with Harvey's complex medical conditions. I went through a highly-regarded agency to source a special needs nanny and found the perfect candidate, paying two thousand pounds out of my own money, but when it came down to it, she wasn't hired. I never got my money back and Harvey's visits had stopped by 2009. Later, Pete would tell an Australian radio station that Harvey was the child who taught him how to be a dad, but the lapse in their relationship when Pete moved away meant that Harvey no longer wanted to visit him.

It is well documented that the beginning of the end of Kate and Pete's relationship led to the demonization of her in the press and, subsequently, an even further downward spiral in her mental health. Somehow, Pete remained the handsome prince while she became the evil snow queen. Those of us closest to her know this was no accident, because she was part of a publicity machine which had sucked her in and was now viciously spitting her out. I first got a sense that something was afoot when I went to Kate's house a couple of months before she was due to record the *Katie & Peter: Stateside* reality show in America in 2009. Kate's house, where they were filming, was complete with turrets like something out of a fairy tale, but in reality, Kate's life was more of a nightmare. Pete had a recording studio in the back garden, and he was in there with Claire and their personal assistant playing songs about a break-up. I suddenly had the feeling that something wasn't right, and that I shouldn't be listening to this music, which somehow felt as though it was part of a grand plan that neither Kate nor I were privy to.

I was asked to accompany them on the trip to make sure everything was stable for Harvey, Junior and Princess, and to look for a suitable nursery for Junior and Princess, as well as for Harvey to visit the Junior Blind School of America. We were picked up at the airport by a friend of Claire and filmed leaving the airport. Somehow the paparazzi had been tipped off about our arrival and the driver made a big thing about going fast and trying to lose the photographers when it wasn't necessary. The children and I were terrified. I said, 'You're going to have to stop this otherwise I am going to get out of the vehicle. What on earth are you trying to do? You are driving dangerously, and we've got kids in here. What is this for?" Things like that really got to me because I was always trying to be protective of the children.

We arrived at our lodgings feeling very shaken and I was shocked to see that the production company had put Kate in lodgings on top of an enormous hill in Malibu, which was really isolated and felt unsuitable for the children. Meanwhile, Pete spent most of his time with Claire who had much better-appointed accommodation at the bottom of the hill. Alongside filming, he was recording music and training for the London Marathon. Kate told me that she felt so lonely at times that she had decided to have her horses shipped out but struggled to find instructors as many were men and she didn't want to make Pete jealous. In the end, she was able to find an instructor that they could agree on. I knew this period was the beginning of the end – Pete's attitude towards Kate had become even more dismissive and cold. Ultimately, the US footage, which was edited as always by Claire and her partner Neville, began to cast Kate as the bad one and Pete as the hero – a role he revelled in. I'm sure anyone who watched the series now would notice the tension between Kate and Pete and that Kate always seemed to be portrayed as the villain. Six months later – in May 2009 – the marriage was over.

The final trigger which led Pete to call it a day was a photograph. Apparently, Kate and Pete had made a pact that they would only go out together because he was concerned about her having a drink and not being in control. I can sympathize with his position – one drink does often lead to another for Kate, and sometimes the exhibitionist side of her comes out, which is not always welcome. But on this occasion, Kate had decided to ignore their agreement and attend the Badminton Horse Trials with her equestrian products manager, book agent and make-up artist. They were joined by the international dressage rider Andrew Gould and his wife Polly. A party atmosphere ensued, and they went on to a club where they were of course photographed. The image would later be used to suggest that Kate was having an affair with Andrew, despite the fact that they were part of a group of dressage riders at the same table. All I can say is that I was never aware of an affair between them, nor when this could have happened. Kate had previously shown an interest in learning dressage, and Andrew was the trainer nearest to where she lived. She had had weekly lessons with him and had got to know him and his wife well. He helped her to choose a dressage horse called Wallace in Holland, and Sophie, Price and I went with them on the trip. They spent time training together, that's all I was aware of.

In the beginning, despite my misgivings, I had wanted to believe Kate and Pete were a couple in love. But as time went on, my initial instincts, from the first day that I met Pete in Australia, were being proved right. Kate and Pete's relationship increasingly seemed to be more of a business deal. And now, any semblance of natural attraction was turning sour because they were constantly being intruded upon. In my opinion, Pete definitely didn't want to be with Kate, and it was nothing more than a career move. I even remember having conversations with Claire and Neville saying, 'You know this relationship will end, don't you, and you can't manage both of them?'

I think Pete is a very complex person who at times must feel exhausted trying to keep his Mr Perfect public persona intact. In an interview to promote his first children's book, he revealed how he suffered a nervous breakdown at the age of 25 and experienced brain fog, panic attacks, depression, anxiety, agoraphobia and vertigo. He put it down to being bullied and beaten up as a child. He was, he claims, part of the 'only ethnic family' on Australia's Gold Coast.

He told the newspaper interviewer that he endured six years of medication and therapy, psychiatric units and solitude, until he was coaxed out of retirement and into the jungle. It sounds as if some of his past was very painful indeed and perhaps what he truly needed was to live an ordinary existence close to his family – not re-enter the world of celebrity. But fate dictated otherwise and by the time he emerged from the jungle, his world had collided with my daughter's. She too had endured serious mental health problems and neither of them were destined to be good for one another. But all I had back then was a mother's intuition that the relationship was not being built on solid ground. I had no idea of the extent of Pete's emotional challenges from his childhood bullying.

As the relationship progressed, there were clear signs of Pete's fragile ego impacting his relationship with Kate, not least his continual need to rid himself of intolerable feelings by giving them to my daughter. Time and time again, she was the one made to feel insecure and bullied – not him – so that she became the one on the verge of breaking down. The more insecure she became, Pete seemed increasingly repulsed by her vulnerability and cut deeper with his insults and passive aggressive mood swings. In the interview about his book, he said, 'I genuinely don't get angry' but there were numerous times when I was aware of him shaming and belittling my daughter with cutting, unkind words and shameful public put-downs which still sting even now when I rewatch their old TV show. True, he did not beat her black and blue but his anger manifested itself in other ways. It chipped away at her self-esteem until she was a shell of her former self.

I'm not suggesting for a minute that the pathology in their relationship was one-sided and there were times when Kate also projected difficult feelings into Pete but, in my view, not to the same extent. Ultimately, he was and still is more skilful at separating his private and public self and presenting an out-ward facing Mr Nice Guy persona and it has served him well. Conversely, Kate has always worn her heart on her sleeve and it became an increasingly thread-bare garment.

Since the split, CAN has continued to manage Pete, and Claire and her family have been on holiday with him, so it is not surprising that they have slanted the media coverage in Pete's favour. A further worry for me is bound up in the cycle being repeated. CAN has already taken on Junior's sing-ing career and is now promoting Princess as a fashion model. My greatest wish for my grandchildren is for them to find their own way in life and I sometimes wonder if they might be better off seeking out new management who can offer a fresh perspective on their careers. I've lived on the side lines for years, forced to sit back as lie after lie has been printed about my daughter. Now, as I approach death, it's high time

I speak up and set the record straight. Her marriage to this man left her at her lowest ebb and set the scene for further toxic betrothals.

Chapter 10

ON THE REBOUND

I was enjoying a little slice of heaven when I first heard the news about Kate's split from Pete in May 2009. I'd decided to follow in the footsteps of my favourite film, *A Good Year*, which stars Russell Crowe and Marion Cotillard and tells the story of a British investment broker who inherits his uncle's château in Provence and finds love while he renovates it. It came out back in 2006, but I still love the way the château conjures up sentimental memories for Russell Crowe's character, and the scenery evokes a different way of life – one I would love to have led myself. I was especially captivated by the scenery of lush vineyards and stunning architecture, so I gave a copy of the film to my closest friends for Christmas and suggested we begin plotting a tour of the key locations the following summer. In the end, six of my oldest friends said they were up for the adventure, and we set off from Brighton to Provence via Gatwick airport. Sadly, the title of the film didn't turn out to be a good omen at all – 2009 would be a bad year for me.

One of my pals, Lin, planned the route and arranged for us to stay at B&Bs in villages throughout the South of France.

It was wonderful. We shared rooms, ate delicious French breakfasts and sampled different cuisine at lunch and dinner. One evening at a tiny restaurant in Moujon, Lin decided to be the waiter – just like Russell Crowe in the film – and served the other guests. It felt so good to be away from the pressures of Kate and Pete's life at home. They were working as usual when I left and I put all their trials and tribulations to the back of my mind as we travelled through Grasse, Valbonne, Mougins, Cannes, Saint-Jean, Cap-Ferrat, St Tropez and Nice. The driving got a bit hairy in our Fiats as we climbed the mountains, but it was nothing compared to life at home as Katie Price's mum.

It was such a wonderful trip. When I think back, I can still smell the sublime scent as we drove past endless lavender fields onto the next château. I'd worked so hard all my life to take care of others and now I was finally taking some time out just for me. Except, when you're Katie Price's mum, it's hard to be just 'you'. My friends and I were enjoying one last lunch in a lovely restaurant in Nice on the last day of the trip when a *Sky News* headline flashed up on the small TV screen mounted behind the bar: Katie Price and Peter Andre announce split. Obviously, I knew my daughter and son-in-law weren't getting on, but I felt shocked to receive news of such a big family event in this cold, impersonal way.

In truth, I wasn't exactly surprised. By this point, Kate had become so tightly controlled by her management team she was barely allowed to breathe without asking their permission. And clearly, they were in the driving seat once again with this divorce, by managing the separation their way. Kate had refused to sign another contract with CAN and had given them notice before the break-up. Kate hadn't yet found a new management team, so she'd asked Claire to put out a statement that Pete wanted to divorce her. But this did not happen – instead the statement read, 'Peter Andre and Katie Price are separating after four and a half years of marriage. They have both requested the media respect their family's privacy at this difficult time'. Kate didn't want this but, at the time, due to her emotional turmoil, she'd agreed to it.

Kate then got her book agent Diane to put out a separate statement, saying, 'Pete is the love of my life, and we have children together. I am devastated and disappointed by his decision to separate and divorce me, as I married him for life. This is not what I want, and this decision has been taken out of my hands. I will not comment further or do any interviews regarding the separation. But I will always love my Pete.' When I eventually got hold of Kate on the phone, she sounded completely devastated and, in between sobs, she said, 'I've got to get away mum'. She told me she was making plans to take the children to the Maldives.

Kate and Pete separated straight away. All communication, which was usually about the children, was done through the solicitors. The press statements had been put out there about the separation and the dialogue with the press and each other was kept to that. Although Kate had not initiated the split, I think in a way she was relieved it was over. She could feel free and no longer felt as if she was walking on coals in front of Pete, and there were no more rows.

And that was the end of that – the so-called reality TV

romance of the decade was finished in what felt like a flash. Kate admitted that even she was shocked by the news that they were going to get divorced as she and Pete hadn't spoken about it in person. Price, Dan, Sophie and I were very upset. We knew that Pete and Kate had been having major problems, but we thought he might have been prepared to understand Kate's depression better and find a way forward for the sake of their children.

I had sensed from the very beginning that his career was his main priority. Now, for every negative story that surfaced about Kate, another surfaced about Pete's reputation as a 'Super Dad', which was slowly being cemented by Claire Powell who had journalist friends in high places. Photos of Pete with the kids strawberry picking and taking part in other activities were often being fed to the press. Kate's behaviour might have proven challenging for him at times, but she was, is, and always will be the mother of his children. He had opportunities to defend her as particularly harsh headlines surfaced, but he chose not to. Pete never even bothered to come and say goodbye to us as a family after their divorce; it seemed to me that he had no respect for us, and I felt that my instincts about him had been proved right. Instead, he left a hungry press pack in his wake. After the split, I arrived home to find so many journalists camped outside Kate's house that we had to install a separate bin just for their takeaway wrappers. TV broadcasters had set up big canopies for live pieces to camera and we found some particularly annoying reporters in trees surrounding Kate's property in Woldingham. Thankfully, the journalists learned early on to leave my house alone, because word got round that they would never get any information from me. Plus, I used to call the police, so they quickly lost interest.

Kate was almost immediately vilified in the press for her so-called affair with Andrew; people had believed the headlines and press features about her and Pete, thinking that their marriage was a fairy tale that Kate had destroyed. She was only contracted to CAN Associates until 23rd June 2009, but when the news of the divorce broke it was clear Kate couldn't stay with them until then. Claire offered Kate a new contract with a higher fee, but Kate refused.

I felt so frustrated at the injustice of it all as I tried to protect my daughter from what I perceived to be a biased publicity campaign orchestrated by this woman. It was a really awful time, absolutely dreadful, and once Pete decided the marriage was over, there was no thought or discussion on his part. Kate needed support to disentangle her life from his. She was devastated, particularly at the idea of her children losing a father just like she had. Kate immediately understood that she would have to come to terms with sharing Junior and Princess and not having them at home with her full time. Meanwhile, Pete had written his new album, got the record deal he wanted, and was basking in good headlines from his reality show with Kate. Mission accomplished. He also started a new relationship with someone else only eight days after they split. It seemed to me that there was no love lost on his part by embarking on something new so soon.

Nothing about it felt sporting at all. This was borne out when Sophie and I accompanied Kate and the children to a polo match at Klosters in Switzerland, in February 2011. The chalet we stayed in was very luxurious and I found it quite daunting. It had its own staff, who wouldn't even let us load the dishwasher, and an outside jacuzzi with a fabulous view of the mountains. There was also a sauna, which I was using one day when three-year-old Princess came in and accidentally brushed against the coals. She received a minor burn, which we put cream on and dressed. No further treatment was required – that was that. But a tabloid showbiz journalist had been given a photo by an acquaintance and wrote a story claiming that Princess had been 'badly burned'. The entire story was cynically constructed to portray Kate as a bad mother, but the fact of the matter was that Princess had been in MY care at the time, not hers.

Years later, my instincts about the plot to demonize Kate were confirmed in the unlikely setting of a high court case between ITV2 and Claire's partner and business associate Neville. In 2015, Neville sued the channel for £4 million and won, after his relationship with Claire ended and she tried to cut him out of a series of prolific deals with the channel. Of course, Pete offered to testify for his close confidant Claire, but Mr Justice Flaux was not impressed with this witness. He concluded that, '[Mr Andre] was an extremely unsatisfactory witness. Much of his evidence was exaggerated . . . Regrettably I formed the view that on some issues his evidence was not truthful.' He also noted that, 'Mr Andre and Ms Price split in 2009. The evidence of both Mr Hendricks and Ms Partridge [Nicola] was that the tactic adopted by Claire Powell as his manager was to portray him as the victim in the break-up and demonize Ms Price. In cross-examination, Mr Andre indignantly rejected any such suggestion and it is not necessary to resolve any issue about that aspect of history. Suffice it to say that the split increased interest in Peter Andre.' Finally, there it was in black and white – confirmed by a high court judge.

When I read the judgement, it confirmed all the instincts I'd first had about Pete in the jungle. He wanted to be rich and famous, and my daughter unwittingly became part of the plan. My daughter is no angel, but she became a sacrificial lamb in a celebrity slaughter the moment she paired up with Peter Andre in the jungle. She had flown to Australia as a fun-loving single mum with her life ahead of her. By the time her marriage to Pete was over, and Claire's work had seen her reputation destroyed in the press, an Irish artist called Kevin Sharkey was motivated to merge my daughter's face with Myra Hindley's in a work called *Public Enemy Number One*. Sharkey said he had heard Kate had been judged the most hated woman in Britain and wanted to question celebrity culture – he described it as being like a horse race: 'You watch it fall; you watch it run. It's like a sport.' Although the artwork was using Kate's image to challenge the brutality and warped morality of media exploitation, I still found it desperately upsetting to see the picture. For years I would ask myself, 'Am I over-reacting in her defence? Has Kate played a part in her own downfall?'

Now, looking back, the difficulties in her marriage, at least, are never more blatant than in a series of clips from their reality shows, which are now on TikTok. In one scene, Kate and Pete are in Australia, sitting in the back of a car together heading towards a sign which reads 'Sunshine Coast'. Pete begins to explain how he perceives himself to have better press coverage than Kate in Australia, adding, 'In Australia they go: Peter Andre and wife Jordan aka Katie Price aka slut.' Kate looks very uncomfortable, but tries to stand up for herself, responding, 'Why do you always put me down?' Her head is down when Pete replies, 'They say former Page Three slut and pop pin-up.'

A similar theme continues in another clip where they appear to be together at an event. Pete can be seen giving an impression of my daughter trying to give him oral sex before going a step further and describing having anal sex with her in a derogatory way in front of the cameras. He mocks her voice, saying, 'Is it in yet?' and adds, 'It doesn't mean my knob's small. It means your ass is big.' Another TikTok clip shows Peter Andre responding to Rebekah Vardy's comments about the size of his manhood. Pete was justifiably offended, saying that men would be berated if they made disparaging sexual references about women. I find this confusing, given his previous behaviour towards my daughter, his wife.

So, Kate now needed a new manager that she could trust. In her eyes, there was only one person she could rely on – her brother. Dan had watched the constant stream of post-split stories coming from Pete's camp, including carefully orchestrated photo shoots of him feeding swans and walking on the beach. In contrast, his sister was shown naively visiting nightclubs and holidaying in Ibiza – he knew Kate didn't stand a chance. There was no real structure to Kate's various business ventures at this point. With her books, perfume, equestrian clothing and merchandise sales, there were no clear lines of communication between the various managers. So Dan set up a company called Blacksheep Management so the outside world could have one point of contact with Katie Price. He had already been helping Kate behind the scenes for several years, so had a unique insight and understanding of her career and its earning potential. He set money aside for tax and VAT, and worked closely with Kate's accountants to build her a savings pot. Like all celebrities, she had become accustomed to certain spending levels, but they can't always be sustained and Dan has always done his best to steer Kate in the right direction. For an ordinary working-class person like Kate, coming into wealth like she did was the equivalent of winning the lottery, and due to her poor mental health and her inability to manage her money properly or take on board the advice given to her, she has repeatedly found herself in positions like the one she is in now, where she's having to file for bankruptcy. We are always there to help pick up the pieces, but it's never been easy to see everything falling apart for her, time and time again.

Despite the onslaught of bad headlines, Dan was slowly restructuring Kate's business in a calm way with a close-knit team of experts. We were trying to support her in getting the help she needed and she did agree to some talking therapy. But the constant rows with Pete about the children would trigger anxiety and depression to the point where the weekly sessions didn't seem robust enough to help her make progress. At about this time, Sophie had made the wise choice to enrol at a hairdressing school, which was a huge relief to us all

– Claire had previously made suggestions about her following Kate down the showbiz route and I couldn't imagine Sophie being put through this as well.

Meanwhile, Kate was keen to keep working, so she contacted Zai Bennett, ITV's Director of Digital Channels and Acquisitions, to discuss having her own reality show which would be produced by her own company, Pricey Media. Kate was very positive and happy with the concept of reality television. She had enjoyed doing it with Richard Macey, but she felt that the way CAN controlled it was relentless and over intrusive. She set up her own company with a former ITV executive, Mark Wagman, and began filming *What Katie Did Next*. The series was supposed to be an honest portrayal of her – warts and all – as opposed to the more scripted reality shows she had done with Pete.

There was a lot of sorting out to do on behalf of the children, including custody and care arrangements. The nannies who were already in place needed to be retained so they could go back and forth with the children from one parent to another so there was consistency in their lives. They were brilliant professionals who used to say to me, 'We're not Team Pete or Team Kate. We're Team Kids.' The children were quite young at the time of the split – Junior was four and Princess was two – and having the same nannies keeping their routines in place really helped them. Kate also tried to instil some healthy routines into her own life and began getting fit with a trainer at his gym in Hove.

However, only 12 weeks after her split from Pete, Kate was telling me about a man who the trainer had introduced her to called Alex Reid. She said he was a mixed martial arts (MMA) fighter and an actor from Aldershot, Hampshire; not particularly good looking but softly spoken. I got the impression she was trying to sell him to me – that's what she always does. She knows I see through these men straight away and there's a reason for this. As her mum, it's so hard to trust men who come into Kate's life. Each time, I end up asking myself whether they really love her or whether it is just the lifestyle they want. Do they just want to be famous? Generally, Kate's boyfriends all start off claiming to have a job, but soon end up sponging off her – their work tails off so they gradually start driving Kate to the odd photo shoot here and there.

Price and I say to all of them, 'Do not stop work. Carry on with your life and don't become a kept man'. But of course, they see how much money Kate is capable of earning, which to them looks to be easy. I'm sure that most of Kate's boyfriends have thought, 'Oh, I'm going to have an easy life now and I can be famous if I marry her'. We see this pattern repeating time and time again and it's painful to have to sit back and watch it play out. Before long, they are creating social media accounts depicting their relationship, actually appearing in Kate's photo shoots themselves, and attending events with her and loving the red carpet. Then they want to be paid for the photo shoots or appearances in her shows. They all end up thinking they're famous just because they're in a relationship with Kate. It's beyond me that many of them never pay anything towards the bills or upkeep of the house – with the exception of Pete, who did pay half. Alex would train enthusiastically for his MMA fights, but he wouldn't contribute anything to the home.

Often, Kate's partners don't seem to be real people. They just want free holidays and more followers on Instagram. They never seem content with the simple things in life and she seems to feel compelled to give them material objects as a way of making them love her. It feels to me as though she has to do a lot of work to try to make things happy in the relationship, and I feel sad for her because she is so desperate to be loved by these characters. She buys them all sorts of things, from clothes and jewellery to cars and even horses and gets them work that they otherwise would not have had.

Over the years, I think it's been hard for Kate not having a husband or partner who can be truly accepted by our family. Price and Dan never have any respect for the men she gets involved with and they end up being out on a limb. My feeling is she should be with an older man who is comfortable in his own skin and accomplished in his own right. Kate needs someone to look after her instead of being the provider all the time. Whenever Kate gets a new boyfriend, her fantasy is always that he will be a strong man who can look after her and keep her safe and provide for her. She always picks someone who looks as though they can play the part – but it never happens. This is never who they really are. We've always asked her why she doesn't get on with her life and enjoy being alone for a while, with just the kids, and wait for the right man to come along when she's feeling ready and up for it. I think Kate has always suffered from a lack of confidence and a fear of being alone and that's why she rushes headlong into the next relationship more or less as soon as the previous one is over. She doesn't give herself a chance to heal her broken heart and recover, and she's too impulsive, simply wanting to fall in love all over again.

Kate's life is such a contrast to Dan's. As a teenager, he found a partner in Louise who is such a genuine person and who we have all loved since they started dating. Together, they have provided such a stable background for their twins. Similarly, Sophie dated an electrician called Harry Brooks for 12 years before marrying him in June 2022. Price and I have always shared a closeness with Louise and Harry which we have never been able to achieve with any of Kate's partners.

Alex Reid was just another example of Kate being attracted to what appeared to be a strong 'fighter' man, and in fact one of the ways he earned his living was as a cage fighter. But below the surface, he seemed vulnerable and complex to me. Kate had been dating Alex for a few weeks when I first met him in a park near where she lived in Woldingham. Kate was out with Junior and Princess and had invited him along. My personal feeling was that it was too soon after Kate's divorce to be involving the children with a new man, but the problem with Kate is she thinks she is in love, so believes her family can come together as one and play happy families. Kate also likes to know if new boyfriends get on with her children as soon as she can; personally, I think she should wait a few months to make sure the relationship is working before she introduces them. When the kids were very young, it wasn't so much of a problem, but as they've got older it has become more of an issue. This was just one of the reasons I wasn't looking forward to meeting Alex. Kate was on the rebound from Pete, so this meeting was too soon for everyone. But she was desperate for love and attention and – as usual – not giving herself time to see things clearly.

At the park, I exchanged pleasantries with Alex and thought he seemed softly spoken and polite. We were getting on well and everything seemed normal – until it wasn't! It wasn't a particularly warm day but all of a sudden, Alex took his top off and just laid down on the grass. As usual, the paparazzi were on Kate's trail and started having a field day with this odd spectacle. Kate didn't seem at all perturbed by it and I tried to justify it in my mind by thinking that maybe he was just hot and a bit vain.

A couple of months later, he came round to our house with Kate for a dinner with family and friends. Halfway through, just like at the park, he took his top off and just sat there naked from the waist up while everyone looked at him agog. They were too polite to actually say anything. For once in my life, I too was gobsmacked and just didn't know what to say. I remember he was sweating profusely, so again I wanted to believe that he had removed his clothing because he was too hot. Kate tried to explain it away by saying he got hot quickly, but I could tell she was embarrassed. I thought he might be going through the male equivalent of an early menopause. Anything was possible with Kate's men. He was also socially very awkward and didn't really say much or interact with anyone. To be fair, he was polite but as usual it was clear that Kate's partner was on a completely different wavelength to the rest of our family and friends. But at that stage, I just didn't realize quite to what extent.

Of course, Alex's exhibitionist streak was not the only issue in his and Kate's relationship. I first saw Alex Reid's female alter ego in action when I attended a photo shoot which her publisher and literary agent had set up to launch her new book, *Standing Out*. Press launches are obviously designed to attract as much attention as possible and the idea was that four men would dress up as caricatures of Kate. Three of them were clearly just cooperating and going with the flow, smiling shyly for the photographers. However, the fourth, Alex, was dressed up in a skimpy gold outfit and stared confidently at the cameras. He seemed to be enjoying the event and he suddenly adopted this female persona – his voice changed, becoming very soft and girly. In that moment, it dawned on me just how hard Kate must been finding it when this side of his character came out behind closed doors.

I was sure the relationship wouldn't survive. It was very disconcerting to see this man change his personality and, in essence, become a woman so quickly and without warning. I'm not against anything like this in life – people should be able to feel as though they can be themselves – but it was very shocking, nonetheless. He turned to everyone at the photo shoot and announced that his name was Roxanne. I instinctively knew that Kate was out of her depth. I asked Kate if Alex was like this at home and she said he was. She had met him at a very vulnerable time in her life, hoping for a cage fighter who would protect her from the storm of her divorce. Instead, she got an equally vulnerable individual who needed looking after himself.

I think the relationship might have fizzled out much sooner

if it wasn't for *Celebrity Big Brother* appearing on the horizon around four months into their relationship. Kate helped Alex to secure a place in the show where he lived alongside her ex, Dane Bowers. While he was in the house, Alex told everyone how much he loved Kate. She thought he was her hero for standing up for her at a time when she was so being so heavily maligned by the media. Naturally Kate believed she had found her knight in shining armour – she seemed to forget her previous concerns and became oblivious to Alex's shortcomings.

Kate jetted off to marry Alex in Las Vegas in 2010, just seven months after meeting him. The whole family had been trying to persuade her not to go through with it because she hadn't known him that long and his complexities seemed to be profound. We all told her that it was too soon. Plus, Alex was strange – gentle, believe it or not – but strange. I think he decided to get married to Kate so quickly because he wanted to be Mr Katie Price with all the glamour that brought, and she wanted it because she was still reeling from the acrimonious split from Pete. None of us in the family knew about the wedding until the last minute, so it was far too late to change her mind. When she returned, she insisted on formalizing everything with a more traditional blessing at St Paul's Church near her home in Surrey. I was drawn in to help with the wedding arrangements, and as usual there was a magazine deal with *OK!* magazine.

The blessing took place on 3rd July. Despite my misgivings, I attended the wedding to support my daughter and went into her bedroom just before the ceremony so we could have some time alone. She looked pensive and was gazing downwards in her strapless white dress. Once again, she heard the words, 'Do you really want to do this?' She didn't answer me straight-away. After a pause in which I honestly thought she might turn back, she said, 'Yes'. For the first time, I knew how my dad must have felt when he'd asked me the same question.

In the end Kate did go through with the exchange of vows, but the ceremony descended into a farce. To start with she found it difficult to get out of the windowless van hired for the occasion into the church because of the paparazzi. Then, during the service, they started trying to break the church door down. It felt very threatening and wasn't safe for anyone to leave the church. Kate was very frightened and so was I. Then the drama really started. Alex decided to show off – he called out. 'My fellow cage fighters, please stand up'. They followed his instructions and fought off the paps at the church entrance. We did have security guards, but obviously they have to operate within professional guidelines. The poor vicar looked absolutely shell shocked and didn't know what to do with himself. It was like a cross between a comedy and a horror movie. Terrible, really terrible. Like all the relationships Kate gets involved in, there was no kind of calm or gentle intimacy. It's always this process of crashing together, then crashing into a wedding, then crashing apart. It means lots of people get bruised in the process, not least her.

After the wedding, reality set in. I was still closely involved by picking Harvey up each day from Kate's home and accompanying him to school before returning to help Kate and the nannies out with anything that needed doing during the day, then turning round again in time for pick-up. I lived a fair distance away from Kate so there was not much point in me going home in between.

Once or twice, the nannies complained to me, saying they found Alex's topless exhibitionism uncomfortable around the house, but things escalated to a whole new level when they said that he had been using Harvey's hormone medication Genotropin. I thought that was shocking. How much lower could someone sink than stealing medicine from a disabled child? The fact it was going missing was thankfully picked up on by local doctors who noticed that they were being asked to prescribe more medicine than was needed. Along with Kate and the nannies, I wondered where it was going. One of the nannies actually caught Alex taking the drug out of the fridge where it was stored. He had only been living with Kate for around three months and was already behaving in a very disturbing manner. It turned out that he was injecting it in a bid to enhance his pre-fight physique.

The nannies were there to help Harvey and I was doing the school run and working from the office at Kate's house during the day, so Alex had little to do with Harvey. I went absolutely ballistic when I found out what he had done and confronted Alex, who could only say, 'Well, it doesn't do me any harm'. He really was only thinking of himself and seemed to have no concept of the harm it could cause Harvey if he missed this medication. I couldn't believe that Kate was with a man who would do this. I honestly thought she had lost the plot and asked her how she could let him be around her children if he had done something so awful as steal Harvey's medicine. To begin with, I think the relationship had filled Kate with a lot of hope and promise – here is a fighter guy who's going to look after me and he's even got his own job doing a bit of acting on the side. But very quickly, it turned out that there was actually a hidden side to his character – I think she was trying to deal with it by herself for a long time. As usual, Kate had to work harder and harder to try to keep up the charade.

Initially, although he had not had much to do with them, Alex had been kind to Harvey and to Junior and Princess and there were no real issues. If there were, Kate would not have allowed him to move in with her. After the medication debacle, I became very concerned about Alex being around the children; I was relieved to know the nannies were always around if Kate was working. As far as I was aware, there were never any further occasions when the children were exposed to anything untoward.

After just two tumultuous years, Kate eventually told Alex to leave in 2011 but he said his marriage status entitled him to stay and he claimed he owned the house too. While Kate's lawyers were deciding how to evict him, they drew up an agreement which dictated that he was not allowed to enter her bedroom while he resided at her house. He was only allowed to go in certain rooms. To stop him going into Kate's bedroom, a guard was instructed to sleep outside.

Unbelievably, at the same time, Scotland Yard had made Kate aware of a kidnapping threat against Harvey and her mental health was hanging on by a thread. We had to set up a panic room with food, water and medication for Harvey. Apparently, the kidnappers had planned to target him because his vulnerabilities would mean Kate would quickly pay a ransom. I had to go through kidnap training and look out for cars who might be following us to school, as well as what to do in the event of a kidnapping threat. We had a security guard with us in the car on the way to school, and the guard would remain with Harvey every day until the police informed us that it was all clear. We never told anyone else about the kidnapping threat, and looking back, I wonder if Alex might have thought the guards had been hired simply to keep him away. These were serious, sobering times and we were all relieved when the threat faded. The police who were tracking the gang lost them on the way down to Kate's and we never heard anything more about it after that. Alex also finally disappeared from our lives. In the end, he made Kate's skin crawl. The whole situation was too much for her to cope with. Sadly, it ended up being a mere warm-up for what was to come.

Chapter 11

A PASSAGE TO INDIA

We were all incredibly relieved when Alex was at last evicted. However, Kate was left bemused and bewildered. Yes, she had noticed Alex ogling the ladyboys on their Thai honeymoon and sometimes actually flirting with them, but ITV2 had been making a three-part special about the preparation, the wedding, and the honeymoon. Filming is always frenetic and stressful and so – as ever – there had rarely been time to pause for reflection about what was actually going on in real life, as opposed to in front of the cameras. The lawyers procrastinated about a financial settlement for Alex but whatever they came up with was a price worth paying to get shot of this man. The real cost would be the harm to Kate's reputation when the inevitable kiss-and-tell stories were sold to the highest bidder and the narrative would be manipulated to portray another innocent male victim of the villainous Kate.

Kate put on a brave face for the world but, as her mum, I saw how cut up she was about the collapse of her second marriage. Deep down she was really hurting and blamed herself even though it wasn't her fault that she couldn't cope with Alex's behaviour. She realized that, in her desperation to create a family unit, she had once again fallen too easily and too quickly in love on the rebound. Does she confuse lust with love, I wonder? With her trademark warrior spirit, Kate set about rebuilding her world and began by buying a house just outside Horsham. It had five bedrooms, two bathrooms and a lovely kitchen, with a substantial stable block with horse walker, shower facilities and hair drier for the horses, as well as a sand school and land ideal for grazing. It was exactly what she had been looking for.

The house was just the right size and Kate decorated it to put her personal stamp on it. She transformed the double garage into a cinema room, adorned with sumptuous purple velvet, and created a large, homely kitchen, a snug lounge and a playroom. She also built a three-bedroom log cabin where the nannies could stay when they were working, which she had in mind to extend for an annexe for Harvey later on. There was a separate block which Kate turned into a gym, and I had an office above it. The place had complete privacy; it was a beautiful country home and I felt hopeful she would settle there and find some peace.

At this time, Kate told me that no longer would she allow her heart to rule her head or allow herself to be frustrated by relationships and misrepresentation in the press. She was determined to create her own Pete- and Alex-free paradise and escape from relationship depression. She wanted to enjoy being single and concentrate on her children and her work. However, Kate is a very sociable and convivial person. She needs to immerse herself in company, so she soon became sur-rounded by so-called friends. Often, they were on her payroll as hairdressers, make-up artists, manicurists, beauticians and masseurs. Most of them were genuine, but it seemed that some of them one weren't, and were instead making a living out of Kate and using their connection with her to promote themselves. Often these very people were selling stories about her. They were just 'yes' people. I could see right through them, but Kate would not listen and I became the ogre mum. She never truly got an honest answer from the people around her, so naturally, she believed that she was right. It was only her family who would give a truthful opinion, whether she liked it or not. Kate always sees the best in people, and it infuriated me that there were so many hangers on in this group who, in my opinion, were just sponging off her and sucking up by agreeing with every word she said.

After a break-up, there is always a pattern: Kate concentrates on work and we see her more. Then her friends encourage her to go out and have fun and meet someone else. There is never time to pause for reflection between one relationship and the next, or to allow any sense of an ending. And as always with Kate, where she goes, the press follows. With Pete, Kate had established herself as a family brand, but now the press wanted wild Jordan back in the headlines rather than pausing to consider the mental health of an anxious and depressed Katie Price. I think the press know that negativity sells – positivity doesn't.

Because she is Katie Price, Kate also gets lots of men contacting her on Instagram and Twitter asking to take her out. I suppose when she is feeling very low and lonely it might be hard to resist thinking that just one date can't hurt. And then someone else comes along and she falls hard. Before long, she's thinking, 'Oh my God, they're The One. This is the guy I'm going to build my forever family with, and I won't be lonely anymore.' In my view, she wants to be in love, and so she more or less *makes* herself fall in love with these men. The divorce from Alex really made me realize that Kate was getting into a pattern of eat, sleep, marry, repeat.

It started with a very public relationship with the rugby player Danny Cipriani. His escapades had brought him a notoriety that ensured immediate media interest in the liaison. However, they were together for such a short period of time I never got to meet him. Then came the Argentinian model and TV presenter Leandro Penna. The first I heard of Leo was from Dan and Kate together. In February 2011, they had both flown to the States for work meetings, to do some shoots for the American edition of *OK!* magazine and to attend the Elton John Aids fundraiser party at the Oscars. It was there that Kate and Leo met and were immediately taken with each other. I would say it was lust at first sight; they couldn't have connected about much more, considering that he could not speak a word of English and Kate not a word of Spanish. I was fuming when Kate called me and told me about Leo. She said she had just met this gorgeous-looking guy and couldn't help herself.

This was only a couple of months since Alex had moved out and that relationship had finished – the separation was announced in January 2011 and the divorce was finalized in March 2012. This was only February 2011 – she'd had no intention of meeting anyone after Alex and wanted to be single and concentrate on her children and work, but it had just happened. Dan told me he quite liked Leo, but by now he was cautious of the men that approached Kate and was always on the lookout for ulterior motives, so didn't engage with him too much. She hadn't expected to hear from him again, but when Kate returned to the UK and Leo flew back to Argentina, they remained in contact and texted each other. The language barrier didn't deter her, as she furiously punched phrases into Google Translate.

Kate felt Leo would be more understanding of her as he was in the same industry. This time Kate didn't introduce him to Junior and Princess until a lot later in the relationship, but Leo met Harvey sooner because he was with Kate full time. What's more, they had a lot in common, particularly their love of horses, and she visited his family ranch in Córdoba, Argentina. His father had been a politician and his mother a beauty queen. Kate loved the outdoor lifestyle, and they spent many care-free days horse riding, sky diving and paragliding. Leo was definitely one of the sportiest guys she had been with, and things seemed to be progressing smoothly. She even decided to film her Sky reality show, *Katie*, in Argentina.

Unfortunately, one day at midnight when Leo was driving them back from a trip, disaster struck when he was blinded by the lights of an on-coming car. He was forced to swerve their 4x4 vehicle and ploughed into two wild horses. When Leo and Kate got out of the car they discovered both animals had been severely injured and were dying. Kate comforted them in their final moments. Kate is a very tactile person and has great empathy with the suffering of both humans and animals. The first horse died with Kate stroking its head in her lap, then the same happened with the second. The incident affected her deeply. In desperation, she called me and her brother Dan. We offered as many reassuring words of comfort as we could, but we sensed a little piece of her had died with those horses.

Within weeks of their romance igniting, Leo gave up his TV career to move to the UK to be with Kate. He started taking English lessons and learned a little but was soon bored of the discipline and gave them up. He tried to get work in the UK but because of the language barrier he wasn't successful. He asked Kate to fix him up with something, but she wanted him to be independent. In the end, he appeared – like all her partners – in her reality show and got paid for it. He also did a shoot for the charity Jeans for Genes and I really believe he genuinely wanted to support Kate and Harvey, who he used to take out on the quad bike. But most of the time he did little besides staying at home and helping around the house or going to the gym in Kate's car.

In Argentina, he had been used to working on the land, so assured us he was very practical with his hands. His endeavours in this department provided us with a lot of amusement. He was a handyman of sorts, but whatever he touched, he seemed to wreck. He broke both the sit-on lawnmower and the digger. He loved al fresco dining and was a good cook, but the electrics blew on the lights he had installed around the garden and the barbecue that he had wired up. He took me to a garden centre where he wanted to purchase £5,000 worth of plants to adorn Kate's driveway, but he had no idea that we would have to water them. He was definitely a character and he used to really make me laugh. The whole family were really fond of him and every now and again he still texts me to ask how I am. We took him clay pigeon shooting and he was a good shot but sadly decided to demonstrate his skills by shooting Kate's white doves which lived in her stables. He said he thought they were vermin. She never got over that.

After a while, Leo and Kate found it hard to communicate and they started rowing – sometimes over Google Translate, due to the language barrier. He decided to return to Argentina, but came back to the UK after a few weeks and rented a flat in London. This was a couple of weeks before Christmas and he came to the house with presents for the children, and for Kate he produced a jewellery box with a ring in it that he said was an engagement ring. Engagement was the last thing on Kate's mind, so she wore the ring on her right hand rather than her left. He also went back to language school and seemed ready to make a go of things. Before long, though, he moved back into Kate's house, without a job, and the relationship went the usual way. Kate and Leo spent Valentine's Day 2012 in Prague and he proposed to her with a pink heart-shaped ring surrounded by diamonds. Unfortunately, the ring did not fit and Kate never wore it. Kate's jeweller Bill Foreman had made the ring and he contacted Kate in June to say that the invoice was still outstanding.

Kate was paying for everything and it was clear things weren't working out, so they decided enough was enough. Kate also found out that he had sold their story to the Argentinian press and that was the final straw. They were both miserable so, in September 2012, Leo left again for Argentina

– this time for good. Junior was so pleased he actually cheered. I think he had become fed up with Leo's constant misery and moping around. The whole saga lasted two years. After their relationship, Leo did the usual kiss and tells, but to me he was harmless. Funny, yes, but disastrous. I actually thought he and Kate were good together with their love of horses and polo. They once played polo together at Cowdray Park and Leo introduced himself to Prince Harry and asked for a selfie – the Prince obliged. I thought that there had been the potential for something more lasting this time, but it was just another relationship that was not meant to be.

As Kate's manager, Dan was trying his best to steady the ship but sometimes he would be driven to distraction wondering the same thing we were all wondering all the time – why, why, why doesn't she listen? We all knew what she was doing was wrong but it was as if she was incapable of thinking rationally and acted only on impulse. A lot of the time with Kate, we're talking about things that happen unconsciously. You can ask her why until you're blue in the face but she will answer, 'I don't know', and I believe she genuinely doesn't know. The consequences come after and then we are all left picking up the pieces. 'We' – what an important word that is. Kate and her partners may get the publicity but, in the background, her family has always been there loving her unconditionally.

During the Alex and Leo debacles, Sophie had also become romantically attached – but not at the same breakneck speed as her sister. Kate has always been close to Sophie, who showed the same determination to succeed but in a much more subdued, ordinary way as she carved out a career for herself first as a hairdresser and later in public relations. Sophie had known Harry Brooks vaguely for some time, but it was not until they got talking through mutual friends that they discovered a common love of good food and the comedy series *Only Fools and Horses*. Harry is a lovely cheeky chappy with a warm openness and great sense of humour. When Sophie introduced him to us, we took an instant liking to him. He was polite and funny, and Price and I could see that they were both keen on each other. To be honest though, we didn't think it would last as Sophie was still only 21 and she isn't the impulsive type. She was still finding her way in the world and making decisions about what she wanted to do with her life. We were conscious that men might have been interested in Sophie because of her sister. I don't say that with any disrespect to my younger daughter, but we were wising up to life in the public eye and had to be extra protective of her. Sophie grew up with Kate being in the limelight, so it was normal for her to meet celebrities and attend events that most teenagers could only dream about. But the bullying episodes at school had often left her wishing she was not a famous person's sister.

To our delightful surprise, Harry and Sophie's relationship continued to blossom and he stuck by Sophie when she changed direction in her career and decided – out of the blue – to retake some of her GCSEs so she could prepare to study history at Chichester University. She had worked as a Saturday girl in hair salons from the age of 12 and eventually graduated from hairdressing school. She had a successful career working at top salons such as Trevor Sorbie, Toni & Guy and Headmasters, but she wanted something more in her life and decided to move out of her comfort zone and pursue a passion for the past. Kate began to take great pleasure in calling Sophie the history geek of the family. They are total opposites, but the reality is that they are always there for each other – come what may.

By now, Kate's engagements, entanglements and marriages to random men were being construed in the press as some kind of a joke. As a family we could see how this situation had arisen, but we also saw the serious and deep underlying issues that they couldn't – or wouldn't – see. Mental health wasn't at the forefront of people's minds in those days like it is today, and the press intrusions that have been so prevalent throughout Kate's career, particularly the phone hacking she experienced, have all taken a serious toll on her mental well-being. I'm not excusing my daughter's choices, but I've come to understand that Kate's relationships are borne out of events that shaped her long before she started dating men. It's almost as if her early adverse experiences suck her into traumatic relationships which create even more heartache, until her entire life is just one big, vicious trauma cycle. She was born with a hole in her heart and it's almost as if she has spent her entire life trying to mend it. But of course the media is not usually interested in such things and Kate's antics only trigger higher sales or viewing figures – an arrangement which suits them both. This relentless negative media coverage was harming her career. As usual, in contrast, the narrative around Pete was all about him dating a sensible doctor and being a perfect dad. Pete's new partner was 17 years his junior, but Kate dating toy boys was deemed unacceptable.

Throughout her break-up and relationship with Leo, Kate had continued filming the *What Katie Did Next* reality series while promoting her clothing and perfume ranges and writing books. But no matter how hard she worked, Kate's industry was always secondary to her role as a mum. When Pete and Kate had been together, Kate didn't mind the children being featured on their *Katie and Peter* reality show. But there were many reasons she didn't wish them to be filmed when Pete and she had parted. There was the obvious potential for them to be used as pawns in the quarrel and Kate's instinct was to protect them. She also wanted the children to have the space to deal with the break-up of the marriage. Pete's attitude was different; he didn't accept Kate's approach that filming the children when their parents were together was not the same as filming them when their parents were apart, and his justification was that Junior and Princess enjoyed filming. But they were so young, and I used to worry about how they would grow up thinking they were famous rather than having a chance to live pressure-free, ordinary lives. Of course, Harvey had been filmed for these shows at a young age, but in Kate's mind, the situation here was completely different. Harvey's appearances on camera had been an inspiration to many people with disabilities. I know this is true because I received so many supportive emails from mums and dads who had been struggling with disabled children and felt relieved to see someone championing and highlighting the challenges. Kate consciously wanted to challenge blinkered and discriminatory attitudes towards disability. There was a public outcry when the comedian Frankie Boyle made a distasteful joke about Harvey's condition in December 2010. Kate even decided to knock on his door to ask for an apology, but he wouldn't answer. Gutless!

Kate also insisted on maintaining consistency for the children. Although they moved between Kate and Peter's houses, Junior and Princess had the steadiness of having the same nannies and Harvey's routine continued with me taking him to Dorton House School every day. Pete was also filming his daily life in parallel with Kate but, unsurprisingly, he was portrayed in a favourable light and was very disparaging about Kate's wild lifestyle. Pete never supported or defended Kate when untrue stories came out in the press, and I wonder if all that negativity played to his advantage. This relentless negative media coverage was harming both Kate's mental health and her career. An example of the unfairness that Kate was facing was in 2011 when Kate successfully sued the *Daily Star* for publishing 17 incorrect stories about her. A settlement was reached where the *Daily Star* admitted that the most serious allegations were false. Of those 17 factually incorrect stories, 11 were written by a journalist called Gemma Wheatley. Gemma Wheatley left the *Daily Star* and then went to work for . . . Claire Powell. She was employed as a PA for Pete! Now Pete had someone working for him who had published false stories about the mother of his children.

Pete met his future wife Emily MacDonagh in 2010 and, after a long courtship, they married in 2015. During this five-year period, he was seen out on dates with Frank Lampard's ex-girlfriend Elen Rivas – they met at Claire Powell's 45th birthday party and Pete had to deal with one of his exes –

a woman called Maddy Ford – selling her story to the tabloids, explaining how they were having sex just eight days after Pete and Kate's divorce. As soon as Pete started dating Emily, the narrative became about him dating a sensible medical student – Emily is now a doctor, but she still found time to appear with Pete in his reality show at the beginning of their relationship and she writes a column for *OK!* magazine, so perhaps she enjoys the limelight too? Nothing is black and white.

Pete had become the darling of reality TV, but his shows were well prepared and could be edited to his advantage. He couldn't manipulate live television in the same way as he found out to his dismay in February 2010. During an interview with the presenter Kay Burley on *Sky News*, he seemed to be expecting just a few compliments and some publicity for his tour. But he became visibly angry and demanded that the interview be stopped when Kay asked him to clarify why, when Harvey's dad Dwight Yorke said that it was 'disrespectful' for Pete to make statements that he wished to adopt Harvey, Pete had protested. Yet he would not consider it if Alex Reid had said he wanted to adopt Junior and Princess after he married their mother. Pete was angry and started to cry. I imagine it must have given him some insight into how Dwight had felt all those years before when Pete had wanted to adopt Harvey.

By October 2012, I needed a break from constantly picking up the pieces of my daughter's life. I was also coming up to my 60th birthday – I didn't want a big party or a fuss, so instead I decided to do something I had dreamed of all my life – travelling. I had spent my life as a daughter, wife, mother

197

and grandmother – now it was time to find ME. I wanted to discover what sort of person I really was, learn about my strengths and weaknesses and step outside my comfort zone. But I didn't want to go to luxury hotels and sip cocktails round a pool – I'd seen enough of all that on my adventures with Kate to know it doesn't make people happy. Instead, I started looking at where I could go to help others.

Word got around about my crazy plan and a friend put me in contact with an organization that helps match volunteers with charities, and it suggested a charity called the Friends of Educators' Trust India, based in Goa. It helps children from the slums by trying to keep them from begging on the streets through education, skills building and helping them to live as independently as possible. I checked it out and found that it was a legitimate registered charity and decided to go and meet the Sheffield-based couple who helped with the funding over here in the UK to make absolutely sure everything was above board. I immediately liked them and the charity's ethos. I decided to pledge an initial £500 donation to guarantee a place on the programme and made plans to live in a town called Candolim in Goa.

I wanted to get a real feel for the country, the people, the children and the way of life; to do this, I was determined to stay for three months. As ever, if I decide to do something it gets done; but it wasn't all plain sailing. Although he is always such a brilliant support, Price thought I was mad – going somewhere that far away ... on my own ... for that length of time. When he realized how determined I was, though, he accepted me doing what I wanted, but he still thought it was far too long to be away. So, as an enticement to help me last the distance, we decided that when the three-month period was up, he would fly over to meet me and we would go on holiday together travelling around India's famous Golden Triangle, from Delhi to Jaipur and of course ending up at the Taj Mahal in Agra.

Kate was also worried about me going for that length of time and tried to persuade me to go for two weeks instead, then on to a holiday with her. She was on a more even keel now and I had to explain that the India adventure was something I wanted and needed to do for me. It wouldn't be easy to leave Harvey, but I knew he would be in safe hands. Mark, the driver who had been taking him back and forth to school alongside me for eight years, understood Harvey like I did. There would also be an escort in the car to sit with Harvey so I knew he would be okay. Kate was quite capable of looking after him, so I had no fear of leaving him at all.

I still seemed to be surrounded by family and friends who thought I was mad and told me I wouldn't last the course being on my own, but I knew I would prove them wrong. Fortunately, Dan and Sophie took a different view to everyone else. They were both working at the time – Dan was helping to manage Kate, and Sophie was juggling her hairdressing with studying. They both thought it was a good idea and Dan, in particular, understood completely. The point of this trip was for me to be ON MY OWN, so I limited electronic devices to a Kindle and an iPod loaded up with my favourite books and music – and set forth on my journey. As soon as I got to India, I bought a phone and SIM card and gave Dan my number in case he needed to get hold of me in an emergency. I said that once I had settled in, I would let him know how things were. I knew I wouldn't have five minutes peace if my number was circulated to the whole family, and it would be just like I'd never gone away. I didn't give my number to Kate, Sophie or Price, as I knew I would still be involved in things happening at home, which would defeat the whole object of me going to India. Price wasn't happy about the arrangement, but he accepted it. On the bright side, although Sophie would still be living at home with him, he'd get three months of freedom from me, so he could do exactly what he wanted and live a nag-free life.

The day before I left, we had a family lunch all together at Kate's house, then Price drove me to Heathrow airport. We both cried as he saw me off through the departure gates. I knew it would be hard for both of us to endure the longest separation we'd ever had in our relationship. I was physically shaking with anticipation and excitement as I waved my husband goodbye. Inside my head, my thoughts were all over the place as I tried to reassure myself that I was going to be able to get through this. He more or less pushed me through, and we waved until I couldn't see him anymore.

This was the first time that I realized I was on my own, literally starting the journey of a lifetime. It was strange. I felt so alone. After having been so confident in what I was doing, suddenly what was in front of me felt so daunting, but I pressed on. I had a lot of luggage with me – including toys, clothes, paper, pencils and toiletries for the children – and I must have looked like a weighed-down donkey as I trudged along towards the gate. Thankfully, although my luggage was over the weight limit, the lovely airline staff agreed to let me through once they knew it was all for charity. I boarded the plane and as we took off, I looked out of the window and watched London and my sometimes stressful, chaotic life disappear behind me. I wondered what different countries and sights I would fly over. Flying into the unknown, not knowing what to expect, was both frightening and exhilarating. All sorts of wild emotions were buzzing through my mind. I couldn't believe it was really happening. What had I done? I smiled to myself as I remembered similar feelings when my friend and I had gone skiing without telling our husbands . . . but this time my family knew that I was going away, and for a serious and worthy cause.

I was met at the airport in Goa by Dr Dhiru Mistry and his English wife, Susan. Dr Mistry had worked in the NHS as a doctor in Scarborough and had retired early to return to his native country to do charitable work for the Friends of Educators' Trust India. They took me to a one-bedroom, second-floor flat that would be my home for three months in Candolim in North Goa. It had a lounge, kitchen and bathroom but I was a bit perturbed to see that all the windows had bars on them and the interior interconnecting doors had to be locked when I went to bed. They assured me that the security was needed only for the holiday season when break-ins were common in Goa. Instead I had arrived just in time for the monsoon season, so most things were closed. There were hardly any tourists and I would be safe. How different the ambience of this place seemed compared to the cosy atmosphere of home in The Old Post Office in Sullington, with its incredibly peaceful views across the South Downs of West Sussex.

Very quickly I had to get used to draping a mosquito net – which Dan and his wife Lou had used on their own travels around Asia and had given to me – over my bed each night and scattering mothballs round the edges of each room in the flat to stop cockroaches coming in. I even had to put some around the plug hole in the shower. With Kate, I had stayed in some of the world's most luxurious hotels. Now here I was in a £60-a-month flat that was so damp, the walls ran with water when it rained. The flat smelled when it stopped, and I had to have the ceiling fans going most of the time to cool the rooms down. Rather than feeling sorry for myself, I set about creating a pleasant place to live.

Kate had bought me a pink crystal heart to wear and a dia-mante heart necklace with photos of her and the grandkids, while Sophie had bought me a bracelet with a cross and a turquoise band – I wore these constantly. Dan's more practical gift of the mosquito net reminded me of him and Lou every night. I took framed photos of the family with me, and Junior, Princess and Harvey had drawn me pictures which I pinned on the walls in my lounge. My flat wasn't far from the main street in Candolim and yet it was surrounded by lush greenery, which I loved. I had a balcony that I would hang my washing on, and the windows were covered in reflective glass – every morning a bird that looked similar to a thrush would tap on my bedroom window, looking at its reflection. I used to look forward to that moment each day, even if it did remind me of my former son-in-law Peter Andre who also loved looking at his own reflection every time he passed a mirror.

Outside there were cows wandering everywhere. They are sacred animals in India – the Hindu religion depicts them as symbols of the Divine, so they are allowed to go on the beaches, on the roads . . . in fact, everywhere. Every day I would have to walk through a whole herd of them to get to the bus stop to catch the bus to and from the charity school. One day I even saw a calf being born in the middle of the road and the traffic had just had to stop to make way for the newborn being moved on by its mother.

Because it was monsoon season, the restaurants were shuttered up and the sunbeds all packed away on the beaches. I saw dogs crawling all over the open kitchens where the tourists had previously eaten al fresco – the whole place had a deserted feel. Meanwhile, the rains were torrential and I quickly understood why the kerbstones were about 2ft high: to defend against the flood waters mixed with mud and rubbish, which seemingly had the power to destroy everything. Sometimes, on the way to work, I would have to pick my way through electric cables which had fallen down. There were no safety cones around them, nor were the areas cordoned off – the electric cables sizzled as they waited to be repaired. And there were plenty of power cuts with no warning, so my B&Q stick-on battery lights became my prized possessions.

I wanted to immerse myself in the community as much as possible, so I joined the gym. Even though it was basic, hot and sweaty, I worked out every day to Bollywood music, which I loved. And thankfully it wasn't long before I found the comfort of lovely neighbours, too. There was Jennifer and her husband Bilai, who had given up their jobs in the UK because Bilai had wanted to come back home to Goa. Jennifer worked for the same charity as me. Because they had lived in the UK, inevitably they had heard of Kate but they both knew I was there to 'find myself' and so there wasn't much conversation about her. They were a really accommodating couple and helped me to find the shops and stalls to buy the bits and pieces that I needed. Every week they would invite me for lunch or dinner in their flat.

I also met a lady called Bernie who was in Goa to volunteer, like me. We did yoga together – I had found an amazing yoga teacher at the gym who came to the flat to teach us. He was a large, softly spoken man and taught us ways of moving that I'll never forget. As well as helping me physically, he also enlightened me mentally. Firstly, he introduced me to 'huffing' like a dog on all fours and sticking my tongue out to get rid of the toxins in the body. I learned how to use my breath properly and he made me sit and meditate. It was a completely new experience for me. I felt good and in control of my body, both inside and out. It was a surreal feeling but I loved it. Jennifer, Bernie and I used to go on walks together by the sea and we had many enlightening conversations.

What with the yoga and the gym work, I was as fit as a fiddle and had never felt better in my life. I also began eating healthily. Most of the time I avoided meat and fish, or any processed food. I became more or less a vegetarian and ate eggs and vegetables as well as lots of fruit with fresh yogurt. I lived about 20 minutes from the supermarket and so could walk back and forth every day getting fresh food. And one of the things I loved most about working in India was catching the daily bus at the bottom of my road. It took about 45 minutes to get to the little school I worked at, which didn't even have a name. Basically it was just a small brick building – not much more than an annex – in the back of the garden of a big house with a paved courtyard and coconut trees, next to a lane in the middle of rice fields. At a push you could just about get a car down there. The bus was very reliable, and it would still travel even if the monsoon water was rising to the top of its wheels.

Bollywood music blasted out and incense burned in the front where the driver sat. My eyes were dazzled by the colours that blazed from the bright saris the women wore. The conductor initially tried to make some extra money out of me, charging a higher price or 'forgetting' to give me change, but we soon developed an understanding of one another and he gave up, allowing me to become one of the locals and even shouting at me in Hindi to get off at my stop at the top of the little lane. Then I would stroll through the rice fields and the ladies who tended them would wave to me as I went by. It was by far the most exhilarating commute to work I'd ever done in my life.

The school comprised of one large room with no desks or chairs. All the children, aged between three and seventeen, worked on the floor and ate their lunch there too. There was a toilet and sink, which I took it upon myself to clean every day because I couldn't bear the thought of people using it in the dirty state it was in when I arrived. The children thought they had to stand on the toilet and use it that way, so you can imagine the mess. I taught them how to sit on it and wash their hands afterwards. I even put a towel by the door so they could wipe their feet going in and out. Reading and writing is important, but so is hygiene.

Considering the school children lived in the slums, they looked immaculate coming to school in their charity-funded uniforms, and I quickly learned how nutrition was linked to learning outcomes because the children who had access to better diets were able to learn much quicker than those who were poorly fed. The school was a leveller because it allowed all children to access nutrient-rich daily meals. There was a kitchen which distributed the government-issued breakfast of rice and a milk drink, and a cook who prepared a lunchtime curry. The food was delicious and fresh, and the children used to sit on the floor and eat from tin plates with their hands. They laughed at me for using a spoon.

The teaching was in English so it was challenging for the children, who had to be helped through the use of picture books and phonics to learn. There was also a lot of singing in English and I worked alongside two amazing female Indian teachers, plus any other volunteers who were crazy enough to brave the monsoon season to work there. Each day, I sat on the floor with small groups and loved helping them to read and write. Sometimes they just needed tender loving care but at other times, I was able to provide medical assistance. All the medication in the school's first aid kit was donated by the local doctors and was out of date. Once a shoeless boy limped in – he'd stepped on a sharp twig which had embedded itself and infected his foot. His parents had tried to treat the wound with a lit cigarette to cauterize the infection but it looked awful and must have been excruciatingly painful. I washed and re-dressed it several times until it healed. I had to show the teachers that they must wash their hands before touching a wound and, if possible, wear surgical gloves. Luckily, I had brought some with me. All the children became very special to me and at times the little ones would crawl onto my lap and let me read to them. They were all beautiful children and loved having their photos taken, so I took many pictures of them. They really enjoyed that.

After I'd been there about three weeks, I felt a bit homesick so I spoke to Dan who reassured me that there was nothing unusual in feeling this way and said life would soon feel like normal. Dan is always the steady, calm and composed one and I could tell him how I felt about the day-to-day routine that was filling up my days and nights and share any problems. He told me to call him if ever I wanted to talk or felt low. He assured me everything and everyone was okay at home and that I should take advantage of the special experience I had wanted so much. He asked if it was any different from what I expected. When I told him it wasn't, he told me to just get on and enjoy it. Never once did he suggest that I should come home; he just helped me to cope with being away. Although he never mentioned it at the time, I am now sure he was being pestered at home. Eventually, he caved to this pressure and gave my phone number to Price, Kate and Sophie, who all started telling me I had proved that I could travel independently and should come home. But they had missed the point – the trip was about finding ME (not finding my way from A to B) and I couldn't do that overnight.

So I pushed away thoughts of home and visited the slums where I saw the children's ramshackle tin homes, some of which were incredibly organized. To my surprise, a few even had TVs and satellite dishes. But overall, the poverty was heart breaking and it put my family's first world problems into perspective. I learned that many of the children born in the slums didn't even have birth certificates, so they had to battle very hard just to get their foot in the door of a school because they couldn't prove their age. The charity used to liaise with the landowners to establish when they thought the children were born. If we could help support them getting a place, we would. I also couldn't believe that girls were still regarded as second to boys in the family. I remember one 12-year-old boy bossing his 17-year-old sister around all the time. She had no voice and I tried to educate him that this was wrong. At school, where they were all equal, he began to treat her with more respect. But at home within the caste system, social position was determined by gender and ancestral lineage and it was almost impossible to change so his mother and sister were still second-class people. I sensed he realized and respected that things were beginning to change for the better, and that his generation would have an important part to play in these shifts in attitude.

Sometimes, I would see our pupils begging at bus stops after I had been teaching them at school and it broke my heart. I felt powerless to change this aspect of a culture that has existed for centuries. It was terrible to see them sitting on the ground, holding out their dirty hands, looking pleadingly at strangers and asking for money so they could eat. The caste system is so ingrained it can only be addressed by new generations of Indians – not one woman from Brighton. However, I had definitely caught the charity bug and got involved with another project, renovating a house for abandoned girls. I never saw that completed but helped at the beginning to clean it up. I've often wondered how it turned out.

We are so fortunate in the UK; even though there is child poverty, there is nothing on a scale compared to this. It makes you appreciate what we have and made me realize how lucky my grandchildren were to have such a privileged upbringing. They were young, of course, and it was not their fault that they were totally spoilt and had no idea what life was like outside their bubble. I trust that one day they might experience volunteering, and I mean real volunteering, like I did in deprived areas. I hope that by helping others they will appreciate that real life really is about more than fame and money.

I hope that one day Kate will also follow in my footsteps, and that she will realize the importance of life and what it means, and the real struggles people have in order to just survive. I know she would wholeheartedly love to do what I have done. Even the basic living accommodation would not be a problem to her – she would adore setting up her own little flat, making her own home comforts, just like I did; you don't need much to live on and be comfortable. I know she has the strength of character to embrace it and that the experience would make her whole and realize that in comparison, her problems are small. Thinking of others is the best therapy to help yourself and give meaning to life. Kate would probably end up wanting to buy a home there and take in children, just like Old Mother Hubbard. Deep down, Kate is so kind and good natured I know she would appreciate giving love, encouragement and help to disadvantaged communities. I know how satisfying that would be for her.

After school, I used to look forward to returning home to my ramshackle little flat each evening to contemplate the events of the day, but I found it daunting walking alone at night and I had to be aware of my surroundings at all times. I carried a key alarm and never went out again once I had locked myself in. I had to pass through a green wooded area when I was walking back to my flat and I had been warned to be vigilant. I used to walk back after the gym at 5pm every night, so I always looked over my shoulder or pretended to drop something to let people walk by if there was someone behind me. At weekends I would immerse myself in the local community and the locals got used to seeing me and would help me select the best fruit and vegetables at the market. Sometimes, a fellow volunteer and I would get a bus and make the hour-long journey to Mapusa to visit bigger markets, where we stood out like sore thumbs among the locals who hounded us to buy their wares. It used to make me laugh when the stallholders shouted out, 'We are cheaper than Primark'. Over time, they got used to seeing me and ignored me, which I took as a huge compliment.

I also visited elephant sanctuaries, spice farms, religious buildings and lots of other beautiful places. Sometimes people wanted to take photos of me because I was white with blonde hair. When I had first arrived in Goa, I went on the beach to sunbathe and got chatting to the man who rented me a sunbed. He told me that people who took photos of me were likely to publish them on the internet alongside an untrue statement about the subject being a conquest. So I was prepared for that and used to say that it would cost 500 rupees a time for photos. They soon stopped trying to take the pictures.

In the evenings, I relaxed by doing ordinary things like watching BBC *World News* or old dramas like *Murder She Wrote* and *Columbo*. It was the time of the London Olympics and I wanted to be there, but I had to be content to watch the events on TV. I would have liked to see the English coverage, but of course things were shown from an Indian perspective and they weren't interested in the same sports as we were in the UK. Despite everything, I was very pleased with all the medals we won; after all, I am British and proud of it.

I could have spent the rest of my life helping at the school but eventually – after three months – it was time to come home and I took some satisfaction knowing I had achieved something for myself and others. I knew my last day at the school would be heart wrenching and I'm somewhat ashamed to say that I didn't feel strong enough to say goodbye to every-one. Our days began with the teachers having coffee together and I had become so emotionally attached to them all as well as the children so I knew I would break down and cry if I had to address them all and I couldn't do that. When the last day came and I had to leave my flat in Candolim, I asked Jennifer to take additional items such as blankets, plates, knives and forks, cushions and bedding to the school – in fact, everything I had bought for the flat – in the hope it would all be distributed to the families of the children in the slums.

Now it was time to be reunited with my husband. Despite the fact that I had refused to listen to his pleas for me to take advantage of my open ticket and make an early return home, I was dying to see him and couldn't wait for him to arrive. I had spoken to Price before he came out to join me and given him instructions on how to get to my flat. I will always remember the moment he called from Goa airport. He described how busy it was with the crowds pushing and shoving each other. Even though I was so excited, I casually told him to get used to it and as I was speaking on the phone, I realized just how much I had become part of the surroundings. My head was nodding from side to side just like some Indians do when they speak. More than that, I had learned so much about myself. Away from the hustle and bustle of being Katie Price's mother, I had discovered that I am a caring, emotional and patient person, but also someone who is determined and very independent. I learned the concept of boundaries and that it can be good to say no to people sometimes.

It was around 4am when Price arrived so I told him to get a taxi. I didn't go to the airport to meet him because I had no transport, and it would have meant going out at 2am, which wouldn't have been safe. When I first caught sight of him walking towards my flat down the road, I could not believe it was really happening. My first thought was how fat he had become and when he saw me, he commented on how thin I was. It was funny to me but not to him. In Goa I considered myself to be in perfect health, but in reality I had plummeted from 9½ to 7 stone. I thought I looked good and felt great, but ominously Price said I looked ill.

The next day, I put Price's concerns out of my mind and showed him all my favourite haunts, like the beach and the coffee shop. I took him to the market, on the buses and to the gym. In the evening, we watched a live football match. It felt so strange having him with me. I took him to one of my favourite shops where I had bought lots of silver jewellery and made him buy a silver wedding ring. He wasn't wearing his and I knew it would be culturally frowned upon. He never wore his wedding ring at home when working as it was too dangerous and he had forgotten to bring it with him. Price was mesmerized. He couldn't believe the hustle and bustle of the traffic and just couldn't get used to the fact that no one bothered to queue anywhere. He was also amused by the fact that I had picked up the Indian nodding habit. Naturally, Price wanted me to take him to the school, but I just couldn't do it; it would have been too upsetting.

The time had arrived for Price and me to undertake our tour of the Golden Triangle. It goes without saying that it turned out to be a spectacular and unforgettable experience. We hired a car and a guide, who we always invited to join us for meals, and stayed in five-star hotels. I have to admit that it was an uncomfortable contrast to what I'd been used to. I also struggled to get used to the larger and posher meals again. The Taj Mahal, the forts and indeed all the sights were amazing, but the tourist trail was not the reason I had come to India. As I travelled around, there was always a feeling of guilt at the back of my mind as I remembered the slums and poverty I had left behind.

India was definitely a period of self-discovery for me. It had been heaven to live outside of the celebrity culture which had become more and more claustrophobic before I left. Reality TV and so-called magazine exclusives pale into insignificance when you are watching children just trying to eat, learn for their future and simply stay alive. By the time I came home, the true extent of how meaningless media and celebrity culture are had been revealed to me. Some aspects of it now make me shake my head in disbelief. I wonder what it is all for. Money? Fame? It just triggers greed, envy, jealousy and unhappiness. I much prefer the simple things in life and appreciate them. But life is never simple as Kate's mum. In fact, as we had toured India together, Price had brought me up to date me with news from home, including information about a new romance that Kate was kindling with someone called Kieran Hayler. I had barely touched down in the UK before the rollercoaster's cogs were back in motion.

Chapter 12

MAID OF DISHONOUR

In India I had really learned how to instigate better boundaries, so my main resolution on returning to the UK had been that I would learn to say no, and take better care of myself and my needs before thinking of others. Well that immediately went out of the window. As soon as I arrived home, I was bombarded with to-do lists and quickly had to get into the swing of things. One of my assignments was to start taking Harvey to and from school again. I had missed Harvey, Junior and Princess and was very surprised how much the three of them had grown in the three months that I had been away. I also needed to catch up with Kate to find out what she had been up to. I will admit that I was conflicted about returning to the patterns of my old life, but I also knew that – come what may – I had to support Kate and Harvey. I wondered if things had changed and life would be different now. I hoped I might have a refreshing return to my old life and find a less-stressed daughter. It didn't take long to find out my hopes were in vain.

In October, about a month after Leo had left, Kate had been introduced to a man called Kieran Hayler by her friends

215

the make-up artist Gary Cockerill and his husband Phil Turner. Kieran knew them and had told them he fancied Kate. She agreed that he could have her number, but he immediately started bombarding her with text messages – initially she thought he was too full on and blocked him. But before long, she became restless. In no time at all after her break-up with Leandro, which had followed the finalization of her divorce from Alex Reid – and just days after my return from India – she called me with the words I had come to dread, 'Mum, I've met someone'.

Predictably, she began the usual sales talk, assuring me, 'He's normal, mum, from an ordinary background'.

'Really? What does he do then?'

'Oh, he's a plasterer. And a stripper.' I mean, would that career be normal for anyone other than my daughter?

'Well, he's not stripping *or* plastering in our house,' I told her, before explaining that I would soon be on my way over to check him out. By now, I had come to understand that Kate needed support and protection in relationships. She had always been vulnerable, and fame had only opened up the flood gates for any Tom, Dick or Harry who wanted a million Instagram followers and his own fashion range to infiltrate our family.

I entered Kate's house in Horsham to find Kieran sitting comfortably on the sofa next to Kate. He looked young, I guessed he was about 25 or 26. He was small and seemed embarrassed and out of his depth. I looked him over and noticed he was struggling to look me in the eye. He didn't stand up to greet me. Inwardly, I concluded that Kate had found herself yet another vulnerable, pretty boy. I know it sounds awful to come to these conclusions so swiftly – everyone deserves a chance – but I knew instinctively this was not going to work. Kieran was quiet and, to me, he seemed to have no backbone. He looked like a lost little boy sitting there. I thought Kate must have warned him that I would have reservations about him, knowing that he had been on the scene for mere moments. To be honest, I was sick of meeting her 'loves' as she called them. They weren't 'loves'; they were just dalliances. If I had been introduced to an older man, who had lived and experienced life, and who had had the good manners to stand up and introduce himself to me, I would have been more respectful. There was no handshake, which irritated me. I was sick of the brawn rather than brains.

We soon discovered Kieran was exaggerating his career. He wasn't a plasterer, he was just a plasterer's mate. He was a stripper though. To give him credit, he had his own flat, which Kate was quick to tell me about – she wanted to convince me that because Kieran owned a property, he wouldn't have to live off her. But it soon became clear that this was rented to his sister, and he was living at his mum's. Even if it meant dredging the bottom of the barrel, Kate always tries to find good things to say about her men.

I wasn't so convinced about Kieran's reliability or independence, so I decided to get straight down to the nitty gritty and presented him with a confidentiality agreement, which I asked him to sign. To be fair, he did so without complaint, but I still walked away that day with a sense of powerlessness – Act One of the familiar whirlwind romance drama was

217

already being played out. I felt certain that it would only be a matter of time before the curtain rose for Act Two and the suitcases would be unpacked.

As I had expected, Leandro Penna had barely touched down in Argentina before I received another call from Kate, on Christmas Day 2012, telling me that Kieran had proposed and she had accepted. 'Not again,' I thought. Not only was it stupid, but it was also becoming embarrassing for us all. How many more times could she mistake lust for love? Before Kate was born, Ray used to tease me about the books I used to read and the films I used to watch. I loved Hans Christian Andersen's fairy tales and *A Book of Nonsense* by Edward Lear, and I can't count the number of times I watched *Gone with the Wind* and *White Christmas* – the fairy tale endings enraptured me. But Ray said that these didn't exist in real life – over time I came to understand how true that is, but this is a lesson that Kate has yet to learn.

Kate brought Kieran to see us, and he asked Price if he could have Kate's hand in marriage. Price being Price – and not wanting to upset Kate – gave Kieran his permission, but with the proviso that he had to keep working. Wisely, Price pointed out that as soon as Kieran gave up his independence and relied on Kate, their relationship would be doomed. I was simply flabbergasted that just a few weeks after meeting Kieran, she wanted to get married. I told her, as none of them seemed real, that this would be the last of her weddings I would ever go to. Kate was in love with the idea of being in love, and the men were in love with marrying 'Katie Price' the brand, rather than Kate the person. They seemed to be clones of each other – desperate to sponge off Kate's fame, and in love with the mirror and their bank balances rather than with Kate. They all certainly knew how to take her to the cleaners financially or emotionally when the split came. I just wish she could find a man who could look after her and be a stable father for her children, rather than one who just looks after himself and leaves her to be the breadwinner. I am also baffled by her friends and wonder what goes through their heads when they introduce her to these guys.

I care deeply for Kate, so as well as getting angry, I often feel drained emotionally; this was how it was after she had become engaged yet again. So you can imagine my reaction when she informed me that a psychic had forecast the match. Because there has been so much written about her, Kate is an easy target for quack practitioners who have read up on her life. She has a constant line of mediums and clairvoyants contacting her, wanting to tell her future or read her palm or even saying they have been contacted by a spirit that wishes to speak to her. People are much more receptive when they are vulnerable, and my goodness how obvious it is and often it is that Kate is vulnerable. I have always told her not to listen to these readings, or at least take them with a pinch of salt. They start off as a bit of fun, then the trickster gains your confidence and you begin to reveal more and more to them; before you know it, you've revealed your life story, including everything that's bothering you, allowing them to fabricate whatever they like to make you feel better. This and that will happen, they say, but just be patient as it might take a few months. You can probably tell how cynical I am about them, so you won't be surprised that I just laughed when Kate told me that one particular fortune teller had told her she would meet a man with a name beginning with K, possibly Kevin. A Kevin did come into her life, and I am pleased to say that he remained faithful – but unfortunately it was only a Labrador that she bought for Kieran.

Despite my initial instincts, though, Kieran seemed quite harmless at the beginning of the relationship, and I began to wonder if my judgements had been a bit harsh. Could things actually work out this time? He had made a brief appearance in *Coronation Street* as a stripper but said he didn't want to be famous and had no interest in stealing Kate's limelight. Early on in the relationship, Kieran continued doing some stripping and plastering and Kate even bought him some gym equipment because he claimed he had been a personal trainer and this was something else he also dabbled in.

However, it didn't take him long to be sucked into Kate's world. He didn't seem to have any long-term plans or ambitions, so Kate found him something to do, and he ended up as a paid employee, looking after Kate's businesses with her and taking over Dan's role managing the paperwork and websites. Kieran had somehow managed to convince Kate that he was a financial wizard who should take over her business accounts – a painful period ensued as Dan was forced to step back from supporting his sister, and was also faced with a loss of income. Unfortunately, Kieran was out of his depth. Dan had been meticulous and understood what he was doing: he organized things so that money was kept back for VAT and tax bills and Kate was given an allowance each month. Kieran's approach, on the other hand, seemed chaotic – I think this marked the start of the downward slope for Kate's financial affairs. Kieran also took over the building work at Kate's house. He seemed to revel in the fact that he was now hiring the very same men he'd once worked for as a plasterer's mate, and I think he took delight in feeling like the boss of them.

Although we did not realize it at the time, I think Kieran probably missed the adulation of other women watching him strip. Despite his initial assertions that he didn't want to be famous, photo shoots with Kate started and soon the familiar pattern began to emerge. The next step is always appearing on the front cover of magazines and then they think they're famous and there's easy money to be made. Next come her reality shows and even more money. Then they accompany her on work trips and, all of a sudden, they abandon their jobs and they are in the Katie Price bubble, relying on her for their income. When – as it always does – the relationship finishes there's even more easy money to be made by selling the story to the press, claiming they are a victim of the wicked Katie Price. It didn't take one of Kate's fortune tellers to predict that the man whose name began with a K was going to follow this same path.

I do so wish Kate would listen to us. We desperately try to get her to reflect on previous relationships and suggest that it would be a really good idea to live with someone first and get to know him, rather than rushing so quickly into another disastrous marriage. I think the attraction must be the security of a piece of paper tying them together. We pointed out that she hadn't known Kieran long enough to really understand him. Also, things were moving at such speed there had been no chance for Kieran to bond with Junior who was seven and Princess who was five. They had hardly had time to get to know Alex and had been glad to see the back of Leo. To begin with, they got on well with Kieran, but they would soon be disappointed with his behaviour and the upset and trauma it caused their mother.

As a family, we hate Kate's weddings with a passion. To us they are a farce. This started when she married Pete and the ceremony turned out to be a publicity spectacle. Her marriage to Alex was just slapstick and impossible to take seriously. And now a wedding with Kieran was being lined up. Was this just going to be another joke? There is so often a dark side to comedy and on top of the embarrassment caused by the weddings, there is the worry about the long-term effect the inevitable break-up will have on the children. When Kate's relationships end, none of her partners ever say anything positive about her. Kate has received a lot of bad press – particularly after her break-up with Pete – but one day Junior and Princess will be able to look back and make their own minds up and hopefully see how their mother has been harshly and unfairly judged. I hope by reading this book, they will understand more.

In January 2013, I took another phone call from Kate, excitedly informing me that I was going to have the opportunity to meet Kieran's mum, Wendy. But of course it wouldn't be over a cup of tea and a few biscuits like a normal family. No, Kate instructed me to stand outside WH Smith at Heathrow airport, where Mrs Hayler and I presumably might have time to greet each other and buy ourselves a magazine or two before boarding a flight to the Bahamas. I couldn't believe what I was hearing. Mrs Hayler and I were being invited to meet each other for the first time on a flight to the West Indies and, to make things even more jaw dropping, the flight was taking us to watch our children tie the knot at the Sandals Royal Bahamian Resort and Spa. I was shocked – it seemed ridiculous. Here we go again. Our families were joining and I was to meet Kieran's mum for the first time on a flight to the wedding. I didn't want anything to do with it.

After sleeping on it, though, I realized that Kate would go ahead with the marriage whether I was there or not. I thought the best course of action I could take was to protect Kate in any way I could. So, callous as it may seem, I had a prenup drawn up and decided to take it with me for Kieran to sign. I had already seen the damage done by marrying a guy this quickly and I didn't want it to happen again. Wendy, Kieran's mum, seemed to be a really nice person and we chatted pleasantly throughout the journey. Although she was happy that Kieran was marrying Kate, she was as shocked as I was about the bizarre situation we found ourselves in, and that things were happening so quickly. She was not prepared for the aftermath once Katie and Kieran were married, so I told her what to expect from the press. The flight turned out well, but that was the only part of the trip that would.

In the end, the wedding – which was held on a beach – was a total disaster. It was nothing like the romantic pictures you sometimes see. There were holiday makers everywhere – on the sand, drinking at bars, pestering us for pictures.

When you see brochures of weddings on beaches in idyllic locations there is never anyone in the background, but this is a false impression. At Kate's wedding, crowds of holiday makers were there sunning themselves and watching the ceremony. There was no privacy – anyone could take photos if they wanted. The beach bars were open so there were people drinking, talking, laughing and watching. The press were there, too, taking photos looking down from the hotel rooms. What had been sold to Kate as a private location turned out to be anything but and, as anticipated, this wedding too turned into an absolute farce.

Having spent so much time in India, it was impossible not to reflect on the hollowness and selfishness of this ridiculous wedding and our Western materialistic values; as I took time to reflect, the extravagance of the whole situation seemed meaningless, and I felt really uncomfortable after all the poverty I had witnessed. Here we were among all this greenery and endless bouquets of flowers in a fake setting of love statues which was meant to conjure up the atmosphere of a romantic sunset in Ancient Greece. I hated it, and with every moment the strain became worse. I could read Kate's face and I could tell this was not the Arcadia she had imagined. As I had only known him for such a short while, I could not be so certain what was going on inside Kieran's mind, but he gave the impression that he had won the jackpot, and this was the party to celebrate it. To an observer it was obvious from the outset that, as usual, Kate's wonderful expectations had been completely shattered.

As if there wasn't enough tension at the wedding already,

there was also Kate's best friend Jane Pountney's strange behaviour. She had become gradually closer to Kate over the years, so she was the natural choice to be Kate's maid of honour at her wedding to Alex and also at this wedding to Kieran. Kate had been friends with Jane's husband Derrick since she was a teenager and spent a lot of time with Derrick and his friend Neil. Neil was good looking and worked out at the gym; to be honest, the family had hoped and even expected Kate and Neil to get together one day but, although they were very close, Kate and Neil were never boyfriend and girlfriend. I admire Neil's loyalty and integrity because he has always refused to sell his story – what he could say would be much more authentic and truer than some of the semi-fictionalized accounts that others who don't know her half as well have pawned for their thirty pieces of silver.

I first remember being introduced to Jane by Derrick. She seemed a shy, retiring kind of girl who was happy to remain in the background. Derrick was always round with Neil, but Jane wasn't there quite so much because at the time she was working as cabin crew and would sometimes be away. She was pleasant, unassuming and respectful and she could also be good fun – I'd never had a cross word with her. She had married Derrick and because her children were the same age as Junior and Princess, it's not surprising that the friendship flourished. Jane would accompany Kate to restaurants and clubs. She also began to accompany Kate to a lot of social and work events. If Kate had her hair or nails done, Jane would be with her. Jane seemed to spend more time with Kate than with her husband. Over time they became very close, and

Jane seemed to be involved in all the dramas that beset Kate. As their lives became more and more entwined, Jane became entangled in Kate's relationships and rows.

I remember one occasion that showed how inseparable they had become – when Kate had returned home exhausted after a particularly taxing day, Jane suggested that I should leave Kate alone and not disturb her. Gradually, it seemed that Jane was spending as much time at the house as Kate was. In fact, even the nannies noticed she was there at Kate's house most of the time. She used to feed her children there and they used to play with Junior and Princess. It got to the stage where I had to tell Jane that the nannies were not there to look after her children and that she should clear up the mess they made as it wasn't the nannies' responsibility to do this. I had the feeling that Jane was not only trying to usurp my role as Kate's mum, but she was also beginning to morph into Kate herself. Looking back, I don't know why I so readily accepted this.

This became more evident at Kate and Kieran's wedding. Jane was normally quite plain, unremarkable. I would have described her as being a mumsy character prior to the wedding and I mean no disrespect by this label – in fact, the opposite as I believe it is important to be a mother before worrying about appearances: Jane dressed casually and didn't waste hours taking care of herself. But at this wedding, she had suddenly bloomed – she had hair extensions, she had had her teeth done and whitened, she wore false eyelashes and nails, she had lost a lot of weight, she was wearing a short dress of the kind that Kate would often wear, she'd copied Kate's make-up, and her personality seemed to have completely changed. She was more outgoing and flirtatious. A different Jane. A Jane that was also more critical of Kate. She would say that Kate's hair didn't look right, or her make-up wasn't good enough and she was critical of the clothes Kate wore.

Jane was being quite loud for Jane and at the dinner later in the evening, after too much Champagne, she climbed on top of the table and started to dance. She was obviously looking to attract someone's attention. Derrick was as surprised as we all were. It seemed like some sort of mating dance – looking back, perhaps it really was one! An embarrassed Derrick told her to get down and helped her off the table. Knowing what I know now, it is clear that she was completely infatuated with Kieran. I am not sure if anything was going on between them at that stage, but it seems that she saw how he had fallen for Kate and thought by morphing into Kate he might fall for her too. Poor Derrick didn't know where to put himself. Kieran's mum and our other friend noticed Jane's behaviour and thought it all rather strange. Would you believe it, though, it happened again on the following day at a restaurant we visited for pre-dinner drinks. She was definitely looking for attention, but at the time it just seemed so out of character.

Internally I was shouting, 'For God's sake. What are you doing?' There wasn't even any music playing. Kate and I looked across at one another and instinctively acknowledged that it didn't feel right. But as ever with Kate, things were moving at breakneck speed. We sat down to dinner and there was no time to process what was really going on with Jane before Kate announced to us all that she was pregnant. In a way, that justified her decision to have such a rapid marriage. But if I am honest, I found it hard to congratulate her because everything felt way too soon. Kate and Kieran had barely lived together, let alone tested their ability to parent together. In Kate's head it was wonderful news but in reality, yet again, I felt very concerned about how this relationship would play out and what it would mean for Kate's other children and her career. The children said they were pleased that their mum was expecting another baby – Princess thought she would be able to play with it like one of her dolls. More recently, Junior has said that although he didn't admit it at the time, he did find it hard to adjust.

After the wedding, Kate and Kieran returned to Horsham to build a home for themselves and their expanding family. Jane was still a frequent visitor to the house and I began to think it strange how she would often, unexpectedly, turn up when Kate wasn't there. I'd tell her that Kate was out, but it was unnecessary because she would have known anyway as she followed all of Kate's movements so closely. She never explained on any of those occasions why she was visiting. I wonder now if her visits were in the hope of seeing Kieran. Once, she even brought her dad with her. Soon she and Derrick moved from Hove to be nearer to Kate. We were invited round to their house on one occasion and discovered that she had made it a replica of Kate's style and colours. More and more it seemed as though she wanted to be Kate.

Just two months after the wedding ceremony in the Bahamas, Kate and Kieran tied the knot yet again, in March 2013, at a Somerset venue recommended by her close friend and confidante Andrew Antonio. The couple wanted to have a blessing on home soil. Getting involved with this event was the last thing I wanted, but Kate needed help with choosing her dress and the bridesmaids' outfits. Among the 12 bridesmaids were Sophie, Dan's wife Louise, and various friends of Kate's, some of whom have stayed in touch and some who Kate doesn't see much of anymore, which isn't surprising to me. I refused to get involved in the planning of the actual ceremony. For this one I just kept in the background because this time I wanted to enjoy myself, just like everyone else. Price and the rest of the family were convinced we were about to witness another farce and were determined to be part of the audience rather than participants.

The night before the wedding, Kate wanted me to stay in a room opposite her just in case Harvey became upset. But this never happened because Jane wanted that room and made sure she got it – Harvey's welfare became of secondary importance. She only wanted to stay there to be first in the queue to get her hair and make-up done. She demanded the same style as Kate, looking like a clone of her, and even Sophie who normally keeps her thoughts to herself commented on this weird change in Jane.

Although I had severed contact with Ray, Kate had kept in touch. Ray sometimes attends barbecues at Kate's house or comes over for birthday celebrations. So, Kate walked down the aisle with her biological dad Ray and stepdad Price, as a gospel choir sang 'I Will Always Love You'. It did feel more like a real wedding this time and not as stressful as on previous occasions. Kieran's sister did a reading, then Dan gave a speech suggesting that as this was the third time it might be the lucky one. He ended by playing the Jermaine Stewart song 'You Don't Have to Take Your Clothes Off to Have a Good Time'. That went down well, and everyone laughed, knowing it was a dig at Kieran. It was fun and the atmosphere was light hearted and spontaneous, unlike the tense, staged previous weddings which were stop and start to accommodate the photography and filming. This time everyone seemed to be enjoying themselves and it was the nearest Kate had got to a 'normal' wedding. She seemed genuinely happy, and we were pleased for her. In our hearts, despite our reservations, we wondered if things might work out after all.

There was a Willy Wonka theme at the reception, which had been chosen with Junior and Princess in mind. Just like Kate, they loved the film of *Charlie and the Chocolate Factory* and they were involved in the wedding as a page boy and a flower girl, as were Jane's children. They seemed to be enjoying themselves. Junior got up and sang 'Let Me Entertain You' and Princess, like Harvey, danced the night away. However, there was no way they were going to be the centre of attention.

Jane had engineered a seat for herself at the top table, and gone was the retiring, shy person we had met years ago. She was loud and confident, and even gave a speech about her friendship with Kate. At the time, though, we were content to enjoy ourselves and because things seemed to be going well, we weren't noticing any untoward signs. Kate seemed happy and it appeared that Kieran was in love with her so at the time no one registered the other Kate emerging. In retrospect, it is far more obvious. Looking back at photographs, it is clear that not only had Jane copied Kate's hair and make-up, but she was also imitating her poses and facial expressions. Was something already beginning to heat up between Jane and Kieran? Were they already exchanging secret glances and the odd compliment? Who would even have contemplated such a possibility at this time? This was Kate's wedding. Kieran was her new husband. Jane was her best friend. Even if sparks had not been ignited between Kieran and Jane, they certainly were elsewhere – the evening ended with a firework display which caused a tree to catch fire and prompted a 999 call.

Kate continued to work during her pregnancy and in June of 2013 she published her ninth novel, *He's the One*. Jane was still on the scene as Kate promoted the book – she was more confident than ever, and by now had firmly adopted Kate's dress style. But, while Kate's outfits changed as she developed her baby bump, Jane's outfits became much skimpier and revealing – particularly in front of Kieran. Kate, with that second sense that women seem to get when they know something is happening but can't put their finger on it, asked Kieran if he thought that Jane fancied him. Kieran dismissed the idea and said that Jane was fit for her age, but that was all.

In August of 2013, Kate and Kieran – along with Derrick and Jane – rented a villa in France for a joint family holiday. They planned to travel together in Kate's pink horsebox. Kate's horsebox was very luxurious; it had a seating area, beds and a fully operational kitchen, so comfort was guaranteed. When the time came to pack, Kieran had hurt his shoulder so couldn't help and instead sat in the back of the truck laughing and giggling with Jane while Kate and Derrick did all the hard work. Kieran and Jane couldn't drive the truck so, again, they sat in the back as Derrick and a heavily pregnant Kate were again put upon to share the toils and get the families safely to their destination.

When they had settled in, Kieran continued to spend a lot of time with Jane as he played in the water with her and the kids. Derrick and Kate watched beside the pool and began to suspect something was going on. Although at the time it was still only intuition, Kate was worried enough to call me several times. I wondered if she was just feeling a bit frumpy and more emotional because she was pregnant. I tried to console her and said she was worrying unduly, but deep down I was very concerned. I had noticed in the run up to the holiday that Jane had become much flirtier with men at Kate's house, and she had become more full of herself ordering the nannies and cleaners around as if she owned the place. However, it never occurred to me that anything would happen between Jane and Kieran as she was Kate's best friend and Kate was pregnant with Kieran's first child.

As a dramatic distraction from these anxieties (an event which may have even been caused by them), Kate's waters broke in France, two months before her due date. She was rushed to hospital where she had to undergo a traumatic Caesarean birth. Her son, Jett, needed to be incubated, suffered from sleep apnoea and had to remain in hospital to be monitored and treated. I was receiving frantic and tearful calls from Kate. While she had the comfort of Harvey being driven to see her by his nanny, she was very lonely because she was spending so much time on her own in a hospital in a foreign country. Kieran was not visiting very much and, unsurprisingly, she couldn't understand why. It wasn't until the evening that he would visit, often with Derek, Jane, Junior and Princess. Kate was particularly concerned that she wasn't seeing Kieran alone – after all, he was her husband and the father of their sick child.

As their time at the villa was coming to an end, Kate had to rent another one nearer the hospital. Dan flew over to Marseille to pick up Princess and Junior and return them to Pete as they were due to fly to Australia for another holiday. Derrick had to be back at work, so he drove the horsebox home with his children. I flew over to France, with our nanny, to look after Harvey while Kate was in hospital. Dan told me he thought it was strange that Jane hadn't returned home with Derrick and her children. Kate told me that Derrick had told Jane he was leaving her there to 'play happy families with Kieran', whatever that was supposed to mean.

Derrick and Kate both seemed to be aware something was happening and when I arrived, there was certainly a different atmosphere. Jane was very quiet and so was Kieran. They did not speak much to each other when I was there, and it was obvious something was not right. I visited Kate with Kieran at the hospital to meet my new grandson, Jett Riviera. Kate was eventually allowed to return to the villa, but Jett had to remain in hospital and she and Kieran needed to feed him there in the day and the evenings. I went home and soon after that, Jane finally returned too. With Kate back at the villa, her private time with Kieran had come to an end and six weeks later Jett was allowed home to the UK.

After their return, I noticed the relationship between

Kate and Jane was a little different. Although she still often seemed to arrive when Kate wasn't there, Jane wasn't round at Kate's house continuously as she used to be. She was still full of herself and she had become very sarcastic too, which I didn't like. She would even tell Kate she looked fat and frumpy, but she and Derrick continued to socialize with Kate and Kieran, so besides these differences life carried on with some pretence of normality. However, worrying cracks were appearing in Kate and Kieran's relationship. Kieran had become much lazier and seemed to have lost his enthusiasm for Kate and the kids. He and Kate also seemed to argue much more. I was disgusted that Kieran had left Kate alone in the hospital for such long periods to spend more time with Jane, when he should have been there both celebrating the birth of his son and sharing Kate's concerns about Jett's health.

All of this stood in stark contrast to Dan's happy news. He told us that he and Lou were thrilled to be expecting twins and we were all delighted for them. I will always remember the look of happiness on my son's face when he came to tell me that the love of his life was pregnant, and showed me the scan photos. Just like the rest of the family, I was thrilled. I was kept informed almost daily of the baby's progress as Lou grew bigger and bigger. When the day came for her to be induced, Sophie, Kate and I went out and bought lots of baby clothes and toys to take to the hospital. We were ushered into a room with Lou's mum and dad and were told to be quiet because we were so excited and laughing so loudly that we were disturbing everyone. When we finally managed to get in to see them, we were greeted by two very proud parents and two beautiful little girls. As we left them with the presents, the three of us felt inspired – it was so obvious that we were leaving a family who felt contented and complete, and I couldn't help feeling a pang of sadness for Kate because this wasn't something she had so far been able to experience.

In April 2014, Kate was in the early stages of pregnancy with Kieran's second child and despite what had happened the last time, she again went on holiday with Kieran, Derrick, Jane and all the children to Cape Verde. They hadn't been there long when I received a desperate call from Kate in the middle of the night. She was crying down the phone because she had caught Kieran and Jane together on the beach, kissing. Kate was distraught. She said she just lost her temper and hit Jane and then ran away with both Jane and Kieran chasing her, denying what had happened. I was shocked but not surprised. I knew this might happen. Everything now seemed to add up – ever since Jane's behaviour had changed and she had been morphing into Kate, I'd had a niggling feeling at the back of my mind that disaster seemed likely. What could I say to comfort my daughter when I was so far away? Words would not be strong enough, so I told her to come home. Try as she might, though, there were no flights available for eight days.

So, there they were, all stuck together – it must have played out like the plot of a film. The cast of characters included a wife who still loved a husband, who she finds has been having an affair with her best friend, whose husband had been having misgivings about his wife. How many times do such shenanigans happen in novels or movies? But this was for real and it was causing excruciating pain. The next day, Kate told me that they had all talked about what had happened. Derrick revealed that there had been good reason for him to be suspicious during the previous fateful holiday in France – Jane had shown him flirty texts that Kieran had sent her during the trip, telling her he fancied her. It's not clear why Jane would have shown her husband the texts – perhaps to prepare an excuse of innocence for herself if the deceit was to come to light. There was also another bombshell – Jane admitted that she no longer loved Derrick. When Kate asked Kieran in front of Derrick and Jane about the texts, rather than facing the music, Kieran tried to take the easy way out by walking away. Jane shouted out to him, telling him to come back. Kate asked her why she was doing this as Kieran was her husband. Jane screamed that he wasn't, Kieran was now HER boyfriend. Kate just lost it again – she lashed out at Jane and was hitting her, so Kieran and Derek had to intervene. That was the last time she saw them until the day they were due to fly home. Although she couldn't alter the flight, Kate managed to change seats so she didn't have to sit next to Jane on the plane. Kate was devastated and heartbroken.

When Kate arrived home, I immediately went to see her. I couldn't face Kieran because he made me feel sick. Eventually, I did speak to him, and calmly and quietly asked him why on earth he had done what he had. I wanted to throw him out of the house, but I knew that that it wasn't going to be as straightforward as that, because I knew that Kate was already beside herself. She was upset and crying; she just could not understand how her husband and her best friend could do this to her. This vulnerable side of Kate is the part that the public never gets to see, but it's the part that we as her loved ones have to keep the closest eye on, knowing how fragile her mental health can be. When Kate's therapist arrived, I asked her what she was going to do about the situation, and I wondered if she was going to be able to sort it out. She told me not to worry and assured me she would be able to get to the bottom of things and put them right. I couldn't understand why Kate was planning to give Kieran a second chance and put it down to the fact that her hormones were probably all over the place because she was pregnant. Kate's therapist helped to calm her down, and Kieran also started having therapy. The therapist was coming every day and it seemed the more Kate cried, the more Kieran strayed from the truth. Initially, after Kate's prompting, the lie detector used on the Jeremy Kyle show was brought to the house, but Kieran wouldn't accept it when it showed that he was lying.

Soon Kate's therapist fixed him up with a therapist from Gibraltar who had worked with serial killers and psychopaths – his conclusion was that Kieran had a sex addiction and Kieran accepted he needed help. At last, the truth came out – and with it, all the sordid details. He and Jane had been together for months. They had been at it all over Kate's house – sometimes several times a day – and were not too choosy about other locations, even resorting to a Tesco's car park. I believe Kieran knows how to manipulate people and Jane was an easy target. She was obsessed with him and had convinced herself he was in love with her and would fulfil his promise to leave Kate. Since his return, I had tried to avoid Kieran as much as I could but on one occasion when I bumped into him, I told him that Kate might be gullible, but he didn't fool me – I could see right through him.

I question whether the therapists really helped either Kate or Kieran – Kate was too easily placated, and Kieran wasn't yet satisfied. His infidelity continued: another friend of Kate, Chrissy Thomas, had popped in and out of Kate's life and had recently come back on the scene after Kieran had contacted her via Twitter. After their March wedding, when Kate thought Kieran was stripping and then coming home, he was actually meeting Chrissy for sex before returning to Kate. He also used to meet Chrissy in the gym, supposedly acting as her trainer, but this was just a cover. Chrissy was sitting with Sophie and Kate in Kate's car after Kate had found out about her and Kieran, and Chrissy told them exactly what had gone on between them. It had started with Kieran writing a text saying he was in love with Kate, but there was no sex, and he was down and needed a cuddle. Things progressed from there; I won't go into details because they are x-rated.

Other friends of Kate, who were fortunately stronger willed and less duplicitous, told her about similar texts they had received from Kieran. Even Kate's PA received one, but she just ignored it. I found all this easy to believe because before it had all come out into the open, I had been sent one as well. Once, after we had been for a meal at Kate's house, Price and I were leaving and – as was our custom when saying goodbye – we kissed cheek on cheek and Kieran 'accidentally' kissed me on my lips. Later, I had a text from him saying, 'That was nice'. I was shocked and tried to ignore it. Until now, I have never told anyone this story. It showed the depths he would go to – I'm a grandmother!

After these discoveries, my relationship with Kieran had obviously reached rock bottom. He'd tried his tricks with me and it didn't work. I wanted Kate to leave him. Unlike Kate, though, who had paid for his therapy and wanted to believe that there was a reason behind his duplicity, I didn't for one moment think he had a sex addiction. I could see right through him, and he knew it, but the more you tell or advise Kate to do something, the more she digs her heels in. To me he was a man who had been caught with his trousers down and, instead of doing the decent and manly thing and facing the consequences, he had tried to wriggle out of the situation by coming up with a lame excuse. I was convinced that a permanent split would eventually be inevitable. He seemed to know how to push Kate's buttons by coming across as if he was genuinely and sincerely sorry for what he had done. He even tried this act on me, too.

Throughout her pregnancy with Bunny in 2014, Kieran was trying to woo Kate back. She wanted things to work out, but she didn't trust him. Who would? Kieran did offer a certain level of support during the pregnancy and when Bunny was born in August. He was also around for a time afterwards, but Kate was unhappy; the stress between Jett's and Bunny's births had been so awful. Perhaps unsurprisingly, Bunny was also born prematurely with breathing problems. The episode in France culminated in Jett's premature birth, then she was pregnant with Bunny during the period when her fears about Jane and Kieran were being confirmed.

Kate was not in a good place at all; I could see she was struggling and was very unhappy. She tried to hide herself from me a lot of the time so I wouldn't see how upset she really was. But I knew. She continued to have therapy and stuck to a routine to try to keep on an even keel for the children – she had a nanny on board to help her with Jett and Bunny. At this point, I was still playing a big role in Harvey's life, overseeing his schooling and medical issues. Meanwhile, Junior and Princess were also at school, living half the time with their mum and half with their dad. Things with Pete were fraught, but life continued.

Jett is a lovely boy. One good thing I will say about Kieran is that he introduced his son to the world of nature. Jett's knowledge and love of the outside world is so refreshing in these days of screens and computer games. He is a very loveable, kind and helpful grandson. Bunny is a mini-Kate – mischievous, crafty and clever. I can see right through her and read her thoughts. She loves the outdoor life, too, but also adores girly things like dressing up, wearing her mum's high heels, putting make-up on and having her hair done. She wants false nails that make a tap-tap noise on the table. Jett and Bunny have been through a lot and have seen a lot, and I do believe it would be beneficial for them to have some form of therapy for this. It may not affect them now, but it could come back to haunt them in the future.

Therapy was certainly prevalent in the lives of their parents. They were both still in treatment when Kate got it into her head that she had to move house. She had been living at the beautiful farm in Horsham for the last few years and it had been perfect for her, but she could no longer bear to be there; it constantly reminded her of all the deceit that had gone on in her home between Kieran and Jane and his other conquests. So in October of 2014, she bought another house, literally a couple of fields away. Kieran gave up any other work he had and appointed himself chief renovator. What a disaster that turned out to be. He engaged a firm of builders he had once worked for, and this proved to be an expensive mistake as the results were unsatisfactory. Of course, Kate paid for all the work; Kieran contributed nothing to the family coffers. As Kate had given Kieran carte blanche, Dan and I had to remain in the background, watching the beautiful Arts and Crafts house turn into a tacky grey glitter palace. Nothing seemed to be finished properly and Kieran, who clearly didn't have the skills he thought he had, became bored with the house and started on the garden. Up came the delightful flower borders and down came the greenhouses. The summer house, which housed the boiler for the swimming pool, also came down and the pool, which had functioned perfectly well when Kate had bought the property, no longer operated properly. The once-beautiful house had been turned into a suitable subject for the *Mucky Mansion* TV show on Channel 4.

As a family, we didn't see a lot of Kate and Kieran during this period. But when I did go to their house, I noticed an alarming number of animals. At one time there must have been a hundred chickens and there were eggs everywhere. Apparently, Kieran the builder had decided to become Kieran the farmer, so there were pigs, peacocks (anything to keep him happy), lambs, llamas and two turkeys, one called Roast and one called Dinner. Kieran tried to pretend he was a country squire so he needed to dress the part with a waxed jacket, flat cap and boots. This is when Kevin the Labrador joined the family. Kieran wanted a shooting dog and a gun, although I have no idea what he intended to shoot. Kate even bought him a horse, but he was never a rider. Although the situation was a bit of a joke, it worried me that there was a gun in the house with the kids around. I didn't question whether he had a licence, or whether the gun was locked up or not, but looking back, I should have done. Apparently, the animals were a substitute for sex addiction so, not surprisingly, he looked after them.

Kate had to finance Kieran's hobbies somehow, so the invitation to appear on *Celebrity Big Brother* in January 2015 came at an opportune time financially, even if it was a disastrous time medically. Problems had arisen with the breast surgery Kate had undergone in another cry for help, shortly before the recording of the programme began and she had to spend the whole show on painkillers and antibiotics because one of her breasts hadn't healed properly. Surgeons even had to visit the set on three occasions to deal with the infection that was creeping in under her breast and once she had to leave the house for an emergency consultation. Although she was unusually reticent throughout the show, not even rising to the bait when runner-up Katie Hopkins made provocative remarks about Harvey, Kate emerged as the winner.

At the winner's ceremony, Kate was left clutching one of her breasts as she left the house. I was sick and tired of all the surgery. Her boob looked like it had a hole underneath, and the stiches would not hold. She was quickly flown to her preferred plastic surgeon in Belgium to deal with the mess.

For some time, my concerns about Kate's addiction to plastic surgery had been heightening. When most people have an off day or are feeling a bit down, they change the colour of their nails or dye their hair, but Kate changes the shape of her body. It's usually her boobs although she has had liposuction, a mini facelift, a brow lift and a bum lift. Kate used to show off the results when she started having enhancements, but as time has gone on, she has hidden them. Attracting men is not her motivation. She does it because she thinks it makes her in control of her body. Over the years, we have all come to accept it as part of Kate's personality, but we have also seen a pattern emerging – relationship difficulties correlate with an urge to change things on the outside, even though it is her inner thoughts and feelings that need attention. Kate's compulsion to have surgery seems to be driven by unhappiness – I've come to understand the process well.

When Kate goes to be measured up for surgery, the doctors put a bra on her and place a dummy implant inside. Kate is never satisfied and wants it to be bigger – sometimes the surgeons let her have her way. One particular surgeon even told her he would squeeze in bags as big as he possibly could, rather than advising her of the dangers of making such a large alteration. Not always have the operations been successful and there have been times when Kate has really suffered as a result of surgery, but she justifies it by saying her body is her job and also that she can do what she wants with it as it's hers. I've begun to warn her that if she's not careful, she will end up looking like the Bride of Frankenstein, but she tells me not to waste my breath. My 17-year-old daughter's natural 32B boobs have got bigger and bigger until I barely recognize the body in front of me.

Once, when she was married to Pete and they were working in America, she had her breasts enlarged and was sent back to recover in her room at the Beverly Hills Hotel. The nurses were incompetent and seemed incapable of looking after Kate, so her PA rang me in a state of panic. I asked to speak to Kate on the phone, but couldn't understand what she was saying because she was under the influence of so many painkillers. I had to threaten the plastic surgery firm with legal action to get them to sort out the situation. So much for the glamourous Hollywood lifestyle the world thought Kate was living at the time – in reality she was alone and writhing in agony in a hotel room. Once again it was her family she turned to for support, and Sophie flew out to be with her.

More recently, she has added tattoos to her repertoire; whenever she spots a wrinkle or a patch of cellulite, she will have a new design inked over it. I tell her she's going to end up looking like a saggy old washing line when she's older. Some of the things she has done to her body are not only ridiculous, but dangerous. To me the worst was having surgery on her beautiful face. She had always said she wouldn't touch her face, but I think someone must have suggested she was looking older. Or maybe she noticed a wrinkle or two, which is natural and I think looks so much better than having a false, stretched-canvas face. It's just another one of the problems that arise when she goes for these younger men and consequently feels she must remain youthful for them. She has little self-worth. We have tried to get her to see that she is beautiful as she is, but she just can't see it. If only she would find herself a mature guy who appreciates her for her – but that didn't look likely in February 2015.

Just as I had continued trying to make my marriage work after I discovered Kate's dad Ray had been cheating on me all those years ago, Kate was trying to make it work with Kieran – going to the lengths of renewing her vows with him at a public ceremony after she emerged from the Big Brother house. I wanted nothing to do with arranging this. I didn't think there was any point in bothering – nothing was likely to change. So like the rest of the congregation, I was left speechless when Kate called Kieran up on stage during the ceremony, saying, 'Some of you are probably wondering why you are sitting here to renew our vows after only being married for two years, this is why.' Then she went on to summarize everything that had happened – including him sleeping with her best friend while she was pregnant. It wasn't a brilliant way to try to make a marriage work, but it was Kate's way; she was attempting to re-set their relationship, in the naive hope that doing it publicly would make it last. She'd also been humiliated by Kieran and, in turn, wanted to humiliate him. Afterwards, Price said to me that this really, really would be the last time he would attend any of her weddings. For Price, it was even worse than for the rest of us because he had to make the speeches.

Kieran wanted to add more and more animals to his collection and, as usual, Kate footed the bill. The place seemed overrun with chickens and eggs, but Kieran didn't even have the initiative to develop some way of selling them. However, at least Kieran's strange animal addiction was visible. I knew something else wasn't right with Kate but couldn't quite put my finger on it. She had stopped coming down to see me regularly and, when she did, she was fidgety or wanted to sleep. I remember going up to her house one day in August 2015 to find her looking absolutely terrible. Kieran's mum and nan were also there and Kate – who was in floods of tears – told me that she had discovered Kieran had been having yet another affair, this time with the nanny. To be honest, both Kieran's mum and nan were devastated too, and we all thought he should leave Kate instead of treating her like this. I really liked Kieran's mum and nan, and I was relieved that we were all in agreement. At that stage I absolutely loathed him – I realized he was such a spineless man that he wouldn't be decisive enough to take such an action by himself. It was then I discovered Kate's tiredness and behaviour were related to depression and the fact she had started taking cocaine and that Kieran was involved with it too. She had also been taking it recreationally with friends, of whom I did not approve – it seemed that they thought that they were above the law. I went to see them and asked them to stay out of Kate's life.

I felt shocked that I was having to have these conversations. I felt like a hard man on a TV show. As a family, drugs had never been an issue. Yes, we liked a drink, but drugs were a definite no-no. I now looked at my daughter for the first time in a different light. Not only was she depressed, but she was also in a downward spiral and I knew then she desperately needed help. The relationship with Kieran was now definitely beyond repair and even Kieran's mum admitted she thought her son should leave. It was awful and I was back to asking my daughter, 'Why, oh why do you put up with it? Why do you carry on trying to make these marriages work?' But, of course, she could not give an answer because the reasons are too complex to convey. Unbelievably, Kate allowed Kieran to continue living in their marital home for some time after, while managing to fulfil most of her contract on the ITV talk show *Loose Women*. But in reality, she found it too challenging. She had so much going on in her life at home, I'm surprised she kept it together. She admits now that she carried on by blotting everything out, by self-medicating with alcohol or drugs. Kate is not an addict, it was a coping mechanism for everything else that was going on in her life. I wasn't aware of this at all at the time – when she came to see me, it seemed she could cope. Later I realized that she only came to see me when she was feeling good so I wouldn't notice the real state of affairs.

I couldn't bear to go to her house while Kieran was there, so during this period I didn't get to see how fast her mental health was deteriorating. She did a good job hiding it from me. Maybe she really, genuinely loved Kieran and thought she could fix him, but she was blind to the fact that she needed proper help too. It's the rejection that gets to her and Kieran's affairs were causing that time and time again. Towards the end of 2015, I did become more aware of her condition as its effects became more obvious. When I did see her, she was always very tired and neglecting her appearance. I used to ask her what was wrong, and she would just say she was tired. I think she was going to bed very depressed and waking up feeling just as low. I wish I had known the reasons behind it then because I would have made her get help to stop her spiralling out of control. Looking back, this behaviour has occurred time and time again. It is only now she is totally honest with us and she's getting help that we understand her and recognize the signs.

Towards the end, before Kieran finally moved out, he was taking Jett and Bunny to school and he met a mother at the school gates called Michelle Penticost. Even though he was still married, and Michelle knew this, they had an affair which seems to have lasted. It's all so shocking when I look back – I feel lucky Kate has survived and is still with us. There were times when I thought about my own relationship with her dad, Ray, which was very stormy – it made me question whether Kate might be unconsciously repeating this early relationship template. I always consoled myself, though, with the fact that I went on to find a gentle, loving man in Price and hoped that Kate could one day follow that example. I thought that if she was able to have more respect for herself, she would disprove Ray's advice to me and show that there could be a fairy-tale ending. But little did I realize that my own handsome prince was about to turn into a frog.

Chapter 13

HOW COULD YOU?

Price's infidelity shocked me to the core because I didn't see it coming. At the time, we were busy in the process of moving house. We had sold our house and were considering our next move, all the while supporting and sorting out my elder daughter's life (which in itself is a time-consuming job). We'd decided to take a well-earned break from it all in March 2015, and had gone out with a group of friends to enjoy a Chinese meal in Worthing. A lot of food and drink had been consumed and we were all having fun. As the evening drew to a close, we decided to share a taxi home with one of the other couples who were staying at our home that night. The wife had been acting a little oddly. She was making strangely irrelevant and outrageous comments – some of her remarks had also upset one of the other couples with us. I was beginning to feel the meal had been a big mistake. I was reminded of Jane Pountney's behaviour in The Bahamas, but I didn't want to develop a phobia about friends' wives, so I didn't worry too much about it.

When the cab arrived, Price sat in the front next to the driver and left the rest of us to cram into the back. It was obvious that the wife had overindulged, and, on the way home, she complained of feeling sick, so the cab had to stop. I asked Price to help her out. Because he has impeccable manners, Price got out and opened the back door to assist her. The cab driver didn't want to wait so, rather than leaving her alone, I told Price to walk with her for a bit – she seemed unstable on her feet and needed to clear her head. She also seemed likely to be sick. Price chivalrously offered to walk with her along the pavement next to the beach to get some fresh air. To this day, I don't know why her husband didn't offer to do this instead, but he chose to remain in the cab and accompany me back to our house. The agreed plan was that Price would call another cab as soon as she felt well enough. I didn't think any more of it – it was just the sort of kind offer my husband would extend. Unbeknown to me, his offer went way beyond kindness, though, as I was to discover the next morning.

When we arrived back home, the husband and I waited for a while. As time went on, we began to wonder whether we should go to look for them, but we decided they were adults and could look after themselves so there was nothing to worry about. Eventually we gave up waiting and retired to our rooms. I must have been sound asleep because I didn't hear Price and the wife sneak in. I also didn't hear her sneak back out again with her husband early the next morning, and it didn't occur to me that anything untoward had happened. I even received a text message from her saying she was sorry she had had to leave urgently but she'd been told that her dog was in agony with severe leg pain. It even said she was sorry for not making the bed.

The next day seemed as normal as it could ever be in the Price household, and I settled down to tackle some paperwork. I had barely had a chance to focus on the first task before I received what must be one of the most shocking phone calls of my life. I was dumbstruck as the voice on the other end of the line sobbed, 'He raped me'. It was the wife. The woman who had spent the previous night sleeping in my house. I realized that she was talking about my husband. I listened. I didn't shout. I didn't argue. I didn't call her a liar, even though I couldn't believe what I was hearing. She sounded upset, so I could tell something had happened and I had to get to the bottom of it. In a state of shock, I told her she was brave for talking to me, and that I would be there for her. During the course of the call, she asked if she could speak to Price. Having dealt with similar issues myself at the hands of unscrupulous swimming coaches, I could empathize with her feelings, but I was confused. Price wouldn't rape her; he simply was not capable of such a thing. Or was he? I was strangely calm in that moment as I tried to weigh up my options – who should I believe? Who could I confide in? What on earth was I going to tell the children?

Surely there had been some mistake? Some misunderstanding? Why hadn't she said anything when she arrived home last night? She was someone I knew could approach me about anything and talk openly to me. She knew she could talk to me. Why had she left without saying, 'I've got to speak to you about your husband'? Why didn't her husband challenge us? I know if the situation had been reversed, I would have done something and so would Price. I would have been so angered at what had happened that, whether they were asleep or not, I would have flown up the stairs and woken everyone up and said something straight away! Perhaps it was all a dream. But as they say, there's no smoke without fire, so I needed to talk with Price. As I began to reflect, it occurred to me that in the morning before he'd left for work, he hadn't really looked me in the eye, so I rang him. It wasn't that long ago that Kieran had cheated on Kate, and you would have thought that it would still be fresh in Price's mind. If something had happened, where was Price's loyalty to me? I had to uncover the truth.

For years, I had witnessed so-called friends selling stories with some sort of link to Kate so I instinctively thought I knew where this was leading. Am I going to read about this in the press? The calm side of me thought it was good that I had been told, because I was prepared. I thought it was strange that she wanted to speak with Price, but I told her I would get him to call her. As I dialled the most familiar number of my life, I couldn't believe the phone call I was about to make. I had to ask calmly, 'Can you ring her? She says you raped her.'

The conversation was very fraught and Price vehemently denied the rape accusation. I said I wanted to know what had gone on and demanded that he come back immediately and explain to me exactly what had happened. Price was in as much shock and disbelief as I was, and simply couldn't understand the accusation. He was very upset; he knew that there would be recriminations for his actions from me and the whole family, and that our precious relationship could be irrevocably damaged as a result.

Price gave me his version of events. He revealed that as they were walking along the beach, they began to mess around, having a bit of fun and a laugh, which developed into a kiss and a cuddle. Hands began to wander. Both pairs. She told him she was missing sex because she and her husband hadn't had it for a year, and things progressed from there. After they had arrived home, Price let the dogs out and they had a glass of wine together. Before I had time to take everything in, I received a text from her saying she was going to get checked out at an STD clinic. I didn't like what that indirectly implied about me. She also stated that, as I was her friend, she was not going to go to the police, particularly because of the damage it might cause me in my position as Kate's mum. Price tried to call her but she didn't answer so he left a message. He acknowledged what had happened but not how she alleged it had. He said he was sorry about what had happened and the upset that had been caused. Before long, he received a voice message from her husband telling him not to contact his wife again.

It wasn't going to be easy, but it seemed like Price and I would be given the space to sort our relationship out and decide where to go from there. As my mind raced with a million questions, we moved into separate bedrooms. The future suddenly seemed to be on shaky ground. When we did finally buy our new house, would I be moving in on my own? When and how would we tell the children? Two days later, before we had had a chance to contemplate any of this together, there was an ominous night-time ring on the doorbell. I looked out of my bedroom window and saw flashes of yellow and blue lighting up the sky. The back of the house was swarming with people waving torches. It was about 1am. I called out to Price, and he looked out of the bedroom at the front of the house and said there were people at the door. At this stage we had no idea who they were, but it didn't seem as though it was a friendly visit. It was quite frightening. Our dogs were barking, and I told Price to go down and see who it was. I then put on a dressing gown and followed him down.

It was the police. Price let them in, and I arrived downstairs just in time to hear them say that they were taking him away to the police station to interview him. I was surprisingly calm. Deep down I had had suspicions about my friend's promise not to go to the police, so this wasn't entirely unexpected. The number of policemen in my house really felt over the top; she must have painted Price as an aggressive monster. It wouldn't have taken them long to realize that this was a false image when Price was so cooperative – he calmly got dressed and left quietly with them. I was left shaking and felt so alone, especially as I realized that it wouldn't be long before the press became aware of the situation, and the children would see it in the papers. I realized there was now an urgency in telling them about the situation.

I told them all separately that we had been raided in the night and Price was being held in a police cell and being inter-rogated. Sophie was in bits. Kate was really shocked, as was Dan. They all said they knew the rape bit wouldn't be true, but the thought of him being unfaithful to me after all these years was dreadful. As soon as he was taken away, I contacted a solicitor friend as we didn't know the procedure. He talked me through what would be happening at the police station, and what we needed to do to get Price some help.

I waited at home for Price to come back. He was held until the following afternoon, when he was given a lift home. He was shattered and in a state of disbelief. Both of us were in shock about what was happening and where our lives would now be heading. Price was full of remorse and, to make matters worse, the story was in the papers. We do not know how the details reached the press but, obviously, they did not come from us.

I needed to be alone and just couldn't face Price, so I asked him to move out and he did so without complaint. He rented a house a few miles away. I packed his stuff in bin liners and left them for him to collect outside. I even went to Sainsburys with him to buy plates, cereal bowls, a knife and fork and spoon, towels and bedlinen, dog bowls and dog beds. This felt really surreal, as if I was making a new home for him. He apologized to each of the children. To be honest, I expected them to shun him, but they were all incredibly forgiving and supportive. He was a lucky man that they had so much love for him and didn't for one moment think of abandoning him. I think that shows the strength of the family unit we had built together. Dan was the calmest and, as usual, was advising me about the best course of action and asking if I could cope. Sophie and Kate were more emotional. Sophie was still living with us, on and off, so I felt very fortunate that she hadn't been at home on the night that the police had arrived, and was instead staying over at Harry's. She was probably the most affected because he was her biological dad and she looked up to him, loved and respected him and would never have thought something like this could have happened. She was very upset and kept asking him why he would do such a thing. Because we are all so close, everything was spoken about openly. Harry moved in with me and Sophie so they could both be there to support me. Kate was concerned about the possible outcomes and details, analysing what could happen in court. She worried about the long term and offered financial help if I needed it. She also said that, if necessary, I could move in with her in the future when Harry and Sophie moved out. Kate understood exactly how I felt, having gone through the emotional upheaval with Kieran. It was dreadful.

There was now the property situation to consider. Our house in Angmering by the golf course was in the process of being sold before the allegation, but we hadn't started looking for another place and I had to make up my mind whether I would get something by myself or invite Price to move back in. The question of survival also had to be considered. I thought, here I am at my time of life when things should be more comfortable for me, going back to thinking how I could support myself and live. Could I keep a roof over my and Sophie's heads and live within my budget? I still worked and it had never occurred to me to retire because I liked to pay my way and have financial independence. I have had a good track record for supporting myself over the years – I had my two jobs to keep me going.

And beyond the financial concerns, there were the emotional ones; there was a void at home after Price had gone. We had been together for so long. I missed him and everything felt bleak. He was still calling me every day and telling me that he loved me and that he was longing to get back together as a family. The children were in constant contact with him – Kate was particularly supportive to us both, even though she was still reeling from the antics of her own cheating husband. Now, here was her father doing the same thing to her mother. I suppose because of the circumstances she had been through, she had a better understanding of the situation and felt in a position to tell Price what a plonker he had been. I certainly didn't have a clear understanding. I wanted to be with my husband, but I still needed to have respect for myself. How could I allow him back into my life? I was so hurt. But when we did meet up, I could feel the sadness and also the love we still had for each other, and he would plead to be allowed to come back home. After the initial shock had passed, and we were both attempting to restore a routine to our lives, Price and I decided to meet once a week to talk about things. These discussions would start in a civilized manner but gradually I would lose control of my temper and demand answers. I wanted to know how Price could have done this after what Kate had suffered with Kieran and after we had been through so much together. So every week we were going round in circles, but then one day after about four months, out of the blue, we sat down and he asked if he could come home.

I missed Price and every time I saw him, I knew that I still loved him. Part of me thought that perhaps we should be together to face up to things. He looked dreadful, lost and unhappy. But the situation also felt so confusing. Why should I make it easy for him? What about me? Why should he feel I could forgive him that easily? How could I ever trust him again? I was devasted, sick and humiliated. My home had been raided by the police and that was something I had never expected would happen to me. And, of course, it wasn't just an affair, or my husband being unfaithful to me, there was also an accusation of rape. My initial thoughts were that there was no going back. The devastation and disbelief on my children's faces made things worse. They rallied around me and wanted to know what I was going to do. They also wanted to know what was happening to Price, and how he was coping with things.

Eventually, I relented and allowed him to move back in, but I would set the rules. In all honesty, I don't know how he survived – there were no cuddles, just me moaning at him all the time. Every time he went out, I asked where he was going and what time would he be back. I activated the tracking device on his phone and if he was ever late, I questioned where he had been. I realized it wasn't healthy and my behaviour was becoming controlling, which is wrong in a relationship. As time passed, I decided things needed to be a lot more relaxed and I had to learn to trust him again, so our lives began to drift back to normal. This was one of the hardest things I have ever done in my life. I have my principles, and this went against all of them. To me, loyalty and love are important, as are commitment and trust – Price had broken them. But I felt I needed to make a stand for what I really held dear to me, and I had to set an example to my children too.

At this stage, nobody was sure what was happening with the police. My close friends were all very supportive of me but, being a private person, I found it hard that people knew my business and what was going on with my husband. I began to develop a phobia, thinking that people at my work, at the gym, at the local pub – in fact everywhere – were gossiping about me even though, if the truth were known, no one believed he was capable of rape.

In November of 2015, I went away with a friend to have time to think. While I was away, I was told the devastating news: it had been decided that Price was to be charged with two counts of rape and two counts of attempted rape, but we would have to wait over a year until the case came to court. During this time, a permanent cloud lingered over our heads but fortunately none of our close friends believed for one moment that Price was guilty, so we were fortunate to have their support. Character references can be lodged with the court on the trial date, and the number of these that Price had from women, friends and even people we hadn't seen for years was staggering. One of these letters was even from a judge. I was convinced he had been wrongly charged. Something had happened that night, I know, and I wanted to work out in my own mind what it was.

I saw all the reports, including the medical reports, the drawings, as well as the witness statements and I kept reading them, analysing them, driving over the route they took home that night, reliving what had happened step by step, over and over again. As a safety net, I kept my two jobs working as an online payroll accounts administrator and also as a tour guide at Arundel Castle. We tried to maintain a façade for the public by going to the gym and visiting our local pub regularly.

We had to make sure that the press didn't come at us through Kate. We kept going, but every day of those nineteen months between the incident and the trial, we were in a state of shock.

There was a helpful and pleasing distraction during this time, though. Sophie had been studying for a history degree and part of the course involved a one-year exchange programme in Levin, Belgium. Levin is a beautiful town and Price and I visited her there – we could tell she was happy studying the history of the Low Countries. Because Sophie and Harry were saving for a house, he had come to live with us while she was away and provided us with more wonderful support. Harry truly helped me put things in perspective and was a calming influence when I used to have a pop at Price, which – believe me – was a daily occurrence.

A couple of months before the trial, Sophie's graduation was an occasion for us all to forget about the trauma we were experiencing. It was an extraordinary moment watching her take the stage at Chichester University – Kate and Kieran, Harry and Price and I all attended. We were very proud and organized a lunch to celebrate for close friends and family at a restaurant nearby.

As a family, we were surprised at Sophie's transformation into an academic – she was blossoming in a way she had never managed at school. In order to support herself as a student, she had applied for a part-time job as a tour guide at Arundel Castle and the personnel officer who interviewed her spotted something that no one had previously understood – Sophie is dyslexic. This explained why she had struggled so much at school and had often been so miserable. Early diagnosis of dyslexia would have been helpful for Sophie, but it was never picked up. Once Sophie's learning difficulties were diagnosed, she was able to access the right support and flourished, despite the terrible rollercoaster she was on waiting for her dad's trial.

The trial eventually took place at Chichester Crown Court over several days in December 2016. Although most of the family attended, Kate was advised to stay away – the barrister said that her presence might be a distraction and could even influence the jury, but the press were there every day. One of the other couples who had been at the meal on that fateful night gave evidence supporting Price. Sophie was called to the stand to give evidence for her dad, and she collapsed in tears. Even if the verdict was to go against him, Price would have the consolation of knowing how much his daughter loved him, as well as Kate and Dan, and how his friends had stayed loyal.

A lot of other people turned up to support Price and we all agreed that the story our so-called friend had concocted was far-fetched and dubious. It just didn't make sense. But would a jury see it that way? If Price was found guilty, he would be facing a long prison sentence. The barrister had advised he could be behind bars for seven to ten years. If that played out, I knew it would be the end of our relationship because I just couldn't cope with it. He knew this too. In my mind, I'd reasoned that that would be it: I would never visit him in prison and, because he was guilty, I would not be able to face him again, even though, in my heart of hearts, I knew it was not true. I would have to move on with my life. I started making practical arrangements in case Price was sent down, like making sure I could access bank accounts as we were waiting for the verdict.

Each day during the trial we had lunch at a nearby pub. Our friends came every day to support us and we would sit there going over what had happened in the court that morning. After what seemed like months rather than just eight days, someone rushed in to tell us the final verdict was due. We raced back to court. I went to a private room on my own to wait, while Sophie, Harry and Dan sat in the open court.

I sat there alone, lost in thought, still attempting to come to terms with what had been going on. I was feeling sick, cold and shaky, just waiting in the silence, when a friend came in shouting that Price had been found not guilty on the first two counts of rape. He then disappeared and went back to listen for the final results from the jury. Inside, I was pleading for him to get let off the other charges. Then, my friend came back and told me that he had been found not guilty of the other two charges too – he'd been set free.

I just sat there in relief and disbelief. I could hear my friends calling from outside the room, then Price emerged and hugged me. He was hyperventilating, so my niece got him a glass of water – I thought he was going to have a heart attack. Sophie was crying and Dan was in shock as we all left the court speechless and headed on autopilot to our local pub where a friend had organized a get together. It was then that Kate and Kieran joined us, so we were all together as a family. My initial thought was how happy and pleased I was, knowing Price was free to be with us again and we could look forward to life as a couple and a family. I sat there watching everyone cuddling Price and shaking his hand and being so happy for him, but what about me and the rest of the family? I wondered if I was being selfish as I thought of all the suffering we had also been through – I felt all the celebrations were for Price. Was it just accepted that I should stand by him and forget all the trauma and heartache we'd endured? This was wrong. My heart went out to all those women and rape victims who don't get the justice they deserve, and have to pick their lives up again, even though, in this case, Price was innocent. My heart was still heavy with all that had happened, and I knew it would take me a long time to forgive.

It was unbelievable to think what we'd all been put through. Price was a free man but I wasn't sure if our marriage would ever be the same again. Although I began to understand that Price's infidelity was a result of one of those weak moments that can happen in anyone's life, I struggled to shake the fact that when he had been tempted, he could and should have said no. Why didn't he? There must have been an attraction there and that hurt. The kids were disappointed in him, but they had supported him from the start and they accepted his apology. Price and I were a little bit broken in places, but we still got on well and he told me he still wanted to be with me and wanted to make things up to me – as if it was just his decision. After what he had put me through, was I meant to be grateful? Gradually, I had to make my mind up. The events had taken their toll on me, both mentally and physically. At times it had been so bad I had felt physically sick. I couldn't get the question out of my head of how he could do this without thinking of me or the children – just for the kick of a cheap thrill. My head was still spinning and I started to wonder if had I done anything wrong. I began to analyse our marriage and couldn't come up with any reason. The physical side was good.

We've now been together for 38 years and married for 34. For a long time, there was hardly a single night when I let my husband forget his betrayal. Not one night. Even now a random sex scene on the TV can reignite memories and Price has to pacify me as I start asking questions all over again. But we have tried to pick up the pieces and get over the nightmare together. There was no excuse for Price's actions, but I still wonder what caused them. I spent so much time focussing on Harvey and supporting Kate. I believe I was right to do so, but did I lose focus on the needs of others and not give Price the attention he wanted and deserved? Often I had come home late, sometimes after having dealt with Kate, and would pour out my frustrations about how she would not listen to me – I suppose Price might have thought he was playing second fiddle. The pressure of the media and Kate's relationships had taken their toll on me, Dan and Sophie but we never really thought it affected Price. He was the provider and the steady influence, and I suppose all of us just took him for granted. I suppose I expected his parents to support him in the way that mine had always supported me, but that wasn't the case, as they never attended the court proceedings.

Gradually, Price has come more to the fore in the family. He now says what he thinks to our children, and they listen. Instead of just me being there for Kate, he is an equal anchor and she calls him in times of need. He works with Dan and is closer to him and confides in him. He has grown into his role of a dad, and is a super grandad too, stepping up to the mantle of head of the family. Price is great company and he's naive in an endearing way, which does make him attractive to women. Despite everything we went through, I'm very glad he's still mine.

I will add that to this day, Price still has difficulty dealing with what happened. It turned his life around so drastically that recently he is beginning to wonder if he should undergo some therapy. He is grateful he still has a life with a family and loyal friends, but for me it still hasn't completely gone away. Little did I know that as Price's life was being given back to him, mine was just about to be cruelly and abruptly cut short.

Chapter 14

THERE IS NO CURE

Price and I worked out a strategy for rebuilding our lives together. Although the verdict was such a relief, the events of March 2015 were horrific and left mental scars on our entire family. So, we could understand each other's feelings and decided to continue talking openly about things. Price needed to rebuild his confidence and I was determined to support him in doing this. It was evident how much he loved me and the family – he was full of remorse and clearly wished he could turn back the clock.

Shortly after the case concluded, a friend offered us their house in Wales for a weekend break. We loved every minute and it prompted us to book a proper holiday. I had always wanted to go to the Greek island of Santorini so in May of that year, that's where we headed. We stayed in a delightful village called Thira and our hotel was perfectly situated high up on a hill overlooking the island. On some days we just lazed around sunbathing, on others we went sightseeing. One day we visited Firostefani and the beautiful church at Oia, where I lit a candle for my mum and dad. In the evenings we returned to Thira for supper and would sit watching the stunning sunset turn the beautiful white buildings pink. Finally, it seemed, we were regaining a sense of peace together and now had the rest of our lives to look forward to. We had made it to the other side.

Although Santorini is a spectacular island, it isn't for the faint hearted. There are many hills and an inordinate number of steps to climb. I pride myself on being fit as a result of my regular gym work, but I was finding the gradients a challenge and sometimes Price had to push or pull me up the steps. As anyone will know who has suffered from it, or lived with someone afflicted with it, asthma is not pleasant. When I was a little girl, I had problems with my chest and was diagnosed with the condition. It meant I wasn't allowed near feathers, dogs or cats because they triggered wheezing. When I started swimming, the problem seemed to disappear and I thought that was that, but sometimes the aggravating cough came back when I was stressed or if the weather changed and the temperature dropped quickly. Other people's smoke also made me cough so doctors prescribed inhalers. Even though it's been a bit tedious, I've attended a clinic regularly for check-ups to monitor my oxygen levels and, when necessary, I've adjusted my inhalers. But I was having more trouble than usual in Santorini; my breathing was sometimes strained, and I felt like something was wrong. I thought I might have caught some sort of chest infection, and I went to see the asthma nurse at my local doctor's surgery when Price and I returned home.

She didn't seem too bothered or think that there was anything particularly unusual and I've never been one to dwell on illness, but I was convinced something wasn't right. Simple tasks, like going up the stairs or carrying washing, had started to leave me breathless, as did swimming. I shared my concerns and, in the end, the nurse decided to consult one of the doctors who said I should have an x-ray and make an appointment to come back at a later date to discuss the results. When I returned, it was for a consultation with our family doctor – the same trusted individual who had first helped us with Harvey. I was expecting a brief chat about the x-ray results and a prescription for antibiotics – I wasn't expecting anything serious so I hadn't asked Price to come with me. I was alone when the bomb exploded. The doctor got straight to the point, 'It isn't good news I'm afraid,' he said. 'You have something called interstitial idiopathic pulmonary fibrosis.' I had no idea what IPF was so the doctor had to explain. He informed me that the disease involves scarring of the lungs (fibrosis), which causes them to stiffen and, as a consequence, it becomes hard to breathe and get oxygen into the bloodstream. It's irreversible and terminal and gradually gets worse over time. Usually, people with the condition live no more than five years. Ongoing research offers hope and life expectancy may be extended through medication – in some cases a lung transplant is possible, but the qualifying criteria for this are very strict. There are an estimated 6,000 or so new cases recorded in the UK every year. I knew nothing about the illness and I think one of the reasons was because although there were many posters with details of the threat and devastation caused by other killer diseases, there was absolutely no information about IPF on display in the doctor's waiting room. I was very surprised and, on a later visit, told the doctor how I felt about this. To this day, as far as I know, there are still no leaflets or posters about IPF and I believe that greater awareness is needed about this terrible disease.

It was as if time stood still. I was shocked, but also angry. I wondered if the doctor had actually studied the results before I entered the room. If so, why hadn't he suggested I bring Price with me for the support? I clearly needed him when faced with such shocking news. I couldn't believe what I had heard. I found it hard to speak but I managed to ask the doctor how this could have happened to me. I was healthy. I worked out regularly. I had never smoked. I had been a champion swimmer. Surely it couldn't be right. He explained that no one is sure how you get the condition. It could be pollution, dust, birds; it could be passed on genetically. So much is unclear about IPF, apart from one fact: there is no cure. And just like that, those four words robbed me of the future I had dreamed of – the chance to grow old with Price, to see my children and grandchildren flourish and to continue to protect the more vulnerable members of my family like Kate and Harvey.

I felt broken, devastated, yet I still had so many questions to ask. Why hadn't the signs been picked up during my previous visits to the asthma clinics? I appreciate the symptoms – such as breathlessness and the irritating dry cough – are similar to asthma, but surely the nurses should have known what to look for and how to check their patients? After all, the actual *sound* of IPF stands out – activity in the lungs sounds like the scratching of Velcro being ripped apart and I could not understand why nurses hadn't been trained to recognize the symptoms. Later, the doctor told me that this would be changed and everyone would be trained up to spot IPF in other patients.

I had to ring Price. I will never forget that desperate phone call. In a state of panic, I spluttered, 'You're not going to believe this, but the doctor says I've got this lung disease which is terminal.' I was crying and in shock. It was difficult for Price to comprehend or accept such devastating news over the phone, and my state of panic probably didn't help matters. He said I must have heard it wrong and it couldn't be true. He was at work and I was on my way back to my payroll job. This was just typical of us – we'd keep going with our routine no matter what. When I arrived back at work, I walked in like a zombie and didn't tell a soul. It was as if I was floating above myself, looking down on a woman with a terminal illness who definitely wasn't me. When we both got home that evening, we spoke about it on our own. Price was still in a state of disbelief, but agreed that we would need a second opinion.

Coping with the shock of being given the diagnosis on my own had been hard enough, but now I had to tell others … tell the children. I decided to break the news to each of them individually. It took a while for the information to sink in because I didn't look ill to them and I was as fit and active as ever. They couldn't understand it – it was as if I was telling them something unreal. Sophie cried, Kate wanted to research everything, and Dan said he thought we needed to find out more about it. He told me not to panic because it was possible that a cure might be found. We had to take one day at a time. I'm pretty sure the children put the phone down and then contacted each other without me knowing. Sophie is so sensitive like me, and she continued to ask me loads of questions and wanted to meet with the doctor in case I had got something wrong. Kate was the same and said she wanted to come with me to discuss it. Dan, on the other hand, wanted me to report back to him as he would prefer to hear it from me. Dan mulls things over in his head.

And me? Apparently, our brains deal with traumatic situations by regressing to a primitive state, triggering a fight, flight or freeze response. I had initially frozen when I received the shocking news but now I needed to take flight towards my husband. It was only about six months after the trial, but we were well and truly a couple again and at this time, Price was my anchor. It felt cruel that we had regained our dreams for our future, only to have them snatched away. Because he couldn't take it all in, Price went to the surgery himself for a face-to-face meeting so the doctor could confirm and explain exactly what the diagnosis meant. From that moment on, he was by my side and determined that I would never again attend an appointment by myself. To this day, he has never missed a single one of my hospital visits or overnight stays, and there have been many, which continue to this day.

The doctor had advised me not to start researching the illness on the internet, but I wonder if any patient could have followed that advice – and I'm afraid I simply ignored it. I immediately started Googling and researching the condition. It was through this research and with my doctor's help that I first discovered Professor Toby Maher. He was a consultant at the Royal Brompton Hospital, specializing in respiratory problems, and a leading figure in IPF research. My doctor made the referral so I could pay him a visit. I had a CT scan at his clinic and he showed me where the scarring on the lungs was. It looks like short, dark lines starting around the edges and, unfortunately, I had it in both of my lungs. As the disease progresses, the lungs start to fill up with what looks like clouds and the lung capacity reduces. He told me he would refer me to the lung clinic, and I would be assessed properly and told what drugs I would need. I felt safe in Professor Maher's hands and more positive mentally because I was taking some action to help myself. I asked him how long I had to live, and he confirmed up to five years but added the proviso that it could be more if a drug was found, or less if I became ill. The only hope on offer was if I could get a lung transplant, but I knew that luck was against me on account of my age. Nevertheless, I tried to stay positive and to keep myself as fit and healthy as I could.

Meanwhile, Dan, Kate and Sophie had started to look up IPF and realized how serious the situation was. They were as shocked as me. On my next appointment, Kate and Sophie came with me to see Professor Maher and he explained to them in greater detail about the illness. When Kate saw me blowing into the tube to measure my lung capacity, she joked, 'Come on mum. You can do better than that. You've had plenty of practice'. The professor laughed and raised his eyebrows. I looked at him and apologized. It was typical of Kate – she makes sexual innuendos when she's nervous as she thinks it lightens the atmosphere, which it did, slightly, but there was no getting away from the seriousness of the situation. Sophie found no comfort in Kate's jokes and couldn't stop herself from crying.

Professor Maher outlined my possible treatments: it turned out that two medications called Pirfenidone and Nintedanib were the only ones that could be prescribed for me. Before the appointment, I had contacted the late TV presenter Keith Chegwin, who had been on *Celebrity Big Brother* with Kate and was another victim of IPF. He had told me to try to get on the transplant list at all costs, so I took his advice seriously. Professor Maher – and later another specialist called Professor Phil Molyneaux – said I might actually live longer by not having a transplant because there is less chance of surviving the operation as you get older. But I still thought it was worth the gamble. Professor Maher said a transplant could only be considered at a later stage after my condition had deteriorated and I was deemed to be very close to death.

Kate asked more about what I would be like as I deteriorated and what she could do to help me. She showed unbelievable compassion by offering to give me one of her lungs but, unfortunately, as Toby explained, things are not quite as simple as that. The transplant team cannot take a lung from a living person and, in any case, her lung might not be a match. Even if I had been able, I wouldn't have taken her lung as I worry about the condition being hereditary. And, of course, she has her own children who rely on her and want her to be around. But I think the gesture does say something profound about Kate. This kind of heartfelt generosity is at the core of her character, but sadly few people get to see this up close like we do. I was eventually referred, and am still waiting for that call to tell me that a donor has been found as I write this sentence. I fear that when the doctors think my time is up, they will call it a day and I will come off the list. I worry that I'm not too far off that, but let's wait and see.

On reflection, I think I coped with the overwhelming feelings of fear which came with my diagnosis by taking action, *doing* something rather than just sitting with the terror. It was similar to how I sprang into action when Harvey was first diagnosed with blindness. Through the British Lung Foundation, I got to know fellow sufferers and we went to parliament to meet with the drug company that supplies Pirfenidone, asking why there are issues with eligibility. The drug slows the progression of the scarring, but you have to be in a certain lung capacity range to receive it – once you are out of that range you are taken off it as it is no longer so effective. I kept up a daily exercise regime at my local gym and the spin class teachers did a charity event for the British Lung Foundation to raise money. I was so honoured and grateful for the support I received. I will never forget it. I was also very appreciative of Kate when she attempted to raise money for the charity by running the London Marathon dressed as a pair of lungs – unfortunately her knees played up and she couldn't finish it. Professor Maher even came on the daytime TV show *Loose Women* with me to discuss and create awareness of IPF. My hope was that it might help someone else with IPF watching the programme. I also support the charity, Action for Pulmonary Fibrosis, as they have supported me throughout my journey – it is run by a guy called Steve who himself had a transplant.

During the periods when I wasn't doing something to raise awareness, I had to sit with the raw pain of knowing I was going to die much sooner than I wanted or hoped. However, I was determined to take care of myself and stay alive for as long as possible. Early on, I understood that getting a chest infection or a cold would make the disease progress even faster. Once you lose the lung capacity, it doesn't come back; it takes more of your energy to breathe and you get more breathless until your lungs seize up or you have a heart attack as the heart struggles to pump the blood oxygen around the body to the lungs.

Of course, winter poses the biggest risk so in January 2019 I decided that I would rent a tiny flat overlooking the sea in Nerja, Spain until the end of March. Nerja is a delightful town, not too touristy and surrounded by beautiful country-side and stunning beaches. Previously, when I returned from India, Price and I had wanted to continue our adventures so we bought a campervan. In a tongue-in-cheek way we named it the Love Shack because it was a symbol of our renewed love for each other. Now we loaded it up and journeyed through France into Spain. En route to Nerja, we stopped at some wonderful campsites, some in the middle of olive groves. I loved to stop and watch the sun setting over the endless rows of trees and marvel at the way nature seems to have a plan for everything – including me.

Once in Nerja, I joined a gym so I could continue with my spin and yoga classes. I enjoyed feeling the warm sun on my skin each day as I sipped a cup of tea while listening to bird song and the rhythmic push and pull of the ocean. Price and I had agreed that he would return to the UK for work but come and visit me some weekends. During his visits, we took the opportunity to explore Spain and I will never forget our trip to El Rocío, a village famous for its annual pilgrimage, where it is estimated that over a million pilgrims attend during the festival of Pentecost, either walking or in carts pulled by horses. We had never intended our visit to be a pilgrimage, but we found out that many people who went there were hoping for a miracle of healing, like me, so Price and I visited the beautiful church and we prayed with our candles. We went on to Portugal and saw some lovely places there too. We finally drove the motorhome back home in March, meandering through France on the way.

I returned to Nerja again in November to spend the following winter there, coming back to England in February 2020 to attend a check-up at the Brompton. The hospital seemed almost deserted because preparations were being made to combat a new disease called Covid. The doctors advised me that I should stay at home and not return to Spain, where the virus was spreading rapidly. The threat of Covid was particularly petrifying as I knew that if I caught it, it would be the end.

Back in the UK, we ordered our food shopping online to be delivered to the door and never ventured out socially. In retrospect, Price agrees with me that the lockdown period was probably the time we were closest as a couple. We enjoyed staying in together in our own bubble, doing the garden, painting the house and going for walks on the Wiston Estate and along the beach. We joined the family for Zoom calls and quizzes, encouraging the grandchildren to join in the fun too. Covid was strange because although people were physically far apart, emotionally it seemed to bring friends and family closer together. It certainly did with us.

I found the pandemic very challenging and frightening because I was in such a vulnerable state. It was terrible hearing of the poor people who died alone and had to be buried without their friends and relatives. I was scared, almost neurotic, as I watched the awful news stories unfolding each day. But I did what I could to prolong my life. I was able to join in a variety of Zoom classes, including yoga, dance, spin and body pump. Price bought a spin bike which I used to pedal at half the speed of everyone else. I was extra vigilant in avoiding people and meticulous about cleanliness when I was handling food. I am still wary of coming into contact with anyone who has a cold and avoid crowds or going into shops.

As time went on after the diagnosis, I remained under the care of the Royal Brompton Hospital in London and learned that 30,000 people in the UK currently have IPF. For a while I was on a research drug but, unfortunately, it was withdrawn after about a year because of some adverse effects it had on another patient. It would have been great if that research drug could have led to a cure. Nevertheless, I felt fortunate to have been used as a guinea pig because it meant that I had been regularly monitored and recorded, even in the problematic Covid times, and I may have helped to find a cure for IPF by volunteering to take it.

IPF is a learning curve for doctors and patients alike. As my lung capacity diminished and I became increasingly breathless, I learned that I would need a regular supply of oxygen to help me with day-to-day tasks, exercising and walking, and to protect my organs from being damaged through lack of oxygen. But getting the oxygen in the first place was a major task. I had to undergo lung function tests and blood tests, and do a six-minute walking test without oxygen to ascertain what level of oxygen I needed and work out the distance I could walk. Initially, doctors also analysed my lifestyle to decide how many cannisters I required at home. As more oxygen was needed as my condition got worse, I also got concentrators at home. The system didn't seem to be able to cope with the fact that I intended to exercise rather than sit down all day. They thought I was joking when I said I wanted to go out and walk, and try to swim in the sea with Price holding up the oxygen bottle for me. They forgot that people are not all the same. We may be terminally ill, and we may not be able to do much, but at least let us try. I take my oxygen with me everywhere – if I didn't, I could not go out or breathe. It gives me a quality of life. The technician who delivers it thought I was nuts at first because I wanted to exercise, but now we have a great relationship and I look forward to seeing him each week. We swap stories and have a laugh. His name is Ryan and as he leaves, he always says, 'Stay alive then, I'll see you next week.' It's amazing how uplifting human thoughtfulness can be.

The consultants tell me the fact that I'm doing spin, yoga and body pump is keeping me alive. It gets harder and harder, requiring more and more oxygen to get me through it, but I try to do something at least five days a week. Walking isn't easy either. To exercise or not to exercise is the dilemma that confronts me. Too much is physically exhausting. Too little is mentally frustrating. Too little also means I am reducing my lung capacity and my lungs get stiffer. I am lucky because I live near the coast so I can sit on the beach and watch the sea, but I find it impossible to relax. At home I have an oxygen concentrator machine with a 40ft lead. Sometimes it makes me feel like *I'm* the dog on the lead rather than Derick, our bulldog. It's infuriating when it gets caught under doors, but it does allow me to move around the bungalow and potter in the garden. I have an adjustable trolley which means I can wheel myself along the flower borders, and Price built me a raised bed using old railway sleepers and so I can grow vegetables – proving once again that he is my knight in shining armour. Housework is difficult, and bending down too as it makes me so breathless.

Everyone in the family has played their part in helping me to adjust to life with the illness. Dan has been so brave and a wonderful support to me. Each day he checks how I am and prompts me to put on my oxygen supply when he notices I am struggling to talk. It means we have become really close. He is gentle in his approach to me and understands me well. I usually see him first thing in the morning for breakfast and also for tea if he is working with Price on a local fencing job. Price's knees are bad and he is getting older and can't do what he used to do, so eventually the business will be taken over by Dan who will continue working with Price's partner. I know Dan understands exactly what I am going through because he watches me so closely. Some days I cry and then berate myself, but Dan encourages it, telling me that it's good to let emotions out. I have always been a bit emotional. Anything can set me off – a song that brings back memories, a film, a nice message from my children or grandchildren, something beautiful in the garden, the sight of fields, the sea, animals, birds. As a little girl, I remember seeing a big tree being cut down and that really upset me. Dan helps to settle my mind by letting me talk about the things I worry will happen when I pass away. Most importantly for me, he reassures me that he will step up to help Price and everyone else.

Sophie and Kate also come to see me as much as they can. We still go out on our day trips together, touring the countryside, loving the beautiful sights of nature and dreaming of all the houses we'd like to live in. I love the times when my children and grandchildren visit me early in the morning before I'm up and we all lie on the bed together having a cup of coffee.

Kate's way of dealing with my illness is very different; she spends a lot of time hoping for a different outcome. She continually asks when I will get the transplant and tries to appear strong on the outside, so she doesn't upset me. But I feel her fear. Kate spoils me with nice creams, bath soaks, lovely lounge wear, comfy slippers and warm coats. She is an exceedingly generous person and, over the years, she has given me many luxury gifts, including Louis Vuitton, Gucci and Burberry bags. You name them, I've got them and I've kept every one – but I have hardly used them as they are not really me. I treasure the gifts that Kate has given me, but she knows I am not materialistic. I prefer more nondescript accessories which I don't have to be careful about; I prefer going to a garden centre to buy plants rather than go to Bond Street for fancy bags. The most precious gift of all, though, is spending quality time together, something we are doing more of nowadays. It is something I have wanted for so long because it gives us a chance to talk about Harvey and his future. We have to try to ensure that he lives his life as independently as he can, and decide who will be granted power of attorney to sort out any legal issues in case he outlives Kate. Even though all my children are struggling with the idea of my untimely death, they are managing to come to terms with it, both emotionally and practically, in their own ways. And so are my grandchildren, who are extremely affectionate and loving. I have wonderful cards from them with such amazing words, which make me cry, but know I am loved – what more could I ask for?

My grandchildren come to see me and we have wonderful times together, talking and laughing. I treasure these days. Jett and Bunny look at me and ask me what the oxygen tube is for – I tell them it helps me breathe. When they visit, I try to make things fun and normal for them, so Grandad Price takes them to the beach or they help me in the garden with growing vegetables. Bunny is so caring and tells me she'll run and get her grandad if my oxygen runs out. Meanwhile, Jett and I talk about wildlife and compost heaps. They recently dug over my vegetable patch for me so I could plant my summer vegetables. These simple things in life mean the world to me and, hopefully, have created memories for them.

If we can arrange it, Dan also brings his girls Amalie and Betsy to play with Jett, Bunny and Albert; they are of a similar age and it's so lovely to see them all playing together. Amalie and Betsy chatter away together and I get great pleasure in just watching them. Their nickname for me is Nanny

Big Hair, which I just love. Princess texts me every morning, asking how I am and what am I up to, and Junior stays in touch with me too, sending words of love and gratitude. I love talking to them about their lives and I'm extremely proud of them both. Junior is talented, driven and committed and he plays me whatever music he's recently recorded. Princess has my curly hair, just like Kate has, and she's stunning – but she's also a lovely person inside and I know she is destined to do well in life. Harvey understands that I am unwell and asks how I am. He bends down to look at my oxygen tube, touches it gently and says, 'Get well soon, nanny'. He sends me videos, and paintings which I treasure. I remember having to hold his hand when he was little to help him navigate any uneven surface, but now it's Harvey that tells me to hold onto him when he's worried that I might be a bit unsteady on my feet. Who would have thought it possible all those years ago when we wondered what Harvey would be like as he grew older?

As I write this memoir, I am under the palliative care team from St Barnabas House hospice in Worthing, and they keep an eye on me. I now have only 15–20 per cent lung capacity left so I am heavily reliant on oxygen most of the time to keep me going. It is very difficult for Price to cope with my deterioration, and I continue to lose more and more capacity. He knows from close-up how poorly I am but doesn't usually say anything, except when I start coughing – then he starts to ask how he can help. We've been living in an end-of-life way for five years now and both of us have had to learn to deal with it. Even our marital bed has been compromised because of the risk of me getting so much as a basic cold. If Price has even a hint of a sniffle, he has to stay in a separate bedroom, or even check into a hotel if it's bad. We can't even have a hug before we go to our separate rooms. He has another bathroom to use too, and we eat separately. Then he rings me up from his bedroom asking me what I'm watching on TV. But this is only on rare occasions as we both love sharing our bed and watching the TV together. I hate him sleeping in the other room so he has to avoid getting colds!

As well as adjusting our everyday lives, Price and I have had to adapt our holiday style too. The motorhome allows us the freedom to go on mini-breaks, which we greatly look forward to. It means that, if things are getting us down, we can always make a spontaneous escape somewhere, although going away takes organization. Before we arrive at a campsite, I get eight oxygen cylinders delivered and I have my concentrator from home, which provides me with oxygen 24/7, which I can use in the motorhome. The motorhome has to be well equipped with kitchen and bathroom facilities so I'm able to enjoy some quality of life. As there is no chance of any more exotic trips to countries like India or Spain, our excursions are now limited to within a four-hour radius of Harefield hospital, just in case I get the longed-for transplant call. Price and I have revisited some of our favourite beauty spots in Devon, Dorset and Cornwall. We escape like a couple of teenagers and still haven't worked out how to set up the motorhome correctly, which means we often arrive at a new place and struggle to put all the attachments up. It would probably remind anybody watching of a *Carry On* film. Sometimes our journeys are just as chaotic as our arrivals. If the mood takes us, we just start

283

driving randomly and we never seem to learn our lesson as the roads get narrower and narrower until we can go no further. We stop, look at each other, and don't even have to say the words, 'Why do we do this?' We find ourselves having to reverse backwards for miles. Our tumultuous road trips seem to be symbolic of the Price family's journey through life, but our misadventures in the West Country fade to insignificance when they are compared to the ordeals of a journey other members of the family would be about to make.

Chapter 15

DOWNWARD SPIRAL

In some ways, my rollercoaster life with Kate had prepared me for coming to terms with a terminal illness. There were brief periods of slower-paced stability, when I could look around me, take stock of things and try to steady myself. Then, occasionally, a moment of almost deadly calm would prevail before – whoosh – the rug would be pulled from beneath me and yet again I felt as if I was hurtling downhill at breakneck speed. Experience has taught me that this part of the ride with Kate is nearly always precipitated by the ominous sound of an iPhone ringing some time after dark. There is some part of me – a *numb* part of me – which has got used to this way of life, but the call that came in March 2018 was particularly shocking. To me, it symbolized a life now seriously compromised by almost two decades of reality TV.

At first it was hard to make sense of Kate's words crackling through the phone amid heart-rending sobs, echoing down the line from South Africa to West Sussex. I knew Kate was there with Junior and Princess filming her latest reality show, *My Crazy Life*, which was screening on a free-to-air channel called Quest Red. In my view, the title itself was dubious food for thought – Kate had lived almost all her adult life through the lens of reality TV, which was what had fuelled her so-called 'crazy life' in the first place. During her first reality TV series with Richard Macer, Kate had been in control – they'd had a laugh together, a natural bond. But over the years, filming with new crews had become continuous and permeated every part of her life. During the most intense period with Pete, Claire and Neville, my sense was that the production team would start creating dramas to make the series more compelling, which had a tangible impact on Kate's life outside filming, and likely contributed to the worsening relationship with her partners – particularly Pete. There needed to be drama in every episode but, in reality, life isn't like that. It's not all drama, drama, drama. In fact, much of it is refreshingly ordinary and routine – boring even. But that doesn't achieve profitable viewing figures. A lot of Kate's life has been dictated by film crews saying, 'Let's do this' or 'Let's do that', and then she thinks it would be fun. But because the cameras rarely stop rolling, Kate's entire life became scripted in this way – nothing was real. Her reality TV shows had resulted in her not living a 'real' way of life. But this time, the drama had become dangerously real.

The reason for Kate's trip to South Africa was to film a family holiday with Junior and Princess. Following a safari trip, which everyone had enjoyed, the production company decided to try to cross the border into Swaziland at a time of day that wasn't safe, along a road that wasn't safe. Through her tears, Kate managed to tell me what had happened. She said the three-car convoy was driving down a road in darkness as they approached the town of Chrissiesmeer in Mpumalanga province on their way to Swaziland. The film crew led the convoy and Kate was in the second car with Junior, Princess and her long-term friend Neil Tawse, who grew up in South Africa and agreed to use his knowledge of the country to help with the project. The final vehicle, containing equipment and luggage, somehow got separated from the convoy so it was just the film crew in the first car, and Kate and the children in the car behind, that pulled into a layby when Junior said he needed the toilet. Kate and Princess joined him, along with one of the female crew members from the first vehicle.

Neil, who had been driving Kate's car, decided to use the brief stop to go to speak to the crew about his unease at their decision to travel down that particular road so late at night. As he did so, he felt a tap on the shoulder and heard someone shouting at him to hand over his money. Neil was convinced the robbers would be armed and thought it meant big trouble. He heard Kate and the children screaming for help. No sooner had they returned to their vehicle, another member of the gang had appeared at their window, yelling at them to get out. Kate's attacker was part of a four-man gang of robbers who forced his way in and began slapping them all. One of the men also put his hands down Kate's trousers and sexually assaulted her before touching her all over and hitting her hard. Junior, Princess and a crew member were being attacked in the back seat by another robber and everyone was screaming for help. Kate told me she had yelled at the men to do anything they wanted to her, but pleaded with them to spare her children. At one point she recalled holding a pillow up in front of her because she was convinced she was going to be shot.

Neil bravely fought off his assailant and raced back to Kate's car. But after getting in, he realized that he couldn't start it. The attackers were not deterred by his presence and continued to hit him with a pole on his arm, leg and across his face. They smashed the pole down on top of the roof as Neil again tried to fire up the ignition. Neil was eventually dragged out of the car and knocked unconscious. The vehicles were robbed of their computers and other valuables before the attackers finally fled.

Neil's actions were heroic, but Kate felt shocked that the film crew had done nothing to help, only re-emerging when the attackers had gone and the police and ambulance were finally called. They should have had a security team travelling with them from day one, but it clearly hadn't been thought through by the production team with any care. I think it's hard to see these things clearly when you are so caught up in them but as Kate's mum, I was a worried bystander – as I had been so many times before. It now seemed that Kate had come dangerously close to being robbed of her life. I knew she needed to do these shows to earn a living, but the risks felt bigger than the rewards.

As my daughter off-loaded yet another traumatic episode of her life on to me, I began preparing myself mentally to fly over to help, but Kate was adamant, 'Don't come over here mum – it's not safe'. She was clearly in shock and said she didn't really know what was going on but would get back to me as soon as possible. She just kept telling me, 'All I wanted to do was protect my kids'. The phone line eventually went dead and I realized I was now also in a state of shock. Over the years, when I have been confronted with bolts from the blue – like my diagnosis, Price's rape accusation and other incidents that have happened to Kate – I go numb. It must be the freeze element of shock that I feel. Again I found myself in that familiar place I had learned to retreat to in traumatic moments. As usual, I was thinking what I could do for her. The reality was, I couldn't do anything. Feeling powerless, I called the show's producer and told her what had happened. I could tell by the panic in her voice that she had not yet been informed. I asked her what she was going to do about it and questioned the absence of proper security on the trip. She soon got off the phone but I never heard back from her.

Kate and the children finally found a safe retreat with some of Neil's friends in Durban, but unbelievably the cameras kept rolling. Here she was again – like a performing seal – reinforcing her crazy life and continuing to give the public a ringside seat as her trauma unfolded. The crew had planned to film Junior playing football with underprivileged children in Swaziland, but following the incident they decided to change this to a more low-key storyline of horse riding on the beach. Reality TV was no longer being viewed as light-hearted entertainment in our family, but this trip felt to me as though it had a precedent. It was the most unprofessional crew I had ever come across.

For me, it brought back memories of the airport car chase in America, which had been completely unnecessary and had compromised the safety of Junior, Princess and Harvey.

As Kate's mum, I have tried to understand and stand by her choices, but as her children's grandmother it is sometimes hard to reconcile this position. I do worry about the impact reality TV has had on Junior and Princess, particularly when they are exposed to something as traumatic as the attack in South Africa. I sometimes consider the possibility that Junior might have felt guilty for needing to stop the car that day and hope that, somehow, he can be reassured that it was absolutely not his fault – he and Princess were just children, and it was up to the adults to keep them out of harm's way. Neil and Kate did their best and were also hurt and very disturbed in the process. They have both received therapy for this event. I am sure that in the future, the aftermath of the drama will rear its ugly head again and the children will require therapy as well.

When Kate eventually touched back down in the UK, she reunited Junior and Princess with their dad, who was surprisingly understanding for once. She then did what she often does after a traumatic event – glosses over the enormity of it by letting her hair down at a party.

She headed for the most spectacular party so far: dinner at a luxury palazzo near Perugia, Italy, owned by the billionaire son of a former KGB lieutenant colonel and controversial owner of London's *Evening Standard*, Evgeny Lebedev. Kate had previously met Evgeny on the party circuit and he summoned her and a select group of friends to join him there, courtesy of a private jet. Kate is very modest in her conversations with me, but she had told me that one person who had been extremely complimentary to her was Lebedev himself. She had known him for a while and was frank in her summing up of her Russian friend, telling me that they got on so well because he thought that she was so down-to-earth. I was therefore shocked and somewhat annoyed with her in 2022 when I subsequently read about her so-called drunken antics in the press, years after the party. DD-OWNING ST was the undeniably clever headline in *The Sun*, followed by the explanation: Katie Price flashed her boobs to Boris Johnson at dinner party in Italy, reveals Piers Morgan. After reading *The Sun* headlines about her so-called antics, which supposedly included being escorted off the premises of Lebedev's palazzo and flown home early, I demanded to know the truth. She told me how Lebedev had introduced her to everyone, including our then-Foreign Secretary Boris Johnson and his then-wife, Marina Wheeler. Kate ended up doing shots with everyone and promised to invite Boris and Marina back to hers for a Sunday roast. According to Kate, Boris and Marina were the life and soul of the party, and a buoyant Boris joined Kate in putting on clown fancy dress outfits which they found from a huge selection on the top floor of the building.

Leaving aside the political implications, it sounded like a great party and I don't understand the sour grapes towards my daughter. I know that Piers Morgan likes Kate, so I couldn't understand why he would choose to write about her in that way in his column. I am so bored with reading this kind of narrative, some of which is true but most of which isn't. Was everyone at that table meant to be sipping tea and eating cakes? Everyone who attended knew what was in store and many famous actresses, models and other personalities enjoyed a lively time. But what I have increasingly come to reflect on is why Kate is singled out. After all, there were dozens of other people at this party, letting their hair down in a highly confidential atmosphere, so why was my daughter the fall guy, the scapegoat, yet again? Only her detractors know their motivation for denigrating her, but I think it says more about them than Kate. However, it meant that, yet again, Kate was construed as the outsider who wasn't really welcome at the ball.

Kate was not asked to leave the party and indeed flew home with all the other guests – on the private jet, not separately as was reported. The day after the party, she had breakfast and lunch at the palazzo and was seated next to a famous actress, who has had her own fair share of scandals, and they flew home together. Sadly, The Tall Tale of the Lebedev party is just another example of how Kate is always scapegoated by bullies ready to set up another salacious headline. For the record, though, the boob flashing part is true. Even when sober, Kate will happily talk about her boobs if asked and even show them off. Frankly, the number of people who have seen them is mind-blowing. The person who was quite free with her condonation of Kate in her version of events went to bed early, leaving her husband at the party. I could say more about her, but won't – I shall leave her to retain her dignity, though I know that, in the past, she hasn't always been perfect herself.

Kate – it seemed – had starred in the ultimate unreal reality show in Italy, but underneath the party girl façade she was struggling, both with the final act in her disastrous marriage to Kieran and the cumulative effect of one literal and metaphorical car crash after another. Despite suffering years of humiliation in her relationship with Kieran, Kate still wanted to believe it was repairable, but she was eventually defeated after returning from Italy to discover that he had had yet more trysts with their nanny, which had taken place all over the house. Now, another safe home space was contaminated and there was nowhere left to hide.

For years, Kate's life had been filled with noise and drama but behind the whirring of reality TV cameras, the unravelling of post-surgery bandages and the constant drone of hairdryers, lurked unimaginable mental pain. Few elements of Kate's private life had been kept away from media scrutiny but for some time we, her family, managed to keep boundaries around a series of deeply worrying suicide attempts, the first of which was after her split from Dane Bowers. Occasionally people would ring me up and say they were really worried about her and thought she was going to do something 'silly'. We would then of course try to explore the problem and she would usually respond defensively, claiming her friends' concerns were untrue or unfounded. We've always known that night times are particularly hard for Kate, so Price and I sleep with our phones by our pillows. For years, she has been used to having a film crew around her during the day but when everyone leaves, she tends to get low and that's when everything goes haywire. Her brain starts processing things at 100mph and she overthinks every aspect of her life.

Kate's state of mind has not been helped by her attempts at self-medicating with drugs and alcohol. Like any model, she was offered drugs on multiple occasions from an early age but understood the policy of zero-tolerance in our household (until her relationship with Kieran), instead seeking dopamine highs through natural sources like her children and horses. We have always been more relaxed about the ordinary consumption of alcohol, but it became apparent from her teen years that alcohol didn't suit Kate. It triggers a quick change in her mood and she morphs into an outrageous exhibitionist who has no filters whatsoever. This transition has landed her in trouble so many times and is dreaded by us and her partners. At other times, if she drinks when she's depressed, she just cries and cries – and one thing leads to another. Alcohol is not a friend to anyone, in particular Kate.

After her return from South Africa in 2018, Kate's mental health deteriorated in parallel with her will to resist the chemical and alcohol highs which had become a major part of her lifestyle with Kieran. I received some troubling text messages from her friends, some of whom I suspected were users themselves, saying they were worried about her mental state and thought she was drinking or drug taking to excess to escape from the unhappiness in her life. I received phone calls from an ex who was concerned about Kate and told me about attempts she had made on her life. A few months after the traumatic incident, one of Kate's friends rang me to say they had found her trying to hang herself. Another time, in the early hours, I received a phone call from her saying, 'Mum, sorry, I can't take any more. You know I love you a lot.' I turned to Price – not for the first time – and said, 'You've got to go to her at her house.' On that occasion, like many others, Kate said the call had come in a weak or drunk moment, but I knew she was downplaying it because she didn't want to upset me. We were worried sick about her.

Each time I saw her I noticed further decline – the way she talked, the way she looked. Kate avoided seeing me and would call up to make all sorts of excuses about being busy. When I did manage to pin her down, she looked tired, fidgety and wanted to sleep. Normally, she would come into the family home like a whirlwind, heading straight to the kettle and the biscuit tin. But not anymore. When I questioned her, she would snap back, 'Not now mum. I'm just so tired – let me sleep for an hour.' The hour could go on for two or three hours – that's when I knew something really wasn't right. Like when she had first found out about Kieran and Jane's relationship, she looked dishevelled and no longer took pride in her appearance. I was so worried, we all were. It was like waiting for a ticking time bomb to explode. The stress for us was dreadful but we had to tread carefully because we didn't want her to retreat from us completely.

I was at a loss to know how to address the drug taking with Kate, so I simply used to ask her, *plead* with her, 'Why? Why? Why? Why are you doing these things? How could you do that? What about your kids? Why aren't you thinking of them?' On one level, of course, she was. Every time she attempted suicide, she stopped that little bit closer to the edge of death, seeing her children's faces, thinking of how they would feel knowing what she had done and how they would face a future without their mum – especially Harvey. No one loves Harvey like his mum. He would be totally lost without her. Kate couldn't answer me, but would often sob and tell me, 'I get close to the edge because sometimes I just can't cope'. We would cry together and I would cuddle her tight, hoping, praying, that one day she would be understood by others – but most importantly, that she would understand herself. So often she feels conflicted because she wants to be a good mum and tries to do everything right, yet she still realizes that her lifestyle can distract her from this aim. I see her bursting with happiness when she is with her kids, but I know they worry about her and want her to get the help she needs – it's heart breaking.

During this dark period of depression, the kids just wanted their mum back even though they could see things were wrong. She knew she shouldn't be doing those things but she couldn't help herself because, wherever she turned, there was negativity. How can any individual deal with that day after day, year after year? We, her family, understand the pain that she has experienced. There have been many times when we've wanted to intervene, but a therapist would step in and things would quieten down for a short time. There were times when things felt so hopeless, I considered having Kate sectioned so she could finally get the robust mental health support she needed – although, as her mother, I just couldn't bring myself to do that to my own child.

In September 2018, Kate spent 28 days in The Priory hospital in London after her break-up with the fitness trainer Kris Boyson. She was self-medicating with cocaine and drinking heavily to the point of becoming suicidal. She had returned from a binge in Mallorca, where she had been on a hen do, and was so unwell that Sophie ended up having to call 999. She was eventually seen by a psychiatrist who helped to calm her down. We were at our wits' end and decided to call The Priory to get her booked in somewhere long-term. Sophie followed her there by car to make sure she actually went through the doors. Inside, Kate was literally shaking and in a very distressed state but the lead doctor refused to treat her until she had paid the bill. She stayed for 5 weeks and we visited her every week along with Junior and Princess.

It would be easy to pinpoint the beginning of Kate's downward spiral to the carjacking fiasco. But in reality, I think my illness was understandably triggering a lot of fear and anxiety. For years, she had relied on me as her protector, confidante and first emergency service and there must have been times in the dead of night when she wondered if she would be able to manage without a mum. I think this added to her secrecy with me; she just didn't want me to feel any more stress. I had many sleepless nights pondering the same question: how would Kate cope? Dying in the knowledge that my daughter is at peace with herself would be one of the greatest accomplishments of my life. Thankfully, Sophie is now primed to take my place as Kate's chief supporter, backed up by Dan and Price, and to be there for Harvey too. Somehow, her life has remained on an even keel; in fact, while Kate was battling yet more mental health demons, my youngest daughter was continuing her studies, this time for an MA in history at Birkbeck College in London. As ever, we were delighted by the surprise emergence of another academic in the Price clan. Dan had already achieved his degree in European Business Studies and a Higher National Diploma in International Business Management.

However, Sophie's success led me to worry about Kate's perception of herself as the black sheep in the family. She was genuinely pleased for her sister but, at the same time, I sensed she didn't want to be the odd one out in the family and needed to show us she could also achieve something on paper to make us proud. I always tell her we are proud of her for being her. She would joke with Sophie, saying, 'How do these brains come from a hairdresser?' and she started to think about training as a paramedic. She asked Sophie to research it for her but was shocked when her sister told her about the four years of training required that would include her retaking her GCSEs, which she had struggled with at school. For years, I have suspected that Kate has a neurodiverse condition like ADHD, which made it very hard for her to learn conventionally at school – she could never sit still. I bet any money if she'd been properly screened and given appropriate support, her life might have turned out differently because she is naturally very intelligent but struggles to focus on things for long periods. There just wasn't the same knowledge of those conditions back then as there is now. If I'd been more aware of the symptoms, I would have tried to get her help years ago and it is a journey I am supporting her on now – better late than never.

Kate's response to Sophie's research was, 'Can't I do it quicker?' She doesn't realize how long people train for these jobs. Instead, Kate told me she wanted to learn to do beauty treatments like eyebrows and nails, and went on to get qualifications in these skills. In my opinion, though, a qualification shows you can achieve a certain standard in your subject, but

life events demonstrate the same. Despite her trials and tribulations, Kate has proven to be a successful businesswoman
who has also brought disability to the forefront of people's
agendas. She has even visited soldiers in war zones, and is
brilliant with people – old people in particular. There is much
more to her than YouTube clips and salacious headlines.

But the empire that Kate had worked so hard to build for
her children was now falling apart after the downfall of her
third marriage and her poor mental health. She had started
to get herself into serious financial trouble. Kate had never
been good at the management of money. People continued
to take advantage of her and she was spending beyond her
means, which hadn't been helped by the hefty divorce pay-outs
and legal fees, or by Kieran's management with Kate of her
finances. By November 2019 she was declared bankrupt after
failing to pay a series of debts. She had agreed to pay back a
certain amount each month to her creditors after taking out
an individual voluntary arrangement a year before – but had
failed to do so. She now faced losing her £2 million home and
having her assets taken and sold by an appointed trustee to
pay her debts.

In the build-up to this bleak financial state of affairs, she
had become vulnerable to a very unsavoury circle of so-called
friends and businesspeople. There could be no quick comeback from the emotional and financial black holes Kate was
in, but these people tried to convince her otherwise at a time
when she was at her lowest ebb. One of them persuaded her
that he could turn her house into a profitable wedding venue
and horse-training yard for yearlings. We told her it was an

impossible dream, but she wouldn't listen and he played on her vulnerability. He began to dig up the land on the pretext of creating an area to lay the foundations for a training track. The actual building of the track was delayed, he said, because the plans were with the council. Kate was away for a lot of the time while this was going on and this so-called businessman turned out to be a conman who dug up Kate's land and used it for landfill, charging lorries a fee to dump their hardcore, chalk, earth and other contaminated soils from building sites on her land. My daughter was literally being used as someone else's dustbin and she was blind to that fact until a bill for £90,000 arrived to rectify the unsolicited change of land use for which there was no planning permission. Attempts to trace the guy proved to be unsuccessful and we found out that he had previously done the same thing to others.

Kate has accepted that although she isn't the academic one in the family, her intelligence manifests in other ways – she is the one who's been able to make a lot of money and with that comes a certain self-esteem. So this fall from financial grace was very hard for her. At the time of the horse-training-yard fiasco, the rest of the family did not realize quite how serious were the dire financial straits in which she found herself, but we sensed things were not right and as her mum I was obviously very worried. Until she realized he was a conman, Kate had absolute trust in the ability of this 'builder businessman' to straighten out her money situation and rebuffed any help or suggestions we attempted to give. Everything felt like it was falling apart and Dan had to sit back, powerless, watching it all unfold. He began to focus more on his sports management company and occasional work alongside Price in his fencing business, knowing that Price needed help in order to take time off to support me.

Then Kirsty Shaw-Rayner came onto the scene – a celebrity agent I had first heard of when Kate was with Alex Reid. Kirsty managed a few personalities and had been on the periphery of Kate's social circle. Unusually for someone who socialized with reality TV stars, she seemed to have one foot in a more elevated door, through her marriage to Alex Rayner. Alex is an old Etonian who manages a country estate in Essex called Braxted Park, and was appointed to the government's post-Covid economic recovery task force. Kirsty is quite a pretty lady who talks a lot and seems to revel in being the person who organizes and controls things. As had now become my habit whenever anyone put themselves forward to help Kate financially, I made a cursory Google search and gleaned that she had a close connection to Tara Palmer-Tomkinson and had been photographed out socializing with Amy Winehouse. This made me uneasy due to their widely known use of drugs – something my own daughter had been grappling with. I didn't think she needed any more temptation put in her path.

I had no particular axe to grind with Kirsty when we had first met in 2009, but I had been told by an impeccable source that she had a habit of selling stories to the press without permission from subjects. So – despite the fact she had been invited by Kate – I asked security to bar her from the bus hired to take people to the ceremony at Alex and Kate's wedding. She disappeared after that and didn't reappear on the scene, as far as I am aware, until Kate got together with Kieran. She helped him to organize a birthday party at a restaurant called Gilgamesh in Camden, North London, and I remember catching a glimpse of her and thinking, 'Oh my God, she's back'. She came over and asked me how I was, to which I replied quite coldly, 'I'm fine thank you'. Then I went straight over to Kate to ask what she was doing back on the scene – Kate was placatory and begged me not to cause a scene, 'Oh, she's organized it so don't start now mum. Just leave it'.

I didn't hear anything about Kirsty again for ages, until Kate came out of The Priory in the Spring of 2018. Kate had heard through a mutual friend that Kirsty was not in the best of health and contacted her to see how she was. This led to a rekindling of the friendship and then a meeting where Kirsty and her husband Alex presented Kate with a strategy to help get her career back on track and offered to help her in return for a commission-only fee structure. By 2019, Kate had mulled over the idea and decided to work with Kirsty. My heart sank when I heard they had come to an agreement because I didn't think Kirsty was good news for someone like my daughter – who, in my opinion, wasn't capable of making good friendship or business decisions at this time in her life. I also knew that Kirsty and Pete's manager, Claire, were on speaking terms, and I could only imagine the conversations that took place between them.

After Kate and Kirsty decided to work together, I started to get texts from Kirsty in April 2020 suggesting we meet up. She knew about my illness, so her messages were all about sending healing light – that sort of thing. Perhaps in my own vulnerable state of mind, I began to wonder if I had misjudged her. There did appear to be a kind side to her, plus she was now helping my daughter so I wanted to understand her better. I think she was more than aware of my negative feelings towards her and wanted to get me on side. I have to admit that Kirsty was good at dealing with the press when problems cropped up but I was wary this time round – as opposed to plain gullible – and saw the signs. And while I might have become cynically adept at keeping potential enemies close, I drew a line at Kirsty's attempt to employ Sophie. I instinctively told my youngest daughter, who by now had a steady PR job, 'This isn't going to last with Kate, then the last thing you want is to be around Kirsty'. I could guarantee her employment would cease when Kate disappeared.

As it turned out, I wasn't the only one who wasn't keen on Kirsty. Kate's new boyfriend, a plumber's son from Essex called Carl Woods, wasn't a fan either. After the fall-out from Kieran, the usual pattern had played out for Kate, except this time it was Eat Sleep Party (and occasionally Date). Repeat. Kate had been really hurt by Kieran sleeping with her friends and the nanny – all of whom she had at some stage trusted implicitly. So we were really worried that she might get damaged again. Thankfully, when she met Carl, a used-car dealer, at the upmarket Sheesh restaurant in Chigwell, Essex in June 2020 – just under a year after her divorce from Kieran had been finalized – marriage didn't seem to be on the agenda, at least to begin with. Kate knows the owner of the restaurant, who was friendly with Carl and alerted him to Kate's presence at the venue, allowing him to turn up and scope out the woman he had previously admired as a pin-up in his teen-age years, and later studied on social media and reality TV shows. We later learned Carl had made a brief appearance in the 2016 season of *Love Island* but had failed to find romance and was dumped from the villa.

Kate was flattered by the attention and, once again, fell hook, line and sinker for his baby-faced boyish looks. I heard the usual when she told me about him – he works, he's not interested in fame, he comes from a good family. Blah blah blah. She also told me she thought she was 'punching above her weight' in their relationship. I felt sad to think that my daughter was still feeling insecure and inferior to a man like this. Because of everything she had been through, and because Price and I were fed up with these younger men, needless to say I did not think it was a match made in heaven. We were also worried about Kate being hurt again, so all the usual alarm bells were ringing with this young man.

Despite him initially being polite, I remember him saying to me that if Kate wanted to be with him, she would have to play by his rules. His sales patter was strangely convincing. He was straight talking and, like me, seemed to be able to see through insincerity; he said he didn't suffer fools gladly. He actually listened to people and, at the time, I thought it might be good for Kate to have someone who could keep her on the straight and narrow and potentially make her feel secure in a relationship. He also – predictably – said he wasn't interested in fame, appearing in Kate's shows, or being in magazines. Of course, it was only a matter of time before he hired his own manager to promote himself and soon he was appearing in Kate's reality shows and has graced the pages of magazines with her. He also regularly appears on social media and OnlyFans promoting himself, so this so-called publicity-shy man soon changed his tune.

Like his predecessors, he ended up moving in with Kate very quickly, but he owned his own home and she used to stay at his house too, which I thought was potentially a good sign. However, before long the usual signs of jealousy started to surface. Their relationship seemed stifling to me. I'm sure this behaviour was all borne out of deep insecurity on his part, but it's still unacceptable for a man to be like this with any woman.

Price, Dan, Sophie and I quickly saw that this new partnership was simply a repeat of pretty much every relationship Kate had ever been in. Fairly early on in their relationship, on one occasion, Kate and Carl had a disagreement and she stayed at my house. She was really upset because she thought their relationship was over. To my horror, Kate was so terrified of being rejected by him and went back. When I'd first met Carl, I had hoped that he might be a steadying influence on Kate and help her to have better boundaries, but unfortunately, that didn't seem to be the case.

Now there were two people vying for control of my daughter. As Kate's so-called manager, Kirsty wanted to be in charge, but Carl was proving to be a spanner in the works with his own dominant attitude. It wasn't long before it was apparent that he was preventing Kate from doing certain jobs, or at least heavily influencing her choices. He and Kirsty had a big fall out and she would text me constantly asking me what good he was doing Kate. In Kirsty's eyes, Carl was holding her back, and I had to agree with her. I sensed Kirsty wanted me on side more than ever, in order to try to persuade Kate to see the light and dump Carl, who was trying to manage her client. I was in a difficult position because I felt Kate's relationship with both of them was toxic.

The tension was building, and it seemed to be developing into a clash between the unstoppable and the immovable, but we had a wonderfully light reprieve from all this when Sophie's firstborn Albert arrived on 28th May 2021 and lit up our lives like a ray of sunshine. Sophie was pregnant during Covid, which had made the whole family anxious but excited about the birth. She and Harry had decided not to find out Albert's gender before his arrival, so I had been furiously knitting neutral baby clothes along with my friend Lin, while choosing nursery decor and toys. It was wonderful watching Sophie's bump getting bigger and bigger and Harry getting more and more excited as time passed. Family Zoom calls gave us all something to look forward to, and the imminent birth gave me something to strive for, making sure I lived long enough to welcome my latest grandson to the world. In the end, Albert was delivered by Caesarean in a London hospital and we first glimpsed our little 'Tom Thumb', as he became known, through photos and video recordings that Harry took at the hospital. He is an amazing mixture of his mum and dad, with the strawberry blonde hair Sophie had as a baby and Harry's big brown eyes.

It wasn't long after Albert's birth that Sophie, Harry, Albert, Price and I were invited to visit Kirsty and her husband Alex in Cornwall, in August 2021. From the outset, Albert loved to engage with people so we decided to accept the invitation out of curiosity more than anything. On reflection, I think that Kirsty's own attempts to control Kate through me were part of the reason for the invite. It might seem strange to have accepted this invite, but there was room to park our motorhome nearby so in my mind we would be visiting rather than staying, which felt more appropriate. However, there wasn't room for Sophie and Albert in the van, so she did accept Kirsty's invitation to stay in a guest room.

I think the first thing that struck me on arrival at their home was how wealthy Kirsty and her husband appeared to be. It didn't seem as if Kirsty needed to work, so I wondered what motivations were behind her helping Kate. Polzeath is one of the most exclusive areas of Cornwall and Kirsty and Alex's stunning cliff-top holiday home dominates the landscape. Alex told me it had been in his family since the war and still retains many of the original fixtures and fittings, like the large windows and flagstone floors. Once, it provided a safe war refuge for his mother and her family, but had become a hotspot for their friends – like David Cameron and Gordon Ramsay – two individuals who Kirsty was keen to tell us 'might pop in'.

Kirsty liked to name-drop, particularly when the individuals were linked to government, and she told me that her husband would have a word with Priti Patel about backing the campaign for Harvey's Law, my and Kate's initiative to combat online trolls. Harvey had been trolled and we had been to Parliament putting forward our case for stamping out online abuse towards those with disabilities. We had also worked with charities trying to help keep children safe. We had suggested a register of abusers, so that employers can search names of people who had trolled those with disabilities – the law needs to be changed to protect vulnerable people. Social media users under the age of 18 should have to have their accounts verified with the ID of a parent or guardian to provide traceability and prevent anonymous harmful activity. Kate was invited by Siobhan Bailey MP and Andrew Griffith MP to attend the Select Committee debates.

To be fair, we were greeted warmly by Kirsty and Alex, and Price received a beer while I settled for a cup of tea before we all retired to the garden overlooking the bay. Otherwise, everything seemed surprisingly normal and homely, with Kirsty bustling round the kitchen washing clothes and drying out surfing gear. It was not unusual for Kate's managers to offer us hospitality and Kirsty and Alex seemed to have genuine concerns for Kate and the state of her health. I was beginning to think I had completely misjudged her and that my concerns about her malign influence on my daughter were unfounded.

We trundled home to our cosy bungalow. However, unbeknown to me and Price, the war between Kirsty and Carl was hotting up and was about to have devastating consequences for Kate and her children.

The dreaded early morning phone call came in late August 2021, from Carl's dad. 'My son's been arrested,' he told me in his thick Essex accent and mumbled something about Kate alleging Carl had hit her in the face. 'But my son would never hit anyone, and I just wanted you to know that the men in our family are not like that,' he added, somewhat defensively. I felt utterly confused and told him I would try to find out what was happening. I thought, here we go again, another person calling me for something I have no knowledge of or control over – of course I was worried stiff. I tried to call Kate, but she wasn't picking up, so I rang Kirsty who confirmed that Kate had been in trouble the night before. Kirsty had invited Kate and the children to her Essex home, which wasn't far from Carl's. Kate had apparently arrived 'destroyed' after a fight with Carl and had an alleged bruise on her face and cut lip. She told me Kate had been to hospital and the police had been called. Apparently, Kate was now asleep upstairs in Kirsty's bedroom, so Sophie made her way to Kirsty's house, and I drove there later in the morning with Price to find out what exactly had happened.

On arrival, Kirsty showed me a video of Kate looking completely out of it from the night before. She was slurring her words and dressed up as if she was going out clubbing, which I thought was odd – she had Jett and Bunny with her at Carl's home, and partying would have been the last thing on her mind after being allegedly punched by her boyfriend. It just didn't add up, and I was disturbed that Kate had been filmed, seemingly without her knowledge.

Kirsty said that Kate had been attacked by Carl and initially fled to a nearby house where Harvey, who was sound asleep, lived with his carer. As Kirsty only lived about ten minutes or so from Carl's house, she suggested Kate should come to her home and she had given Kate some stuff to calm her down on arrival. Kirsty claimed that Kate went 'haywire' afterwards and began getting ready to go clubbing with the help of one of Kirsty's daughters, using her daughter's clothes. Kirsty said the police had to be called because Kate lost the plot and was running around the house and garden not knowing where she was or what she was doing. Then Kirsty showed me a very disturbing video of her daughter putting make-up on Kate while she was completely out of it. Kate was slurring and trying to get off the bed. I couldn't understand why someone would want to film another person in such a state.

But this wasn't the worst of it. Another video had been made in which Kate was talking to Jett who was just eight and Bunny who was seven in a slurred voice about what they had seen at the house. They said Carl had punched Kate in the face; they were looking up and laughing at whoever had filmed the video as they said it. It was as if they had been prompted to answer in a certain way when Kate asked the questions. When I saw the video, which was on Kirsty's daughter's phone, I told Kirsty I thought it was awful and asked her to delete it. She was placatory, but obviously copies had been made. I kept asking myself why anyone would make a video like this. For what reason? I felt very uneasy about it.

After a while, Kate came downstairs and seemed relatively fine to me. She admitted that Carl had pushed her while trying to grab her phone off her, but she said he didn't hit her. She had put the phone down the front of her trousers in an attempt to keep it from him, but he persisted. So – in order to avoid further confrontation – she ran across the road to Harvey's house with Jett and Bunny, but Carl had followed them there so she got Harvey's carer to take her to Kirsty's house.

I asked Kate if she was aware that Kirsty had taken a video of her and she had no recollection of it. She could remember sitting with Kirsty and having a drink, but nothing more.

Jett and Bunny told me they had been in the video and Kate became worried about what she had been given, and what the children had seen when she was in a comatose state.

Ultimately, Kate refused to press any charges against Carl, but the police still conducted an investigation into the incident at Kirsty's house. Unsurprisingly, Kate fired Kirsty. She was still in contact with Kieran and, at a later stage, began managing him and his partner, Michelle Pentecost. She also became a godparent to their son Apollo.

One result of the police investigation – in which Kirsty and her husband were required to show police the videos she had on her phone – was that Jett and Bunny were placed in the full-time care of their father Kieran and his then-fiancée Michelle. Now Kate had been robbed of the one thing she valued above all else – full responsibility for her children. This was devastating for everyone involved.

Towards the end of May, Kate was allowed supervised contact with Jett and Bunny at my house. She was initially allowed to see her children for an afternoon once a week where possible. When the visits went well, this built up to them staying at mine overnight with Kate as much as possible, until things eventually reverted back to normal with the children back in Kate's full custody.

It was also a worrying time for Princess and Junior, but I reassured Kate that they were coming to an age where they could make their own decisions about their mum and when to see her. No one stopped to think about Harvey and how Kate had continued to love and care for him through her darkest times. Strangely, she was regarded unsafe to look after all her children except him – yet he demanded the most attention, the most monitoring and the most safeguarding with his strict medication regime. Like any grandparent, I had to accept the situation and try my best to support my grandchildren and their mum. It was hard but I had to do it, to put aside my pride, to rise above the stigma attached to the situation and work through it.

Behind closed doors we were coming to terms with a seismic split in our family, while outside the predictable onslaught of negative headlines began to roll off the presses. Kate's bankruptcy, her relationship with Carl, her work – anything and everything were presented as being entirely Kate's fault. Claire had been firmly in Pete's camp ever since the split, and now Kirsty was working for Kieran, so there was a powerful and united front which Kate was struggling to battle against and had no chance of competing with. After that fateful night at home with Carl, when it seemed as if Kate had run from danger into more danger, the world felt like a very unsafe place for her. Deprived of her role as a mum, and fuelled by relentless negative media coverage, it was only a matter of time before her thoughts took her to the darkest places so far in her life.

The next time the jarring notes of my iPhone's ring tone cut into the early morning silence like a knife was September 2021. It was 6:30am, and the usual feeling of dread landed square in the pit of my stomach. Calls this early usually meant one thing: really bad news. I pressed 'accept' and listened in horror as my daughter's shaking voice crackled through the airwaves. 'I'm sorry Mum,' is really all she could say. 'I've had an accident and I'm still alive, but I don't want to be here. Why have I survived?' How had it come to this? Who was this shell of a woman who had once had everything to live for? Kate kept repeating that she was sorry because she had let me down. Apparently, she had accidentally flipped her BMW X5 while under the influence of alcohol and cocaine – but deep down I knew it was no accident. This was proof that Kate's inner world was now propelling her dangerously close to death.

Price leapt out of bed and began to make his way to the accident scene while I hooked myself up to my oxygen supply and sat on the edge of the bed trying to steady my rasping lungs. I knew it would be some time before Price would be able to call me again and my mind began racing. Where had it all gone wrong? How dark had my daughter's world become to risk leaving five children without a mother? My troubling thoughts were interrupted by a call from a lovely, gentle-sounding man called Lee who had been driving down the dark road towards Partridge Green in West Sussex, when he saw Kate's overturned car. He went to take a look and heard Kate crying out for help, so he got her out of the side window of the car as it laid upside down, and cuddled her as she sobbed, telling him she was sorry and that she didn't want to be here. He then helped her into his car and called me with the number she had given him, and we kept talking until the police and her dad arrived.

For the first time in years, Kate had found a decent man. Lee was brilliant to both of us, talking to her to keep her calm while reassuring me she was okay. He just couldn't believe a mum of five wanted to end her life, but he didn't know all of the external circumstances that were affecting Kate. He called the police and ambulance and even later told me that the photograph of Kate's car which ended up in the press the next day was the one taken by the police themselves. Lee proved a rare species because he never spoke to journalists – despite being offered money. We asked him to appear in a documentary Kate later filmed about mental health and he agreed. We still text each other to this day.

The morning of the accident, Dan and Sophie came to my house and we all sat in the conservatory in shock. We instinctively realized the implications of what might have happened to Kate and knew she had been lucky to survive. All three of us sat in silence to begin with, all with our own private thoughts and the collective knowledge that this was literally an accident that had been waiting to happen for years. We realized Kate was in a dark, dark place and put out a statement asking the press to please give us space.

Unbelievably, when Carl was told about the accident, he seemed more concerned about what had happened the night before, rather than how she was doing now. I was gobsmacked and told him I had nearly lost my daughter, while Dan and Sophie had almost lost their sister – and was that really what he was most concerned about? We told him to leave us alone and give us space. Dan told him in no uncertain terms, 'This isn't the time to talk about that.' It was clear that Carl's first concern was Carl, and Kate's welfare – even after her brush with death – was not high on his list of priorities. I decided there and then that such an attitude was not going to be welcomed by the family, and Carl left.

Meanwhile, Price was giving us regular updates. He stayed with Kate directly after the accident and followed the ambulance, which took her to hospital for a check-up. After that, the police put her in a cell where she stayed overnight before appearing in court. She was let out on bail and Sophie made arrangements for her to go directly to The Priory. Price took her straight there. He said he thought it looked like a hotel, where you book in at reception, sit and wait and then have your belongings taken to a bedroom. Whatever the arrangements, Price now had to say goodbye and leave her alone to sort out her demons.

I think I was at my lowest ebb that day. I cried a lot, yet I still felt numb. I feared this day would one day come, after all the years of failed relationships, betrayals by friends, duplicitous managers, and the painful loneliness she had experienced all her life. It had all come to a head. I felt for her because I knew the only happiness she really had in life was linked to her children, her horses, and us as a family. At the time she wasn't riding which was always therapeutic for her, and with her children gone – even with the strong family network backing her – she had been unable to stop herself from making a serious attempt on her own life. We knew she had suffered from depression for a long time, but to reach this depth was so, so sad.

I cast my mind back to Kate as a little girl, the one that

liked nature and simply wanted to be loved. Where had she gone? A million thoughts raced through my brain. Did I do the right thing splitting up with her dad? I wasn't happy but should I have stayed with him and given up my happiness for the sake of my children, or even waited until they were older and left when they were teenagers? But that would have meant raising them in an unhappy house. Then there was the episode in the park. I don't think I realized at the time how badly it had affected her. She should have had counselling, but it just wasn't widely available back then. Did we naively think she was so young she would just have forgotten it? And what about the paedophile photographer? Should I have insisted on being in the room with my daughter rather than drinking tea next door? On and on the thought processes went, eventually taking me back to Ray. I genuinely wish I could have helped to create more of a bond between them. Ray is not an unreasonable man so why didn't he see her more often and how has that felt for her? What more could I have done? I honestly don't know. I had left them to see each other without me interfering. I listened to the concerns of friends and managers about Kate, and, as her mum, I tried everything I could think of, but her attempt to end her life in that car accident proved I did not do enough.

I wish I could have spotted the patterns earlier in Kate's life and helped her think about the way she has allowed herself to be controlled by husbands, boyfriends and managers – always for their own benefit. Of course, they would argue they were trying to get the best out of Kate, to make money for Kate, but in reality, it also lined their pockets. In the early days, I was naive and listened to their points of view too much. I felt annoyed at Kate when she seemed to do the opposite of what they wanted and when she spurted things out in interviews as though she had no filter. I had been influenced by the way that I had been brought up, to gain approval by conforming to the expectations of others, and I wanted her to be a 'good girl' and do what other people were telling her. At times she has behaved badly and has told me lies to cover things up. She is to blame for some of her behaviour and its results. But she has never truly understood herself or why she acts the way she does. When I have looked back at my younger self, I have seen how Kate's behaviour has reflected my own life and how so much of her behaviour has been about trying to break free from control.

Instead of me texting her at night, begging her to be good and listen to people, I should have realized she was mentally unwell. Instead of thinking she was being destructive, obstructive and not taking advice, I should have tried to understand her behaviour more. She was reaching out, but I didn't listen carefully enough. When she used to say, 'Mum, I want you to be my mum, and not interfere or listen to my managers. Be there for me not them', I should have heeded her plea. By going through me, people knew they could manipulate my daughter. While there were times that I could see I was being used as a pawn in her life – like with Kirsty – there were other times – like with Claire – that I hadn't realized this was happening. At times, I was totally played. We all were.

Our whole family should have stopped lecturing Kate a long time ago and really paused to consider why she was behaving that way, what she was doing it for, what was she really trying to tell us with her actions that she couldn't say in words? From the very beginning at school, it felt like Kate was a round peg being forced into a square hole. I now believe there is a reason she has a different mind to others in our family – it's not a worse mind or a bad mind, just a different one. It causes her pain and I want her to be able to understand why, so we are finally taking steps to seek out the right expert clinicians who can give her a full assessment. For too long, she has been trying to help herself through self-medicating and that can't go on. She has also tried to make amends after difficult episodes by buying expensive presents for people; spoiling them one minute to show her appreciation and then being totally awful to them the next. The stress has broken relationships because not even her husbands have understood, had the capacity to understand her, or even wanted to try. The ultimatums, the control, the upsets – Kate has had a rough ride from people at times, me included. I hate the thought of that. It hurts.

Kate has moved from relationship to relationship through-out her life, and I think that her desire to find the perfect family environment for Harvey has at least partially motivated the enormous pressure Kate has felt to do this. She desper-ately wanted that loving relationship to bring her son up in, but she has never found it. Instead, she had to face raising Harvey alone. In many ways, I think she has seen herself in Harvey – someone who is vulnerable and often pursued by bullies from every walk of life.

As this book was poised to be published in April 2023, eight serving and former Metropolitan Police officers were found guilty of gross misconduct after sharing 'toxic and abhorrent' discriminatory messages in a WhatsApp group, including frequently making fun of Harvey. Six officers involved had already left the Met and the remaining two were facing the sack over the 'Secret Squirrel Shit' group, which also contained racist, sexist, homophobic and transphobic messages. A disciplinary panel heard that between 2016 and 2018 the officers, who were attached to a safer neighbourhood team based in Bexley, southeast London, used the group to make discriminatory slurs and share derogatory comments.

The officers involved were former Sergeant Luke Thomas, former Acting Sergeant Luke Allen, former PC Kelsey Buchan, former PC Carlo Francisco, former PC Lee South, former PC Darren Jenner, PC Glynn Rees and Officer B, who has been granted anonymity. The disciplinary panel said that Thomas, the most senior officer in the group, should have shut it down but instead became one of the most active participants, mocking Harvey's weight. Meanwhile, Rees described an image of Harvey riding a child's train as 'genius', which the panel found to be 'obviously sarcastic' and 'making fun of him behaving in a childlike manner because of his disability'. Allen, who resigned in January and said he felt 'ashamed' of his comments, posted a photograph of himself in the chat attempting to imitate Harvey, with the caption: 'Hello you c***'.

As a family, we were sickened by this. The very people who were supposedly trained to serve and protect our society were using Harvey as a receptacle for their own pathologies. We have seen the best and worst of humanity through the lens of Harvey's disability and this episode certainly plunged us into a new low, revealing just how hostile the world can be for people who are different. On top of her profound love for her first-born son, this type of behaviour has meant Kate has had to fight for Harvey ferociously over the last two decades.

So much of her energy has been channelled into protecting him and getting people to accept him despite his differences. Kate has challenged and shamed online trolls and cowardly comedians. She has been nominated for National Television Awards twice and she has been relentless in her pursuit of Harvey's Law – now parliament has accepted that legislation is not satisfactory in its approach to the online abuse of disability. I look at mainstream programmes now, like *Strictly Come Dancing*, and notice how people with disabilities are more widely included. I am immensely proud of Kate and Harvey as I think they have played their own part in making this happen.

Harvey is on my mind now more than ever. Kate does a terrific job, but of course it has occurred to me what might happen if I or his mum isn't around. There is no man or father to step forward, unless Dwight eventually does. Never say never; I like to think there will be a reunion one day but I don't think I'll be around to know about it. If Kate is no longer able to take care of Harvey, Sophie will be given power of attorney to ensure he has a good life, a happy life and a family life. Harvey will never be forgotten by any of our family – ever. We all love him deeply and will be there for him one hundred per cent. None of Kate's exes who claimed they loved him have ever come forward to claim any responsibility, so their names are not there on any paperwork or legal documents, nothing. It's Kate then Sophie.

I need to know that he will always have a good quality of life – not to be shut away and forgotten but continually loved and looked after. I know Sophie will fulfil this role for Harvey with love and dedication. He will also have Uncle Dan the back-up man and Grandad Price by his side.

Kate's other children have their fathers, of course, but seeing Kate unwell and being taken into The Priory was worrying for all of them. I feel that Jett and Bunny have witnessed and know far too much about adults' lives for their age, and are only now beginning to feel happy again in the comfort that they may soon be able to see both their mum and dad, as they've been living in the sole custody of Kate since November 2022. The events with both Carl and Kirsty should never have happened. To my mind, both events were equally shocking for the children and it will take time for them to heal. They must have felt so worried being separated from Kate in the immediate aftermath of the incident with Carl and Kirsty, and then again when she went to The Priory after the crash.

Junior and Princess also feel their mother's ups and downs very keenly. They have both seen her at her best and at her worst and know she has mental health problems, which is a lot for them to cope with. The first time Kate was in The Priory she was visited by them both. But the second time, they didn't come. Princess made it clear she wanted to see her mum, but Junior was unsure, and I worried that he was being influenced by other people in his life. As Kate's mum, I found it hard to stomach. I would have hoped that everyone might have understood that part of what Kate desperately wanted to do was to say sorry to her children for what she had put them through and assure them she was trying to put her life together. It felt important, not only for the children, but for Kate's mental health too. In the end, Kate did not receive a visit from her eldest children while in hospital and, while it was no fault of theirs, she struggled to come to terms with this.

Throughout her life, Kate has met a million different people but sadly – in my view – few of them have been able to offer her the true love and compassion she needs. In the end, we her family are her only true support system. We continued to offer her love while she was in The Priory, even though she attempted suicide again while she was there by trying to slash her wrists with a pair of scissors. How she got hold of them we just don't know. It was another cry for help, another near miss. The nurse on charge found Kate. She wasn't seriously cut, but her actions raised the levels of treatment and monitoring. Thankfully, suicide is a topic that is now being discussed more openly in our society, and as a family, we have tried to open a dialogue and keep it going.

Kate stayed in The Priory for a month in September 2021. She came out more relaxed and happier than we had seen her in a long time, even though she knew it would be a long road back to normality. She was shown how to deal with things one at a time as part of a therapy called Dialectical Behavioural Therapy (DBT). Its basic principles help develop healthier thought patterns and strategies for regulating emotions. Since then, she has seen a therapist regularly via Zoom and in person to help maintain her mental health. She is also being assessed for ADHD.

In December 2021, Kate was given a 16-week prison

sentence, suspended for a year, after pleading guilty to drink driving. Magistrates said they were unable to send her to prison as she had completed a stay at The Priory, having agreed to attend the rehab centre on her first court appearance. She had been given a chance to rebuild her life and Price, Dan, Sophie and I knew she would need our help to do it. We pledged to be there for her as a family more than ever before. So ever since, Sophie and Dan have been there to give Kate advice on work and help with enquiries from the press, but first and foremost, they are her brother and sister, and that will always come before anything else. Dan is also back assisting with Kate's financial affairs. And me, I am concentrating on taking care of my daughter.

Our family Christmas in 2021 could have been my last, so we all got together for presents and lunch. As I celebrated with my children and grandchildren, it hit me that Kate might not have been there and I felt so very grateful that we were both still there, still together, fighting on. We all loved being together that day, savouring Harry's roast, opening presents, playing games and watching TV. We were also lucky to have Albert with us for his first festive season, and Kate enjoyed cuddling him and feeding him just like she had done with his mum all those years ago. I just sat there watching everyone, thinking: all these children came from my belly. They are all different in their own ways, but I helped to make them all. How wonderful is that? I am so proud of them all.

Chapter 16

SOME JOY AT LAST

Kate started New Year 2022 on good form, which was a relief to us all. Her therapy was helping her to adopt a new mindset, even though she was still in a relationship with Carl. She was using strategies learned through the DBT treatment implemented by The Priory and, overall, she seemed calmer and less prone to impulsivity. She answered the phone when we called her and when she felt things were getting too much, she was able to reach out for help, seeking support from the therapist who seemed to be keeping her on an even keel. She was back to enjoying normal family time with us and her children and returned regularly to the great love of her life – horse riding. Because she had been so busy and otherwise occupied, for a while Kate had let her horses out on loan. That had been a mistake as riding had always been good for her mental health. Kate's business affairs were also looking hopeful again with Dan back in charge and Sophie dealing with media issues.

This new sense of self-confidence led to Kate's decision to launch her own OnlyFans channel in January. She had been watching the online platform and app with interest since its creation in 2016 and saw how new glamour models were able to control their own content and capitalize on it through the monthly subscription revenues. Content is mainly created by YouTubers, fitness trainers, model and public figures in order to monetize their profession, but it is popular with adult content creators too. Kate believed there was still sufficient interest in her images to give it a try and with her usual chutzpah she launched her channel dressed in a nun's habit complete with a sash which read My Body My Rules. She told the waiting press, 'I see my OnlyFans channel as a place I can feel secure, confident, empowered and beautiful,' but behind the scenes we saw a different reality playing out.

Carl had denigrated her new business idea and insulted her. It was simply a repeat of a pattern that had played out over and over again. In the past, these types of cruel remarks made in anger had undoubtedly fuelled Kate's addiction to surgery – I was very concerned about what it would trigger this time. Would her therapist be able to hold things steady? Could she find the strength to finally go it alone? I could only hope.

Meanwhile, this partner who had vowed he had no interest in capitalizing on Kate's fame was in the process of using his association with her to set up his own OnlyFans platform, giving subscribers all-round access to his life. Talk about double standards. I was gobsmacked when I heard this and asked myself why she was still with this man. How could she love someone who put her through all this? Her fear of rejection and desperation to be loved were clearly still stronger than her capacity to love herself and we all felt sad about that. But this time we vowed to stay alongside her, listening rather than shouting. I am not happy with the relationship between

Carl and Kate. Price and I both believe it is wrong. We don't argue with Kate over this; it's her choice, but she understands our viewpoint. I have no respect for Carl, and both Price and I have made a stand – since the car crash, I haven't seen Carl, and he knows and accepts that he is not welcome in our home. There's no argument, and no discussion. Like any mother, I would of course love to have a good relationship with my daughter's chosen partner, but in this case, I have to stand by what I believe in, and I believe that Carl knows and accepts this. All I want is for Kate to be happy.

I think Kate is often misunderstood because of the continued persecution she received after the failure of her marriage to Pete. She was compared to Myra Hindley for this. Any rational human being will be able to see how foolish and unfounded this ill-judged comparison is. Such a malicious idea can surely have only been prompted by the greed of the management, journalists, and men in her life who have just wished to exploit her name to line their own pockets. Attempts to make her look evil in the eyes of the public have continued to this day. Just like the rest of us, Kate has her faults and she is the first to admit that. No one is perfect, not even her exes though the perception is that they think they are. She is beautiful – much better without make-up – courageous, impulsive, funny, loving and bold. She wants to make a living for herself and her family and she tries very hard to do this. No one could ever accuse Kate of being lazy, a freeloader, or not being a trier.

I'm going to be perfectly honest here – the truth and not paper talk – people need to analyse who is really causing the problems you read about constantly. Kate doesn't deserve the way she is portrayed. Her exes and hangers-on drag up these stories, many of which seemed to have been made up by the sources – but invariably their management need to use Kate's name and their association with her rather than any achievements of their own to stir up interest and rake in the money for themselves. There seems to be no consideration at all for Kate's side of the story, or any consideration of the feelings of her and her children. I hope this book will have helped to show the situation as it really is. The reality is that many of Kate's exes are still tied to Kate, whether they like it or not. The media will forever refer to them as the ex-boyfriend or ex-husband of Katie Price, rather than the other way around.

Sadly, my health deteriorated in the first part of the year and while I still held out some hope for a miracle in the form of a transplant, part of me was coming to terms with the fact that 2022 might well be my last year. I was given an end-of-life care package by the local hospice and was trying to live each day with as much gratitude as possible, spending time with the family at weekends and going on occasional trips with Price in our motorhome. We made memories together throughout the year, visiting some of our favourite places including Devon, Dorset and the Cotswolds. We had just returned from one of these mini-breaks in April when we received a call which brought us some much-needed joy at last.

Sophie and Harry had been together for 12 years. We knew they would eventually get married but they had been prioritizing their new baby Albert and saving for a bigger house so I was reconciled to the sad but salient fact that I may never see them become man and wife. So, you can imagine my delight when a call came through from Harry while I was in the car with Price saying that, because both me and his nan were ill, they had decided to bring the wedding forward so we could both share their happy day. He was asking Price for Sophie's hand in marriage, and I could hear the emotion in his voice as he spoke of his love for our daughter. Both Price and I yelled, 'Yes, of course. It's about time'. Soon after, he proposed to Sophie around a fire pit at a log cabin in Braintree, Essex, and presented her with a beautiful square-cut emerald ring which had belonged to his grandmother. Sophie was ecstatic and immediately asked me to help her start planning a wedding for June. I felt so privileged to be involved in this life event which I never thought I would witness, and it really bucked me up. I could feel the excitement in my belly as we started to look at venues and dresses together. Some families start planning a wedding years in advance and here we were planning one in eight weeks.

Of course, news of the wedding date eventually leaked and the media spun a negative story, writing that we chose it in case Kate had to go to prison for breaching a restraining order against her ex-husband Kieran's new partner Michelle Pentecost. She had got into an altercation with Michelle and another person in the playground at their children's school in 2019; some three years later, in an angry moment, Kate sent Kieran a message asking him to stop Michelle provoking her on social media, but in stronger words. Her hearing was set for 24th June, the day after the wedding, but the reality was that Sophie chose her day to accommodate the deteriorating health of two matriarchs in the family – not another difficult wobble in Kate's life. By now I'd become almost immune to this kind of nonsense and barely gave it a second thought as we continued to excitedly plan the nuptials.

We heard about a beautiful place in Findon called Cissbury Barns and Sophie, Harry, Harry's mum Lisa, Price and I instantly fell in love with it on our first visit. We immediately saw the advantage of the privacy it afforded in the middle of the countryside and felt it was peaceful – an atmosphere the Price clan now craved after so many years living in the noise and glare of the spotlight. Now we had the venue sorted, we could concentrate on Sophie's dress. She shunned big labels and instead chose a fabulous dressmaker called Velvet Birdcage who fashioned a stunningly simple scoop neck crepe gown. The bridesmaids and flower girls were free to select their own designs as long as the colour was navy. They settled on stylishly simple designs with the youngest bridesmaids' outfits being bought at another shop. Kate took on the role of chief bridesmaid alongside two of Sophie's closest friends, and Harry's sisters and niece. She selected a navy off-the-shoulder creation which was plain and covered her boobs – exactly as she wanted. It was a far cry from some of the more lavish creations she had worn to her own weddings, and I think it suited her beautifully. We were all so excited going for the fittings and would listen to the wedding music in the car to and from the bridal boutique, singing along together.

It felt like Kate was our Kate again and I loved the fact that Sophie had given her this prominent role. Dan's wedding 20 years earlier had been a joyful occasion but also painful for me because Sophie was asked to be a bridesmaid, but Kate was not. She remained gracefully silent about the matter, but I knew she felt the rejection deeply. After all, she was Dan's sister too. Somehow, she rose above it and excitedly drove Dan to the ceremony in her Range Rover which she had adorned with white bows on the handles. Just like she had driven him back home to Lou from university when he was feeling home-sick so many years earlier, here she was taking him to the love of his life once again. After the wedding, we all moved on to the reception and Kate wondered whether she could get up and sing a song for Dan and Lou. It's just something Kate always does, and we all go, 'Here she goes again'. But this time she didn't sing and I could see she felt sad and unnoticed. She went to bed early. I don't know if she had been told not to sing or just decided it wasn't appropriate, but I felt the need to go and comfort her. As usual, she wouldn't tell me what was wrong and I tried to console her until eventually she went to sleep. Only Dan and Lou know the reasons Kate was not given the same status as Sophie at these celebrations, but I think it only served to reinforce Kate's sense of being different in the family and her anxieties around that.

I think Kate still felt some concern about what her pres-ence might stir up at Sophie's wedding and was keen to let her sister know she would remain in the background. She told her the day was all about her and Harry. Sophie just told her not to be silly and enjoy herself. Sophie is a laid-back person and this was reflected in her wedding plans which felt free and easy. We all had fun sampling the eclectic buffet menu, which included Moroccan lamb koftas, falafel wraps, tandoori prawns and Greek salads. Dan's vintage VW campervan was selected as the wedding car – he attached white ribbons and even bought water and Champagne to stock the fridge for the bride and groom.

Price also had a chance to prepare for a wedding in which he genuinely loved and respected the groom. He had suit fittings with Harry and used to come home brimming with excitement. It also meant he could actually prepare a speech from the heart, and it contained some very moving lines – he said he was very proud of Sophie's beautiful personality and achievements and also Harry, who he has seen grow from a boy into a man. He wanted to mention how Harry has supported us, even though his nickname for me is 'String' as in string vest – the Cockney rhyming slang for pest. This is because I always ask him to do things when he visits us, like fixing the TV or helping with the computer or phone.

All the grandchildren were excited too and the night before the wedding, Sophie, Kate and Princess stayed over at our house. On strict instructions from Sophie, we had to watch *Father of the Bride 2*, having watched *Father of the Bride* the previous night. We were all huddled together on my bed, and it just felt wonderful. In the morning, Jett, Bunny, Harvey and Junior arrived and Sophie brought me my usual cup of coffee with two digestive biscuits to help me take the first medicines of the day. Then we had to get up and start getting ready. Having my girls and grandchildren with me and feeling so happy and carefree was magical – these memories will remain some of the happiest of my life. Sophie and I would sing and cry, and Kate would turn to us and say, 'What is wrong with you two?' The sun was shining, and it was the perfect start to the perfect day. It was truly wonderful.

Then, Kate helped Sophie into her dress. It was one of the happiest and most emotional moments of my life seeing my girls together like this. The sun was shining and the weather seemed to be a metaphor for what was now possible in our family – joy at last. Only Price looked a tad nervous with the speech tucked in the top pocket of his dapper-looking suit. I don't know why he felt worried – he'd already had plenty of practice at Kate's hat-trick of weddings. A couple of days before, while typing up the speech for him, in between each paragraph I had added the prompt 'Breathe and count slowly one-two-three' so he wouldn't rush through it. I just had to keep my fingers crossed he wouldn't read that bit out.

We were almost ready to go when the cameraman who had filmed Kate's *Mucky Mansion* series and her documentary *Trauma and Me* faithfully arrived with his equipment and began to capture some precious family moments. He had made us all cry so many times while making those programmes, so I had cheekily asked him if he would film Sophie's wedding as payback – to my surprise he had agreed. We were so grateful for this – he is great at what he does and very unintrusive. Articles emerged saying that Kate was capitalizing on her sister's wedding by filming for her show, but this just wasn't true. It was filmed just for Sophie and Harry.

I couldn't believe the day had finally come, and that I was alive to see it. I had been really ill with chest infections a couple of weeks previously and had lost more lung capacity so, at one stage, I thought I would be too ill to attend. But

I was determined to make it and had my wheelchair and a good supply of oxygen waiting in the wings in case I needed back up. Sadly, Harry's nan wasn't so fortunate and ended up having to stay at home. Carl had also been told by Sophie and Harry that he wasn't invited and gracefully accepted their wishes.

Throughout the morning, Kate had been great at organizing everyone – I was so proud that she was there, calm and on form as she sorted her children out. She was so excited for Sophie and understood how much it meant for her to marry Harry. She was the best sister Sophie could have wished for and it was emotional to see them so happy together. Kate was determined to keep in the background but Sophie didn't want that at all and told her so. After the year Kate had experienced, to see her in such good spirits and so happy meant everything to Sophie and indeed to all of us.

Sophie and I eventually climbed into the back of Dan's bright red VW campervan to travel to the wedding, while Price sat with Dan in the front. I would describe it as one of the most emotional journeys of my life. Sophie looked so radiant and beautiful and we held hands and looked into one another's eyes; in that moment I think we were each sending an unspoken message about the love we have for one another, which transcends life itself. In the end, we had to tell each other not to cry. It was so special to me and a moment I will never forget. Even the waiting press couldn't spoil it. In a way that felt so liberating, I simply told Sophie, 'Forget about them. Just wave,' and we carried on.

Arriving at the venue, I reflected on how different this felt to my own first wedding to Ray, which my mum had organized with very little input from the bride or groom. We hadn't had a chance to live together before getting married, and we were so young. We were like so many couples of our time – naive and hopeful that we would be married forever. My marriage to Ray lasted 13 years in the end, so we had a good pop at it, but we outgrew one other and I was so lucky to find the love of my life in Price. Sophie's arrival in a more modern age meant she'd had a much better chance of knowing what she really wanted from a man and a marriage; I was confident she had made the right choice and was excited to see her walk down the aisle.

I could feel my spine tingling as Audrey Hepburn's velvety voice crackled to life through the loudspeakers and the silky tones of 'Moon River' began washing over the congregation, moving many to tears. I turned my head to see my youngest daughter as I'd never seen her before. Looking radiant in her stunningly simple dress, she began to take slow, careful steps down the aisle holding her dad tight. For the first time since Dan's wedding to Louise 20 years ago, we were witnessing an event where true love was the star – not the headline or cover photo. The venue, outfits, flowers and food were all what the bride and groom wanted, not a magazine-sponsored circus (Sophie had been offered a deal but declined). We were at a wedding that really meant something to us all, a wedding where no one had to replay a poignant moment for a reality TV crew, and where no one had to worry about the groom's motives. This was such a landmark for me because it demonstrated that my family was still capable of something beautifully ordinary.

Throughout the ceremony, I could see Kate and the brides-maids sitting alongside me on the pew and I thought how pretty and happy they all looked together. Most special of all was seeing Harvey – as usual right next to Kate – with his iPad in hand recording Sophie and Harry exchanging their vows. At that moment, Princess took one of my hands in hers while Price held the other. For better or worse, I thought to myself, this is *my* family, my beautiful, crazy, imperfect family and I love them all. And when the priest declared Harry and Sophie man and wife, she was trumped by our amazing Harvey who chirped up, 'Well done!'. Everyone laughed – it was a perfect comment and so brilliantly timed.

From the moment Sophie and I first started discussing the wedding, I had a plan in mind for Harry. He is such a family-orientated man and can get very emotional, especially when music is played. We always rely on him to do a playlist for our dinner parties and share music on Spotify too. Harry once bought me a portable record player for Christmas and knows all about my old collection of LPs, including some Beatles albums and 45s from when I was a teenager. Recently, I played one of the LPs for the first time in years and heard the familiar crackle and the scratches I had made on certain tracks from playing them over and over, including my favourite *Tamla Motown Hits*. I cried as all the memories came flooding back. I've made it clear I want Harry to have my record collection when I die because I know he will appreciate it and look after it. But the wedding was Harry's music moment and so I thought, I'm going to surprise you Harold. I arranged for bagpipes to be played outside the church on guests' arrival and departure as a tribute to his Scottish granddad who had passed away. I also invited the London Gospel Choir to sing and join in with the hymns and songs – they sat unknown among the audience. As soon as Sophie and Harry had walked down the aisle, they rose from their seats, jumping up and singing the Marvin Gaye and Tammi Terrell version of the song 'Ain't No Mountain High Enough'. The rest of the congregation joined in, singing and clapping, and I could tell that Sophie and Harry were thrilled. It made me feel all tingly inside and the hairs on my arms stood up. It felt as if the church had come alive with these rousing notes as the sun streamed in through the leaded windows. It was all just meant to be.

Guests ate and danced through the afternoon and into the evening to the chilled tones of French jazz café music sung live by a French duo, and Junior sang his new song 'Slide', later teaching the words to Bunny. I'm usually in bed by 8pm but I didn't want such a perfect day to end so I stayed up late. I had brought these children into the world and held their hands long enough to give them wings to fly. As a young girl, I sometimes sensed I was allowed to take off too soon without supervision. At other times, with so much hope invested in my chances of swimming glory, I felt my wings were clipped. I have tried to find a balance for my own children and always thought I would live long enough to see if I got it right. Sophie and Dan seem to have taken flight in the right direction, while Kate is still in search of a safe place in the world, but she is edging closer to better places. Sophie's wedding showed me that when we come together as a family, away from the superficial world of fame, we get it right. It was a special moment in time when we felt complete happiness, with no stress for anyone. In my memory, it is frozen in time and will sustain me through the last chapter of my life. And if I die tomorrow, I know I'll die happy in the knowledge that I experienced that very real and happy wedding.

We were all still buzzing throughout the following week and also relieved when we heard the news that Kate had avoided a jail sentence for breaching her restraining order against Michelle Pentecost when she attended court the following day. Judge Stephen Mooney rightly disciplined Kate, but also seemed to understand her. He concluded that the offence was committed in anger and added, 'In my judgement, balancing the aggravating and mitigating factors, the appropriate sentence is a medium-level community order'. Kate's own solicitor told the court quite accurately that his client '. . . has two different personalities. The public one, and the vulnerable one of being in the public eye every day no matter what she does. It's a case of building someone up only to knock them down'. Kate received an 18-month community order to carry out 150 hours of unpaid work with an additional 20 hours for breach of a suspended sentence for driving matters.

After the long, hot and happy summer of 2022, I was left to face the reality of my declining health. The medical trials I was engaged with had ceased as I was no longer well enough to go on them. I fought tooth and nail to be kept on the active transplant list but, having turned 70 in October, I fear I shall be taken off it shortly. I have deteriorated I know, but I desperately hold on to a glimmer of hope that the call will come. During one memorable trip to Cromer in September,

Price and I were in our van when we received word from my co-writer Sharon Hendry that a very eminent heart and lung doctor – who is a friend of hers – had agreed to speak to me. Professor Sir Magdi Yacoub just happens to be the person who performed the first combined heart and lung transplant in the UK back in 1983 and whose portrait I see hanging in Harefield Heart and Lung Hospital every time I visit. He had heard about my plight through Sharon and his daughter Lisa, an education and healthcare education charity manager, who is also a close friend of hers. Words cannot express what I felt when I heard that a man of such eminence was taking the trouble to think of me, and I was shaking with emotion when I took the call. Tears were streaming down my face while Price looked on, imploring me to pull myself together.

There have been many memorable phone calls in my life but this one stands out as one that was truly remarkable. Professor Yacoub told me he totally agreed with Professor Dunning, whose care I was under at Harefield Hospital. He said I was an ideal candidate for transplant and still healthy enough. I said I was concerned I was now too old, but he told me that as long as I kept myself fit and healthy, and my muscles were still working, there should be no reason why age should come into it. He reaffirmed what Professor Dunning had told me, that one lung should suffice. Professor Yacoub also explained that if I was lucky enough to get a transplant it would make such a difference to my life. Even if the dice does not roll in my favour, I will die in the knowledge that I was shown such incredible care and compassion by a truly great yet humble man.

Since becoming ill, I have reflected on transplantation a

great deal. If I were to live due to a transplant, the reality is that somewhere else a family is coming to terms with the fact that their loved one has died. A momentous act of selflessness has taken place by the donor and their family – a decision has been made to give the gift of life. The law now states that all adults in England are considered to be an organ donor when they die, unless they have chosen to opt out. I and many others are at the mercy of people who willingly donate their organs and how fortunate we are that there are such people in the world. But even if I get that call in time, there may be someone else who has received it too. We would both get prepared for the operation and the person with the better organ match would get the organ. The other would have to deal with the disappointment and hope that one day there will be another call before it is too late.

At times it's felt unbearable living on this knife edge each day and I could not have done it without Price by my side. We've had our challenges, but I wouldn't change my husband for the world. He's been there when it has mattered the most – in sickness and in health, encouraging me to get up in the mornings, to do my exercises, and bringing me a cup of coffee in bed so I can take my tablets. In the medical meetings, it's the opposite to how things are between us normally. He listens and always tries to come away with something positive, whereas I hear the reality which is sadly negative. We haven't yet reached the point when we've had a good cry together, although we've been on the brink a few times and Price is clearly in so much pain he has to turn his head away and deflect by saying he has to make a phone call. In very tough moments, he leaves the room and goes quiet, re-emerging to ask, 'Do you want a cup of tea?' A typical British man I suppose.

Sometimes – my favourite times – we just sit on the beach or take the dog for a walk. Price likes to explore, to go off the beaten track, and I always say, 'I'm not bloody following you because you always get lost', but I follow him anyway. Now, he always makes sure I've got enough oxygen in my cylinders, and we set off for a walk with him telling me, 'Come on, you can do this; you've got to do this'. I am not able to walk very far, so Price pushes me in my wheelchair when I have to admit I am too tired. When he pushes me past shops (he hates shopping) I have to say, 'Stop! I want to look'. He aways comes to a halt and usually spoils me by buying the thing I've seen, perhaps something for the house or a lovely item of clothing. Always by my side, always making me believe it's possible – that's Price.

I am prepared for the end because I know it is going to happen. I wait every day for a sign that I am more unwell – I check my oxygen levels and my temperature. I check in with the hospice nurses and take their advice. I want to die at home, not in a hospital or a hospice, and I don't want to be resuscitated. I see no point. I wonder if, on my last day, I will be doing something ordinary like making a sandwich or doing a spot of gardening. Perhaps I will be sitting in my chair in the conservatory watching a film on the TV. Or sitting in the garden. I would simply like to go to sleep and never wake up – the sort of peaceful ending many of us hope for.

It's daunting facing death. I know we must all do it, but I've reached the stage when I can no longer dismiss it as something on a far-off horizon. Every day when I wake up my first thought is, I am still here. This is a bonus day. I have come to terms with the illness; I have had no choice. I try to keep things as normal as possible. There are good days and there are bad ones. Some days I feel so tired I don't have the energy to do anything, yet on other days I forget myself and overdo things. Although I don't mention it to them, I look at my family and wonder if this will be the last time I will see them. I try to protect them and make memories for them to preserve. I also have to prepare Price for the inevitable and encourage him to get ready to put things in order and take over from me. I have bought bulbs and plants for the garden ready to bloom in the spring, knowing I might not be here to see them. They will be resplendent with all the colours we both like, so when he looks at them he will think of us buying them together and he will remember me and how he asked for instructions on how to keep the garden looking good; it has been special for both of us. There will be a tomorrow and maybe I'll be there but, if not, someone will have to be at the helm as further exploits of the Price family continue to unfold.

Chapter 17

FINAL REFLECTIONS

I have often thought about my family and the history that goes with it. 'Normal' is a word that certainly does not apply to my lineage. I often look at my children and my grandchildren, sometimes with a smile and sometimes with a shake of the head, but so often it fascinates me as I see in them characteristics of past generations. When I look back at my roots, I see a lot of interesting people and very few boring ones. It would be such a shame if the tales I have been told were forgotten. From an early age, I have been impacted and influenced by events and happenings, and I have often spoken with the family about these episodes. I thought it would be good to create a written record of the legacy – the family pedigree if you like – though I still have many more tales to tell!

There is a spirit of independence, determination and enterprise that has been inherited by each of my children. Kate's entrepreneurial streak is well acclaimed. Dan has a very competent business head on him, and Sophie has carved a path that has given her the financial platform to achieve academic success. Junior is following his mum and dad as he sets out on a musical and acting career, and I don't think it will be long before Princess makes her mark in showbusiness. Sport is another gift that runs through our family. Dan has his dad and stepfather's footballing abilities (Price played for Brighton and had trials for Aston Villa) and his daughter Amalie is already showing talent with a ball at her feet: watch this space! Swimming has figured prominently for all my kids – they've all competed for their schools in swimming teams, and now Amalie is doing the same. Running has also played a strong role, with Kate and Dan both completing marathons, and Sophie has also proved herself to be a talented javelin thrower. I hope that future generations will be able to look back and trace the origins of their individual personalities and talents.

As well as providing a record, this book also has a purpose. When I received the diagnosis of IPF and my impending demise, it prompted me to turn thought into action and set pen to paper. As well as providing a history of my family, I hope that the book will draw attention to an awful disease which doesn't seem to have the necessary publicity or funding for research to combat its terrible effects.

Writing this book has made me question myself as a mother, a wife, a daughter, a grandmother – in short it has helped me discover who I really am. I have a strong sense of what is right and what is wrong and, even if it has not always been popular, I have always done what I felt was right ... but were my choices always the correct ones? Have I always done right for my children and husband? The decisions that seemed right at the time might, on reflection, not have been so. I listened to other people's opinions but did not act on them if I felt they were misconceived. Looking back, I have been wondering if perhaps it was me who was in the wrong. Writing the book has prompted me to talk over things with my children and my husband. It has been very reassuring to hear from my children that they always come to me if they need advice, and they tell me that I'm right most of the time – most, but not all the time.

Price and I have had some deep conversations and I feel I have developed a deeper understanding of him and learned things about him that I never knew before. Recently I bought a print by René Magritte – *The Lovers II* (1928). The picture is of a man and a woman kissing each other, but their heads are covered with veils. This reminds me of Price and me. You can kiss someone, but underneath do you really know them? After 38 years together, and after writing this book, I think I finally do know him. Writing the book has also helped Price and me talk about our marriage. Whenever tensions have occurred, it has usually been when we have struggled for money. But as we look back on those times, we realize that so often something positive emerged from the situation. When you struggle together to survive, it makes you appreciate things further down the line.

I've also come to admit that sometimes I have treated my husband as second fiddle to my children, especially with my commitment to Kate and supporting her and Harvey, although I do always believe that children should be the first priority. I thought Price would pootle along and just be there, and I have taken him for granted. When I was studying way back, he would support me, making the dinner and helping with the children – and he has done the same again as I have been writing this book. The book has given us both a deeper understanding of our relationship and we are very close. I'm lucky to have him and he is lucky to have me. It has confirmed that we do love each other through thick and thin.

I've chatted with Dan about his younger days and how he's always been a support in times of need. I've been able to talk about and admire his strong work ethic and how his labours have been a reassurance when we have struggled to keep a roof over our heads. I've been able to say how grateful I was when he supported us financially during the last recession, even helping us one month to pay the mortgage because we couldn't afford it. Dan has always been incredibly generous and, even when he was a student, he used to let us use his Asda discount voucher. We couldn't help smiling together when we remembered how I used to read his student assignments and scribble on them 'Why?... When?... How?... Where?' How things have changed – as I have been writing this book, Dan has done the same to me.

Conversations with Kate were cathartic. As we've sat together and gone over her life and dug up things that had been buried and forgotten, the chats have sometimes been uncomfortable for us both. We faced up to things that we had sometimes previously ignored. When I would ask her why she had done things, Kate would try to explain the reasons why some things happened and why some things shouldn't have happened. It always ended up with me thinking she needed help to cope. We did have some pleasant heart-to-hearts as well, like when Kate reminded me of how much she used to love it when I watched her learning to ride at Ditchling Stud.

And how nowadays she is doing the same thing with Jett and Bunny as they have their riding lessons.

Sophie has kept up a regular interest in the progress of the book. She was constantly reminding me of things and made suggestions about what I should include. We have a laugh when we remember things, like the time she promised Price and I that she had stopped smoking, yet we kept finding cigarette butts on the ground beneath her bedroom window.

Because it has prompted us to talk about so many things together, writing the book has helped to draw us closer as a family. Often, bringing things out into the open has brought about a different take and a greater understanding between us. We developed a kind of ritual. Every morning Dan would pop in for breakfast – three boiled eggs and toasted fingers – before going to work. He would ask me what I was writing about that day, then he would remind me of details that I might well have forgotten because he has such a good memory. If the memories brought tears to my eyes, Dan would tell me to let everything out whereas if there was any crying when Sophie rang on her regular morning call, she would tell me to pinch my bum and count to ten. It works. When Kate rang and asked what I was writing about on any particular day, the answer was usually . . . about her! Although the conversations with Kate tended to be stressful, particularly for her, we never argued. It made Kate think about things in her life and it hurt her. I felt her pain too. I discovered things about her that were new to me. Kate and I opened our souls to each other like never before and I think it's done us both good.

We've talked about things that have never been discussed

before, simply because there was no need. We have dug deep into our inner thoughts with no holds barred. I think, with me writing the book, I've had the best overall view and understanding of the family as a whole, but many things have been said that haven't been before and this has increased our understanding of each other. As I have listened to the others, I have realized that they probably know me better than I know myself. I have also realized that my children are each brilliant in their own way and that they're not so different from each other; it's just a few different traits they have.

I think I have always been able to see myself in Dan and Sophie because they both have similar traits to me. What has surprised me are the similarities between Kate and me that have emerged. Maybe it is because of my own experiences in younger days that I am able to spot the dangers so quickly in Kate's relationships. So much has happened to Kate and to me that we have become emotionally resilient and numb to events. Stress definitely has an effect; it has certainly taken its toll on Kate, and it may also be why I am unwell.

Kate has created a Marmite personality for herself. Like her or loathe her, the public just do not ignore her. The more people try to run her down, the stronger her support seems to grow and the fascination with her life seems to balloon. Over the years I've come to understand Kate's fan base a little. I think, by and large, they tend to be working-class people or at least people who have experienced ups and downs in life. They include single mums, mums with disabled children and independent, feisty career women. And there are always the men who fancy her of course! Consequently, there is always some project in the offing and Kate never seems to be out of work. She is a workaholic. She pays her own bills and supports her children financially and – believe me – when Kate divorces, the fall out costs her a fortune.

Kate has been fortunate that she can work and make money. Without a doubt she is an earner and a provider and she doesn't stop. She isn't afraid of trying different business ventures too. Some are successful, some fail. But she tries and she lives by the motto 'you have to speculate to accumulate'. Admirable though these qualities are, there is a down side. When she becomes obsessed with a project, Kate tends to bury her head in the sand. She will create or launch a product and then put the full force of her personality behind promoting it. It's an activity she uses to distract her from issues in her personal life. During these periods of intense hyperactivity, any sensible advice she is offered about business, relationships and hangers-on tends to fall on deaf ears and time and time again we, her family, are left to pick up the pieces.

That includes dealing with the media – and what a steep learning curve that has been for us over the years. We have experienced all kinds of media, from glossy mags through red tops and paparazzi, to the digital revolution of 24-hour news feeds and TV production. We have learned the hard way how they build you up, knock you down, scrutinize, sensationalize and mock – all in search of that shareable click-bait article.

Don't get me wrong, we understand the process. Kate has wanted and needed exposure and she has pushed the boundaries further than most in terms of opening up her private life for public consumption. But the media is a fast-paced world and is no longer controllable through trusted relationships. In the early days, audiences would only know about a celebrity's private life through pre-arranged interviews. In particular, magazines would pay handsomely for the privilege of exclusive insights and images, but these deals reduced Kate's right to privacy and were sometimes scuppered by leaked information.

Long before Coleen Rooney was on the case, we were noting down who we told what, to see if the story filtered through to the press. If it did, we slowly excluded those people from our lives but it was never a perfect solution because there was always the next deal. Sadly, we learned that money too often trumps loyalty. And Kate has always made it easy for people by being too open and having few boundaries for herself. I think everybody deserves some privacy, particularly in their own home. There have been times when fences or trees have been scaled and hedges climbed in an attempt to position a lens for a lucrative picture. Price has done well over the years helping Kate with perimeter fencing, but it can no longer outsmart the drones which hover menacingly over her home. There are times when Price has put on a blonde wig and driven Kate's car so the photographers follow him, allowing Kate to go in the opposite direction and have a few hours of freedom. Other times she has hidden in a footwell or in the boot to be out of sight. Being in the eye of the storm can be a scary thing – the paps on motorbikes are the worst.

But no one is saying Kate hasn't courted media attention. Like many other celebs, she has set up her own pap pictures in the past in an attempt to regain an element of control over her life and image. Do you ever wonder how that pap could have been so lucky to happen to be in the same park as a celebrity when they were feeding swans, or in a strawberry field picking fruit, or lounging by that luxury swimming pool? It's a lucrative business and you would be surprised to know how many people in the entertainment industry work with picture syndication agencies to set up their own images. When the press report that Kate is on yet another holiday, the truth of the matter is that Kate is on a working holiday – she's being paid to be away and is selling the photos to the press, but they choose to portray her as being reckless and irresponsible.

The press is like a game. No one likes a bland character – a villain is far more interesting than a Goody Two-shoes. But sometimes I think those with the power forget they are impacting the lives of real people. At times, the vilification has been too much for Kate and now we, as a family, recognize the signs that signal she is retreating to a dark place. More recently, Dan has reached out to a couple of well-placed journalists and politely asked them to ease off the constant barrage of bullying headlines. In fairness, they have obliged. They know who they are and we are grateful for their humanity. When Kate puts her life on a plate for public consumption, she opens herself up to be mocked, in particular where her relationships are concerned. I think she sees herself as a modern-day Elizabeth Taylor. As I've said previously, I just see her as someone who wants to be loved and be happy. She has always had a love-and-hate relationship with the press. She needs them and they need her but sometimes the narrative is beyond reasonable.

I hope my perspective will help to balance the scales. This isn't a kiss-and-tell book – you can read about Kate's relationships in her books. I hope it comes over as factual. I have tried to put across my views and opinions about events that I know happened because I lived through them. I hope this book gives the reader an understanding of my family and its history, and puts into perspective why Kate is troubled. Kate has been beset with pitfalls from an early age and they have affected her deeply. As we have revisited these traumas and gone over how she has been treated in her relationships, it has become obvious how significantly they have impacted her mental health. In the media she is portrayed in monetary terms as the working-class girl that did good and had everything, then lost everything. But to me, the sad thing is she lost herself too along the way. I hope that you've come to understand my worries, and why I think this happened – especially as I've spoken from a mum's point of view. I think this book has brought Kate and me closer together and I have learned more about her. I feel I now have a better understanding of her and why she is like she is. She has become more aware of things and is getting the right help. I know now she will look forwards not backwards anymore.

I think the book has helped to keep me alive as I have been writing it. There have been days when I have felt so ill or tired, I've thought I might not be able to write – but then something inside prompted me to do it while I still could. I wanted to unload my thoughts. Once they were down on paper, I knew I had done my best to show people My Kate, My Sophie, My Dan and My Price and the truth that I know hasn't been printed or said before. I wanted to ensure that nothing could be misconstrued. It's all from me and me only.

351

I want to keep the book as a surprise for my grandchildren. Normally they see their nan sitting in a chair with an oxygen tube up her nose. I want to challenge any preconceptions they might have because of my age or my physical condition. I want them to realize that anything is achievable at any time of life: feel the fear and do it anyway – that's our family motto! I also want to show them that I've had a life – and quite a life too! And so did other members of their family. I want them to be proud of me having written a book. I never in a million years thought I would do such a thing. I want them to know about my life, and their family, about when I was growing up and about their great – and great, great – grandmothers and grandfathers. I want them to learn more about their parents too, especially when they were younger. It's a life story, a reference book, a history lesson. They can retrace my footsteps where my family and I used to live. They can discover landmarks where I went to school, walked and played as a child, and a teenager. The hard times for me and their grandad won't be forgotten. I won't be around for Amalie, Betsy, Jett, Bunny and 'Tom Thumb' Albert when they grow up, so this book is for them to keep and know about their Nannie Big Hair. I want Princess and Junior to know there are two sides of their family for them to be proud of. Most of all I want them to read about their mum, know how much she loves them, and how her life has been affected by the hands of others.

They say the best thing about knowing you are going to die is that you can get things in order. I've done that and left instructions about my funeral, and the music too. I've kept everything secret – even from Price and the children. I have left instructions written in a book and this book contains letters to my children and grandchildren. They will have to hunt to find it. I have another book that contains personal things they have given me over the years, which have brought a smile to my face. I want them to have fun finding them – it's my last bit of child-ishness as an old woman, just like putting a pillow on the top of a door to fall on someone's head when they open it. It's childish but funny! I want these books to be kept secret, but I want them to be a celebration of my life. I have already created some mementos – bracelets and necklaces engraved with words. They will have other mementos too, but they'll have to wait and see.

If I regret anything in my life, it was not competing in the Olympics. I now see that if Ray hadn't been there when I got back, life would have just had to move on. Other than that, I wouldn't change a thing. I have lived a life of ups and downs, a journey of sadness and love, challenges and rewards, and I have lived life to the full. I have been lucky to have wonderful children, grandchildren and a partner I love and who loves me – what more in life could I have wanted? I would like to be remembered for being a fun person, a generous person, a loyal person, a good mum, wife and homemaker. I don't want it to ever be forgotten that I love them all.

PS What has kept me going while writing this book is the desire to bring to the fore an awareness about IPF. I have helped in the past with research into IPF but now I wish my body could have been used more to further research into this awful disease. Sadly, I have been informed that that is no longer possible as I am too ill. I am disappointed about this because I believe the search for a cure is so important in the fight against killer diseases. I would ask people to put themselves forward for research projects and to be organ donors too. Although my body can't be used, I am happy that the proceeds from the sales of this book will go to the charities and the hospital that has helped me and so many others. And finally, if you're unsure about anything concerning your health, don't let anyone fob you off until you've got answers! Always, always, ask for a second opinion if you are not happy with what you have been told. You have one life, so please look after it. x

AFTERWORD

Yet again, it was the familiar sound of an iPhone ring tone that dramatically changed the course of my life – but this time it also *gave* me life. The call from the transplant team at Harefield Hospital came out of the blue at 8:35am on Monday 7th November 2022 against the backdrop of an otherwise routine morning at the Price residence.

Dan had dropped in to assess the week ahead with Price. In recent years, he has helped him with his fencing business, partly because Price is finding it harder to do the bigger jobs alone and partly to give us the freedom to enjoy precious days out during what I honestly believed would be the last few months of my life.

Dan had arrived as usual at 8am for breakfast and a cup of tea. Price was at the gym working on strengthening his knees (he will need new ones soon), so we began chatting about what the family had been up to over the weekend. Sophie dialled in on a video call as she does every morning to check up and say hello and, as usual, we discussed the latest dramas in Kate's world.

Dan started to boil the water for eggs and stuck the kettle

on while I sat in the chair watching the TV news relaying updates about the Just Stop Oil protests taking place on the M25. Demonstrators from the environmental group said they wanted the government to halt new licences for the exploration of oil and other fossil fuels in the UK and had climbed on overhead gantries in multiple locations causing major disruption. For once I was grateful to be stuck indoors without having to contend with the stresses of the outside world. But then the call came.

I answered the phone to a lady called Jo who introduced herself as the transplant co-ordinator and told me a lung had become available and it might be a possible match for me. She added that there was a window of approximately three hours for me to get to Harefield Hospital in Middlesex for preoperative checks. Any longer and the lung might not be viable as organs can only last outside the body for a certain amount of time. I simply said, 'Okay, thank you' and put the phone down with my head spinning and my heart racing. Then I looked across at Dan and told him that that was the call I'd been waiting for. I had to get my bag ready. I'd got three hours to get there. It reminded me of being pregnant when you have a bag packed and ready but you don't know when you will be carrying it out through the door.

My breathing started to become more shallow and rapid as the realization set in – this was the moment I'd waited for, for so long. As always, Dan was a calm, reassuring presence and told me to focus on controlling my breathing and organizing my bag – I even packed my trainers, because I honestly believed that I would be working out straight after the operation – but first I had to text Price to tell him to come home. It felt like everything was moving at supersonic speed as I began getting ready to embark on a journey that could save my life. Poor Dan must have felt overwhelmed as I started to blurt out the login details to access this book, my emails, financial and insurance files, my bank accounts. Although I was feeling hopeful, I had to work on the premise that I might not ever return home.

At that moment, I took the very difficult decision to tell Dan not to let Sophie and Kate know where I was heading until the news was more certain. I didn't want to worry them and I needed to protect Price from being bombarded with constant messages while he was focussing on getting me to the hospital. I asked Dan to be the central point of contact and assured him that Price would provide him with updates as soon as he could.

Unbelievably, amidst all the panic, Dan helped me to settle down and eat my boiled eggs while we waited for Price to return. He arrived just after 9am shouting, 'Why haven't you left? We are running out of time! Bloody hell Daniel!' Price was very flustered but once again, Dan stepped in telling him, 'You need to remain calm as mum will feed off your emotions and behaviour. Go and get the van started and warmed up. She has literally just had some food and packed her bag. We couldn't have done anything different because she wants to travel to London with you.'

While Price started the van, Dan gathered up my oxygen tanks for the journey ahead and carried my bag out. I pulled myself up into my husband's humble, trusty van and turned to my wonderful son knowing it could be the last time I saw him. I will never forget the moment he looked into my eyes and told me, 'I love you, good luck'. As we pulled away, he gave me a thumbs up and I was able to give him one back. That was the last I saw of him for a long time. I was on my way to Harefield at high speed. In hindsight, I don't know why he didn't come with us – it was all happening so quickly!

Price must have broken a million traffic laws. He drove on the hard shoulder and over mounds as far and as safely as he could, but eventually we encountered the devastating effects of the Just Stop Oil protests and ground to a halt 45 minutes away from the hospital. We were queuing on the M25 near Cobham services so we called the police to say I was in transit for a transplant and asked if they could help by blue-lighting us through the traffic, but they said they no longer did this and suggested calling the ambulance service. In true, dramatic Price family fashion, Price and I sat there together waiting for the sight and sound of a blue light which would ultimately seal my fate. But even in this devastatingly tense moment, my husband had the ability to make me laugh. The ambulance service had asked for our postcode so they could come and rescue us and Price had to run into a nearby garden centre to find out. It made me chuckle when I saw how his running style had become very unique with two bad knees – more of a straddling hobble than a streamlined jog.

While I glanced out of the window waiting for Price to return, the events of the last few months flashed before me. It was now five years since my diagnosis but I had tried to control my decline as much as possible – such as by staying fit and healthy. For a long time, I'd been conscious of a conversation I'd had with the TV presenter Keith Chegwin who had appeared on *Celebrity Big Brother* with Kate. He had sadly passed away from the same illness as me in December 2017 and in his final weeks, he told me, 'I have this big house, wonderful family and friends around me, enough money – but I simply can't do anything apart from sit in this chair. If I was given the opportunity, I'd take a transplant.'

I too had been waiting for the moment when I became confined to a chair. Weeks after I had that conversation with him, Keith was dead and his mortality was a big wake-up call for me and the downward spiral that lay ahead of me. I became focussed on transplantation and was determined to remain on the list even though it was becoming increasingly less likely as I approached the ripe old age of 70 in October 2022. The doctors have to be responsible and ask the question, 'Would you be able to survive such an operation if the opportunity came about?' and provide evidence for it.

During my birthday month, I had undergone another round of rigorous health tests. I had pushed myself physically and thankfully – and I think much to their disbelief – the consultants conceded that my heart function matched that of a 50-year-old. I was still fit enough for an operation if I was lucky enough to be considered and I made it very clear to the doctors that it was my wish to remain on the transplant list even though I knew time was ebbing away.

In many ways, this book became my lifeline. On the days when I would otherwise have been reduced to sitting in a chair awaiting my fate, the book gave me the additional drive to get

up and out of bed, walk across the garden to our small conservatory, check in with my co-writer Sharon and start typing
away. As we neared completion of the manuscript, I could
sense my drive and enthusiasm waning. I developed a heavier
cough and there were more frequent episodes of struggling to
take in air. My mobility began to decline and I was wracked
with self-doubt and worry, knowing that the literary journey
was coming to an end. I had fulfilled my wish to write this
book and now all that was left was to wait for my last breath.
In reality, I probably had around two weeks to live.

Somehow, during this process of emotional decline, I managed to find the willpower to remain fit, doing daily Pilates,
resistance-band training, breathing exercises and mobility
routines. I still needed hope but in order to maintain it, I
knew I had to stay transplant-ready – a decision I had not
taken lightly. As a family, we had discussed our thoughts and
feelings about whether I should go for a transplant or not.
Ultimately, it's an extraordinary opportunity to accept the
ultimate gift of life but we also knew the risks. The main cer-
tainty was that without the operation, I would die. But there
was also a chance I could die during the operation, or afterwards if my body rejected the lung. Even if I got over those
two hurdles, it had been made clear to me that rehabilitation
could take many, many months and I would have to take a
huge quantity of drugs every day for the rest of my life. Given
my age, recovery would be no walk in the park – a huge battle
for survival with my whole family on the journey with me. All
of these thoughts were buzzing through my head as I sat next
to Price, my rock, waiting for the ambulance. I still had no

idea if I would even get the opportunity of having the lung on arrival at Harefield, but to be asked felt like an extraordinary gift.

I had only just left Dan in the driveway at home, but was already thinking about how he might be feeling. I was also wondering about my girls Sophie and Kate. I know my decision not to inform them will seem strange to some people, but I didn't want them to start panicking and have that stress. Dan later told me that the chaos that had reigned in the house after the phone call soon ebbed into an empty silence when Price and I left. He said he was tempted to let his sisters know, but Kate was in Thailand and Sophie's son Albert was poorly so he adhered to my wishes, which included instructions to help Sharon finish writing the book. Amazingly, he got to work straight away, explaining to Sharon that the task was helping him take his mind off the fact he might have just said a last goodbye to his mum.

As the wait for the ambulance continued, I could feel my heart beating faster and I became more breathless in anticipation of what was to come. I thought to myself that I might be able to breathe again properly after this; I might be able to get back some quality of life – but then I thought about everything I would have to go through to get there. However, I was certain of my decision to take the gamble. If I died in the operating theatre, at least I would not be in pain and my loved ones would know that I had tried my utmost to live.

Then I began to think about the donor. Somewhere, in the midst of my chance to live, was a grieving family processing a death. Their selfless decision meant I could have the chance to see my grandchildren grow up and I knew that if I made it through the op, I would want to thank them personally if I ever had the opportunity. Initially, I would have no idea who the lung came from but after six months, I would be allowed to reach out to the donor family via the hospital. However, they would not have to respond to any communication and could remain anonymous. I would of course respect their wishes either way.

But time was going against me now, ebbing away on a motorway. I was just beginning to think the Just Stop Oil protestors had robbed me of my chance of life, when the familiar sound of an ambulance siren echoed in the distance and two lovely paramedics appeared like knights in green armour. One drove while the other sat in the back with me because Price needed to make his own way to Harefield in the car in a frustrating journey which ultimately would take him another hour. All I could do was chat about all the equipment they had in the back of the ambulance – it was small talk which helped pass the time.

On arrival at Harefield, a chair was ready and waiting for me and the paramedic whisked me onwards straight into the pre-op waiting room. Once there, I had to shower and get gowned up ready for the opportunity to take the lung. They said it was a good match for me and told me I was the only possible recipient in the building. Generally, up to four people might be called in and it's pot luck if you are chosen as the nearest match. At this point, I met with the surgeons who were already gowned and ready to go. Thankfully, Price had arrived before us and we were able to spend a couple of hours together while we waited for the surgeons to make their final preparations and open the doors to the theatre and what fate held in store for me.

Finally, shortly after 5pm, I was wheeled down to the operating theatre where I knew there was nothing more I could do other than place my fate in the steady hands of highly skilled surgeons who would need several hours to perform the transplant.

It was at this point that Dan let his sisters know where I was. Kate was in Thailand and felt helpless. She immediately cut her trip short to return to the UK. Meanwhile, Sophie was at home in the bath with Albert and she was apparently so shocked to hear the news, she started crying tears of happiness and disbelief that the operation was actually happening.

I was in surgery for several hours. I have no idea exactly how long I was under and I really don't remember what I first thought or saw when I woke up as I was under the influence of so many drugs. Even when I finally regained full consciousness, I just remember a very fuzzy, unclear, dazed feeling. There was no clarity or sharpness. Apparently I was delirious, talking nonsense and slipping in and out of dreams. My hospital psychologist has since told me this is a very common post-op phenomenon.

The day after the operation, I was conscious but hooked up to every machine possible to assist with my breathing and monitor my stats. Then, through the night of Tuesday and into the early hours of Wednesday, I took a turn for the worse and went into cardiac arrest. My breathing began to gargle and blood was seeping into my tracheotomy so I was placed in an induced coma and remained in this state for a week, allowing staff to monitor, x-ray and care for me 24/7.

Since then, I've started to make progress but I soon realized the road would be slow and painful. Breathing with the new lung has been no walk in the park and frequent panic attacks have left me physically tired and emotionally drained. More recently, I have managed a few steps down the corridor with the help of a Zimmer frame – I felt as though I had climbed Everest! Price has remained by my side throughout, a reassuring and constant presence – especially during Christmas when I badly missed my children and grandchildren. It was really difficult not being with my family but Price was by my side watching films all day and the hospital staff were in hats and tinsel. A fantastic member of staff played Christmas songs on his violin in full vocal and he even took requests. The hospital also provided small gifts to bring some festive cheer to patients. I will never forget their kindness on that day, or on every other day that they have cared for me with a combination of genuine tenderness and professional expertise. The NHS might itself be in need of tender loving care, but it is still one of the main reasons I am proud to be a British citizen.

Now, as I close this final part of *The Last Word* in early 2023, I am still fighting – fighting for the chance to live, fighting for the chance to show my appreciation for this ultimate gift, fighting to hold a copy of this book in my hand. Whatever happens next, I can rest easy knowing I have had my chance to set the record straight, to write the truth about my family, to have *The Last Word*.

TRIBUTE

by Sophie Price

'No one in your life will ever love you as your mother does. There is no love as pure, unconditional and strong as a mother's love. And I will never be loved that way again.'

The above quote by author Hope Edelman best describes my relationship with my mum and the bond we share; complete love and devotion for one another, and a friendship indulged in lattes, the countryside, and being able to speak openly to one another without fear or judgment – something I've always felt immensely grateful for and that I wish to replicate with my own children. This book is the true story of my mum's life – her happiness and tribulations, and I'm so proud of her for speaking up as a mother, as woman, and for sharing her story, her family's story and her side of things in her own words. Many will, I'm sure, have their own opinions on this book, but I for one am proud to see my mum's legacy in black and white (and I can't wait to see this book sitting on a Waterstones bookshelf alongside all those authors, as I look on with glee).

I would best describe my mother as a cheeky little girl

– there are moments when she gives me this look from time to time: a cheeky look that makes her seem like a mischievous little girl with curly blond hair who's about to do something they know they shouldn't but do it anyway. That's probably why my mum's motto is 'feel the fear and do it anyway.' I love this playfulness and forwardness about her – she is never afraid to say what's on her mind, and I know exactly what she's thinking just by looking at her face, which I think is an endearing quality and gets to the point of things, shall we say! My sister, brother and I have all confided in our mum at some point, whether that be about relationships, work, or just clearing our minds and getting things off our chests, and although she is a good listener, her advice is normally to 'Stop moaning and just get on with it,' or, 'If you're not happy, then change it.' She's always very blunt, and her straightforward advice normally does the job...

Now, as I get older and my mum's illness progresses, she says to me, 'When I'm gone, you will be taking over my role in the family...and sorting out your sister.' I don't think I fully understood the pressures put on my mum as a parent when it came to my sister's mental health challenges, the people Kate has surrounded herself with in the past, and the media. In recent years, though, this is something I've come to fully understand, and I feel my mum is preparing me for any tribulations that are yet to come our family's way in her absence. Alongside my mum and sister, we all like to make sure we spend time with each other – this, I think not only benefits Kate's mental health and wellbeing, but it's quality time together that we all very much value, even if it's going for a quick coffee, or a drive around the countryside talking about anything and everything, and listening to *Return of the Mack* by Mark Morrison – a favourite of ours. It's easy, pleasant, and conversation flips from one thing to another. I adore spending time with them both; they're funny, thoughtful and we can be frank with one another, which is a rare quality with families, I think – nothing is off limits, let's just say that!

My mum always says I'm most like her – we often think the same and we're into the same things: interior decorating, driving around the countryside, the seaside, and Christmas. Christmas is a big thing for me and Mum – we watch *The Snowman*, look at Christmas lights in different villages; even in the summertime, when we drive around looking at properties, the first thing that often comes out of our mouths is, 'That house would look lovely at Christmas.' Mum and I first started driving around the countryside during the pandemic; she was nervous about going outside and mixing with people again due to her illness, so to encourage her to get out of the house again, I suggested that we get a drive-through latte, and go for drives to different villages around Sussex to get some air, have a change of scenery, and to have a look at the cottages. Up until this day, we've continued our little drives out to the sticks, and I absolutely love them – it provides a sense of freedom, of being able to explore, seeing different landscapes, and enjoying life's simple pleasures, something I love, as does mum.

I hope the readers of this book enjoy and take in what my mum has to say; her thoughts and feelings on various subjects and past experiences have very much shaped us all as a family and she has been a pillar for us all. I love my mum deeply and will always support her as she has supported me as her daughter. She is an amazing grandmother to all her grandchildren, and I cherish the time she and my dad spend with Albert and of course, our little drives out to the countryside all together – these are memories that will never be forgotten.

TRIBUTE

by Dan Price

Typically, nothing is straightforward within our family – I even feel that writing this tribute is looking backwards. I'm supposed to be letting you, the reader, know about the author as I know her: who she is, what she is about, and what this book will bring you. Sadly, in a not-so-straightforward way, this book was due to be released upon my mother's passing, and this tribute is a kind of reflection on who she was and what she meant to us, so that I can shape in your mind who 'mum' really is. I'm afraid I have no idea what has been written in these pages, as it was written in secrecy – typically, Amy, my mum, or Nanny Big Hair, as her grandchildren called her, had the last word.

Our family has some characters who I'm sure my mum has introduced to you by now – Uncle Henry with his architecture, Cousin David with his musical genius, Essie, and of course, my younger sibling Kate, whom I think some of you may have heard of. But mum was also her own character. As I type this, it's starting to feel like the kind of thing that I would say at her funeral. I'm going to go with it though – I can only imagine that I'll be too sad to even speak at her funeral, so I'll type my words for all to read.

Mum is colourful, wonderful, and I'd say borderline eccentric.

Nothing was ever magnolia in any aspect of her life. She was a swimmer at national level who swam with the best, even gave Sharron Davies a run for her money and was close to Junior International Olympic selection. She loved her cars; her beige MGB GT was her true baby, but her British racing green VW Beetle 1303S (Amy's Baby) wasn't far behind. Musically, she loved Alexander O'Neal and Luther Vandross, early Madonna – but she'd comfortably listen to The Chemical Brothers, Swedish House Mafia. Back in the day, I would tease her ear drums with The Prodigy. In her later years, she settled for Café Del Mar and French classical jazz café music.

Her varied taste in music was matched by her interior design expressionism (I called it 'Amyonism'). Vintage antiques sat alongside her own 'self-stressed' shabby chic units, with shockingly awful parrot wallpaper and diamante-esque chandeliers all together in one room. I think it said, 'chaos, character and individuality, yet highly sociable and endearing' to all those who knew her.

From sunbathing topless in the Alps, to writing political party conference speeches, to working in the big smoke, to Rocky Horror dress ups, to caring for Harvey full time (nobody knows how much she really did in supporting Kate), to working in Payroll, to volunteering at an Indian orphanage on her own and to then being diagnosed with an incurable lung disease (which all along, she thought was asthma from her youth), I think it's fair to say she has learned a lot, lived a lot and seen a lot, but said very little. Until now.

Mum's always been there for me. I've not always gone to her, but when I needed to, she was there . . . she's not going to be soon . . . she isn't going to be now.

She would be a welcome ear, but she would say it straight. As colourful as mum is/was (I'm struggling to write in the past tense now), she could sometimes be very blunt and black and white (but always with colourful language). There was a stubbornness and she would sometimes refuse to believe there could be another opinion. But sometimes, days later, she would soften and understand the other side.

I don't like to write anything negative, but this resistance has become ingrained in all of us. We've had to, as a family, become very thick skinned, resistant to the point where I think we have become desensitized after almost 30 years of Kate in the limelight. What is written in the press brings negativity, hurt and, ultimately, emotionally draining fatigue. I would say about 20 per cent has had some truth in it, but the majority has had no substance – and this really affected mum as she saw it as an injustice.

Mum was the worst affected, only because she loves her family ten thousand per cent. She is naturally very protective, she cares, she worries about all of us. We have our early morning chat every day and late night text exchanges. I think she just wants everything to be settled, calm and smooth before she goes – but she knows this will never happen in our family.

It's been a tough few years watching her slow steady decline. Mum was a strong swimmer, fitness fanatic and an aerobics master – in truth, this foundation of fitness and strength put her in good stead; without it she would have passed away ages ago. Seeing mum walking around with an oxygen tank trying to do her own spin class and daily yoga shows her determination, fight and strength to remain positive. We have had deep conversations with me looking into my mum's eyes and seeing the tears forming. Those tears told me she is scared, she is worried, fearful of what is on the horizon – she wouldn't say it in words, she didn't need to – I understood. This is another sign of her strong-willed, brave-fronted stubbornness to avoid showing weakness. It's admirable to remain strong in the light of fear, adversity and inevitability.

We once did the London to Brighton bike ride as a family – it's a memory I'll never forget as it typifies mum. She was the last rider in the race; the only ones behind her were the road sweepers, an ambulance and a cycle sweeper picking up the stragglers at the foot of Box Hill. But she didn't relent. She walked up the hill with her bike – she conquered the hardest part of the course, then grudgingly retired. As I write this, she is at the foot of that hill in her life. I think this tells you all about who my mum really is.

I know you will read this mum – I want you to know that I will remain strong for the family. I'll help Paul as much as I can and I will always try to help guide, steer and advise Kate behind the scenes as always. Sophie and Harry have their own family unit with Albert, but I will always be there for them. With Louise at my side, I can only aim to be as good a parent as you were to me for our girls Amalie and Betsy, who (along with Princess) carry forward that strong family gene of your curly hair.

Give nan and grandad a big hug

Dan x

TRIBUTE

by Paul Price

What a lucky man I am to be Mr Amy Price. I knew Amy's first husband Ray and first saw her with him in our local pub. I just thought: what a woman. She was and still is so funny and bubbly. I knew almost immediately that she was the only woman I would ever want to be with, but first I had to see if I could actually win her over. Somehow, I managed it and I'll always count my blessings for that.

We started out as friends and eventually built a relationship. The more we got to know one another, the more laughs we had together, and the rest is history. We've shared so many special moments both at home just doing the simple stuff but also travelling abroad to places like Zimbabwe, India and Mauritius, which will always hold really special memories for me. Our holiday to Santorini in April 2017 was also beautiful but it was also the place where I sadly realized Amy was unwell. She has always been super fit, but one day she just couldn't make it up a flight of steps while we were out walking and I had to pull her up. I remember saying: 'We'll need to get this sorted when you get back.' Neither of us could ever have imagined what would be laying ahead of us.

After the diagnosis, I just tried to take the stress away for Amy and make her life as easy as possible. I hold it together for her, and when I'm struggling, she holds it together for me. That's the way it's always been. Amy's been good for me. I mean, I don't know where my life would have been if I wasn't with her. I just don't think it would have meant as much. When I look at the route we've been on, it's just fantastic. We've had our ups and downs just like everyone else and there was one very bad mistake on my part. I still can't explain it to this day, but she forgave me and when she stopped shouting at me, she pulled me through it and put my life back together.

I honestly can't imagine life without her. She keeps telling me I'm going to end up with someone else but it's impossible for me to think that way. I'll be quite happy keeping busy with my kids and grandkids if they choose to spend time with me. I keep telling Amy I don't need to live with another woman. I have no plans to do that, but she claims she has written me a letter giving me details of someone who has her seal of approval. She will still keep nagging me even when she's gone!

She is just this sort of lifeforce. Even while battling a terrible terminal illness, she has kept an image of a glass half full as her WhatsApp profile picture. I think that says it all really.

Everyday, I pray there's still hope. We've been told that she will only be fully considered for a transplant when she has three weeks to live so it's like living on a knife-edge some days, wondering how long we might have left together. At the last count, there were about 100 people waiting for a new lease of life. Waiting is something we've had to get used to.

While we wait, we tour Britain in our motorhome. We

love being in our own little bubble, cuddled up together going at our own pace. We've had some amazing times in Dorset, Devon and Cornwall where we pull up in a bay and I hold Amy's oxygen tank while she enjoys the freedom of swimming in the sea. Mostly, we are alone apart from the occasional interruption from her phone and one of the kids.

The one thing Amy can never switch off from is being a mum. She's a fantastic mother and while she is able to speak frankly to her children about their choices and behaviour, she is fiercely protective of them in the outside world. There is no doubt that Kate's career choice has put pressure on her because the patterns of behaviour repeat over and over. I think Amy has seen this while writing her book. It's one of the things she has always wanted to do in life, and it's been the best thing for her. It's helped her see how her life has come together.

Each day now, we both live in hope that the call from the transplant team will one day come. If you take that wish away, you might as well give up. I still believe, want to believe we've got a chance and I say 'we' because we have and always will be a team. She tells me: 'Well, this is my last year' and I say: 'But you said that last year'. We're still coming to terms with the situation we're in every day. It is what it is, and we push on. Hopefully, we will get another year and maybe another year after that. However many years we have left together there is one thing that will never change – she is my wife and the best friend I will ever have. I just hope she knows how much I love her and always will.

ACKNOWLEDGEMENTS

When I realized that I could be entering the last year of my life, and that I could therefore no longer put off writing this book, Sharon Hendry was the only person I wanted to approach to help me. Sharon has travelled the world as an investigative journalist and interviewed people from all walks of life. I knew she had a reputation for supporting the underdog and her writing has been nominated and won awards, covering stories that have bravely exposed the evils of society. Because of Kate's experiences I had a pretty good idea how some journalists worked, and I knew I wanted to collaborate with someone who was more interested in truth than sensationalism.

I first met Sharon a few years back when she interviewed Kate, and they worked together when Kate had a column in *The Sun*. I found Sharon extremely honest, principled, and to the point. She is very intuitive at picking up things that others do not notice. She did not suffer fools gladly but was compassionate and had so much life experience that I felt comfortable in her presence. I am conscious that ours is a working-class background, and I was put at ease because Sharon was never

377

condescending in any way. I knew I could say what I wanted to say, and she would understand my thoughts.

I am grateful to her for her patience; I have confided in her secrets I've never before revealed. In fact, I have surprised even myself because normally I am a private person and guarded, but I have enjoyed opening up to Sharon. I have cried, laughed, questioned myself and others but mainly, I have enjoyed writing this book with her. Sharon's advice, not just for the book but on a personal level too, has helped me live, laugh and enjoy the time I have left. I hope she will continue to be a friend to all my family. Sharon, your writing is unbelievable, the way it has made sense of my muddled ramblings and thoughts.

And thanks to our agent Charlie Brotherstone for having faith in us both, and our publisher Lisa Milton at Harper-Collins for agreeing to make this book a reality. Because of you, this book will hopefully end up in Brighton Library where so many hours of my young life were spent. This makes me smile and cry at the same time.

My friend John Hill also became part of our team, helping with book edits at a time when Sharon and I needed some clarity and conviction that we were heading in the right direction. I will always be thankful for his generosity and good humour in this process.

I am also grateful to Price, Dan, Kate and Sophie because they have been very patient and helped me so much in ensuring the accuracy of dates and rekindling memories that might otherwise have been forgotten. We've had so many conversations together that have caused both laughter and tears as we have reminisced and exchanged thoughts about what has happened to us all over the years.

Finally, I want it to be known that my proceeds from this book will go to the following charities and organisations: Action for Pulmonary Fibrosis, Royal Brompton & Harefield Hospitals Charity for lung research (especially Idiopathic Pulmonary Fibrosis, for which there is no cure) and St Barnabas House hospice. There is nothing more certain in life than our own mortality, and the truth written in these pages will hopefully go some way to support those who are currently – and perhaps prematurely – grappling with that fact.

If you are struggling with any of the issues raised in this book, you can seek advice and support by reaching out to the following charities:

Action for Pulmonary Fibrosis
Asthma + Lung UK
Citizens Advice
MENCAP
Mind UK
Rape Crisis
Refuge
RNIB
Samaritan